Ad & Wal

Peter Hain

Ad & Wal

Values, duty, sacrifice in apartheid South Africa

First published in Great Britain in 2014 by
Biteback Publishing Ltd
Westminster Tower
3 Albert Embankment
London SE1 7SP

ISBN 978-1-84954-643-0

10 9 8 7 6 5 4 3 2 1

A CIP catalogue record for this book is available from the British Library.

Set in Caslon and Bentham

Printed and bound in Great Britain by
CPI Group (UK) Ltd, Croydon CR0 4YY

For Harry, Seren, Holly, Tesni and Cassian Hain

Contents

Preface

Their first small steps later became large strides, their modest local actions led to national controversies.

Yet, when they were first asked to help, they gave no thought to where it might lead. Saying yes didn't seem at all fateful. Adelaine and Walter Hain rather stumbled, oblivious, into it all. At the time, in 1953, it just seemed the *right thing* to do, in keeping with their values of caring, decency, fairness and, perhaps equally important, their sense of *duty*.

Staying true to such values, morals, principles was important to them – even if that meant sacrificing the comforts and certainties of job, lifestyle, family, friends, security and indeed country. Maintaining *standards* was fundamental to trying to live a life of integrity where principles mattered. They didn't try to play the hero, they didn't set out with a plan. One thing led to another and, once they had started, there was no way they felt they could walk away or let others down – even though, had the consequences been known at the beginning, they might've had cause to pause and reflect.

Ad & Wal is a story of struggle, of sacrifice, of pain – but ultimately of triumph: not for themselves, but for their cause. They were *survivors* – they came through war, penury, harassment, attacks and bitter loss, still looking on the bright side, chins up, keeping going, making the most of life, living happily at the centre of their close and growing family.

Theirs is indeed a story of their times, their era. Do their values endure? Or have they been lost in a world of personal gratification and celebrity? Could there ever be another Ad and Wal? Or are people simply not made like that anymore?

Not that they were saints – everyone has flaws. I have tried to tell it as I think it was for Ad and Wal, an ordinary couple who did extraordinary things under apartheid South Africa in the 1950s and 1960s – and gave up a great deal as a result. It is indeed the very fact that they were so much like their white peers and relatives – that in their own words they were 'just an ordinary couple' – which makes their story intriguing, and along the way raises questions about why *they* did what they did, why *they* were rebels, when the great mass of other whites – including all but one of their many close relatives – did not and were not.

If you, the reader, were in their situation, would you have done what they did or stayed quietly with the vast majority, 'walking by on the other side'?

Of course being published doesn't make their story more important than those of tens of thousands of other South Africans, including whites like them, who joined the struggle against apartheid. Ad and Wal were, and very much saw themselves as, foot soldiers rather than leaders. They always insisted that others suffered a great deal more and contributed much more, and that their own role was modest.

Above all this is a *story*: I have aimed at readability rather than deep political or indeed psychological analysis. Other whites also brought up by anti-apartheid parents in South Africa at much the same time have written memorable books. Gillian Slovo's *Every Secret Thing* is unsparingly, uncomfortably honest about the personal and the political underlying the leading roles in the African National Congress played by her parents, Joe Slovo and Ruth First. Lynn Carneson's *Red in the Rainbow* is a moving tribute to the bravery and fortitude of her South African Communist Party and ANC parents, Fred and Sarah Carneson. Eleanor Sisulu's *Walter and Albertina Sisulu* is captivating on her inspirational in-laws. There are also insightful biographies of those times, for instance on the leaders, including Nelson Mandela and Thabo Mbeki, where similar themes – and values – arise.

But writing about your parents is not straightforward and I am grateful to both for their cooperation – despite their misgivings (including on my mother's side considerable emotional stress) and even embarrassment that they should be singled out. My thanks to my brother Tom and sisters Jo-anne and Sally for their own, sometimes painful, memories, and to Elizabeth Haywood for both her love and invaluable edits. My good friend and wonderful South African historian, Andre Odendaal, gave me sensitively trenchant and detailed advice without which this would have been a lesser work. I am also grateful for their help and comments to Myrtle Berman, Vanessa Brown, Jill Chisholm, Annette Cockburn, Eddie Daniels, David Evans, David Geffen, Hugh Lewin, Deputy Chief Justice Dikgang Moseneke, Jo Stocks, Jill Wentzel, Ann Wolfe, David Wolfe, Duncan Woods, Jane Woods and Randolph Vigne (whose book *Liberals Against Apartheid: a history of the Liberal Party of South Africa 1953–68* is an important source). Also to my agent Caroline Michel for her sympathetic wisdom on authorship; and to Sam Carter, Biteback's editor, for his enthusiasm for this story. Finally to Joe Hemani for his unfailing support and generosity in friendship.

Above all to Mom and Dad – Ad and Wal – who will always be an inspiration to me and many, many others.

Peter Hain
Ynysygerwn, Neath
November 2013

Prologue

If the end was bitter, at the start they could not believe their good fortune.

It was morning on 21 October 1944 when two army radio operators, Walter Hain aged nineteen and Lanky Brasler aged eighteen, moved to Point 806 high on Monte Pezza in the Apennines. Among some trees they stumbled across a 'slittie' (slit trench) wide enough to take both of them.

It was the only one like that they'd ever discovered. Normally a slittie was a one-man trench, long and deep enough to protect a soldier lying in it from shell shrapnel and flying bullets. Sometimes they had to toil away in the hard, unyielding soil to dig out a suitable slittie.

They delightedly occupied this one. To make it more secure from overhead shell bursts, they gave it a roof of tree branches topped with a layer of soil, and a gap at one end for access. As Walter's meticulous diary recorded, they 'felt as safe as a house'.

Both were soldiers of the 6th South African Armoured Division, part of the British 8th Army which, with the American 5th Army, was driving the German forces occupying Italy northwards out of the country. One of its infantry battalions was the Royal Natal Carbineers (RNC), and they were in C Company.

That morning their C Company took over a frontline position from B Company and they were able to move straight into existing slitties. Although around ten o'clock German shells started coming over a hill to their left, Walter and Lanky 'felt very safe and were trying to sleep'. But, two hours later, when shells began bursting nearby and shrapnel flying, they found the din 'terrifying'.

The two were suddenly trapped in their 'safe as houses trench', the Germans pounding their lines. Then – shockingly – their worst fear: shrapnel tore through the access opening in the trench roof near their feet. It hit the top of Walter's right thigh in the groin. 'I quickly put my hand down to make sure the family jewels were intact – they were. Lanky shouted: "I've been hit, I've been hit."'

'So have I,' Walter shouted and Lanky jumped out the opening of the slittie to call for help. 'Then another shell arrived and Lanky grabbed his back and screamed "Oh Mama, Mama, Mama."'

Pandemonium. Horror. Walter pulled a moaning Lanky back into the slittie and tried to prop him up; Lanky was badly hurt – very badly. The company medical orderly, Dutch, soon arrived and gave Lanky morphine; it seemed not to make any difference. Despite Walter's desperate reassurances, Lanky 'was sure he wasn't going to make it' and asked Walter to see his sister. 'But I told him he'd be alright and the stretcher-bearers would soon be coming.'

Ignoring incoming fire, Coloured[‡] stretcher-bearers soon rushed in to carry Lanky away to the regimental aid post nearby, in a large house, Casa Ruzzone. Limping to it later himself, in shock and in some pain from his injured thigh, Walter came across the stretcher-bearers having a breather. Lanky, they told him matter-of-fact, was dead. Surely not. He was stunned, with a dreadful sense of guilt that it was when Lanky had jumped out, calling for help for them both, that the second shell had killed him. Walter had been through some scrapes earlier since arriving in Italy, and counted himself lucky. But now he was overcome by a dulling, deadening despair.

Forty-one years later, in 1985, retracing his steps through the Apennines aided by his old wartime diary and with family members, he rounded a corner in the tiny village of Castiglione dei Pepoli. There, quite unexpectedly, was a Commonwealth War Graves cemetery for South African soldiers, set in a beautiful glade, a kaleidoscope of green shades with a sprinkling of brightly coloured flowers, birds tweeting in the sunshine: peace and tranquillity.

---

‡ Mixed-race, one of four racial groups, the others being whites, Africans (blacks) and Asians. Only whites in the South African army were permitted to carry arms. Soldiers from other racial groups, though often in danger, could only perform back-up roles.

Both curious and eager, Walter's hopes rose and the family stopped. In a small stone building they found a metal-encased ledger, and in it – yes – the location of Lanky's grave. Elation but also deep melancholy: his emotions swirled as he walked down through rows and rows of white-grey headstones, stark, sombre and dignified. Finding Lanky's, he knelt down on his knees to photograph it, conjuring an inescapable image of fate: had their positions in that slittie been reversed, it could well have been Lanky and his family visiting Walter's gravestone. Instead, through friendships made in action in the Second World War, he lived to meet the love of his life.

❦

Adelaine Hain was frantic. Somehow, anyhow, she had to save the life of a close friend and political comrade, John Harris. For five months after John was sentenced to death by hanging, the shadow of the noose hovered as she was involved in frenzied efforts to save him.

As a member of the African Resistance Movement (ARM), Harris had confessed to placing a bomb on the main railway concourse at Johannesburg station in 1964. With Nelson Mandela in prison along with many other anti-apartheid activists, and internal resistance all but suppressed, Harris, along with his close colleague, fellow ARM and Liberal Party member John Lloyd, planned the bomb as a spectacular protest against apartheid.

Police testimony in court confirmed that he had indeed telephoned a warning to the railway police and urged them to clear the concourse, in order to avoid injuring anyone. But the authorities deliberately ignored that and an old lady tragically died, her twelve-year-old granddaughter maimed for life, others injured and burnt.

This would have carried a life sentence for manslaughter had John Lloyd not turned from co-conspirator to state witness and damningly insisted – against all other evidence – that the act was pre-meditated murder. The judge accepted Lloyd's version with fatal consequences for Harris.

When his legal appeal on 1 March 1965 failed – because no additional evidence was forthcoming – Adelaine rushed about Pretoria helping organise clemency appeals. Repeated pleas to Lloyd, safe in England, to retract the damning part of his evidence were refused. John's wife Ann and his father flew down to Cape Town to appeal to the Minister of Justice, John Vorster. But he was hostile and intransigent and, even worse, asked her questions seeking to entrap and implicate her in the bomb. Petitions from a range of public figures were presented and the matter was even raised in the British Parliament. But the state would not budge and a grim sense of foreboding enveloped them all while John Harris was being held on death row.

Then: a slim gleam of hope. John managed to convey a message to Ann that he had been approached by a warder who wanted to help him escape. At great personal risk, and from the outset highly suspicious of a set-up designed to trap them, Adelaine decided to help Ann, with Walter's support. There were weeks of tense and contorted dealings with the warder. Then he was posted over 1,000 rand to pay for a car and expenses for the escape, Adelaine insisting that Ann had Elastoplasts stuck discreetly over her fingertips to cover her prints.

Beside themselves with worry, they waited for the elaborate arrangements the warder specified were needed to spring John. On the nominated day, two weeks before he was due to hang, he was to be sneaked out of his cell, and climb a rope over a wall.

Nevertheless, as Adelaine had feared all along, it had been a security police trap from the beginning. As John waited in his cell wearing a civilian suit given him by the warder, the door opened as arranged at 2 a.m. But instead of the expected warder it was apartheid's chief spymaster, General H. J. van den Bergh, mocking him. (Together with John Vorster, 'HJ' was a former member of the paramilitary Ossewabrandwag, which conducted sabotage operations against the Allies in the Second World War; both were interned for pro-Nazi activities.) HJ tried to pressure Harris to reveal the identity of his co-conspirators outside. Despite being promised his life would be spared, Harris refused. It was just as well that Adelaine was obsessive both about secrecy and ensuring any evidence of her (criminal) collaboration was concealed.

But she remained distraught at being unable to save him. At 5 a.m. on 1 April 1965 John Harris ascended the fifty-two concrete steps to the pre-execution room next to the gallows at Pretoria Central Prison. Each step was six feet or so wide in a square spiral configuration; there were four landings with metal bars on a side wall all the way up. A Catholic priest, Father McGuinness, walked up the steps talking with him. (John had originally agreed to see a priest because it got him an extra visitor and they became good friends, though John's firm atheism never wavered.) Inside the execution chamber, which had barred frosted glass windows along the top, the hangman waited. So did a medical doctor to certify his death, and a policeman to take a set of fingerprints and check his face against a photograph to confirm his identity. The death warrant was read to him and he was given the opportunity to say his last words.

Ready, he was now led forward by a warder into the large and brightly lit execution room, some forty feet long with white-painted walls, the gallows beam running its length. (Seven black prisoners could be – and often were – hanged simultaneously on this gallows.) It had a low ceiling with barred windows in the top of the wall. In the corner there was a table with a phone on it, in case a last-minute clemency was ever granted. There is no recorded instance of the phone ever having rung – and it certainly did not ring for John.

In the middle was the cruel hole, rectangular trap doors hinged along each edge. Alongside was a rail at waist height so that the warder holding John's arms did not fall down the hole when the trap doors opened.

Above the trap door was the machinery of the gallows. The ropes and fittings had been adjusted to match his height and weight.

The hangman began his grisly routine, tying John's wrists behind his back and attaching a rope around his neck with the knot next to an ear. Then he fastened a hood over John's face with a flap at the front left up until the last moment.

John had begun singing the freedom song 'We Shall Overcome' as the hangman turned down the hood flaps, checked all was ready and pulled the lever, plummeting him through the huge trap doors. In the gruesome medieval ritual the rope jerked with such force that it not only broke John's neck but left a severe rope burn. Christiaan Barnard, South Africa's pioneer heart surgeon, wrote years later:

> The man's spinal cord will rupture at the point where it enters the skull, electrochemical discharges will send his limbs flailing in a grotesque dance, eyes and tongue will start from the facial apertures under the assault of the rope and his bowels and bladder may simultaneously void themselves to soil the legs and drip onto the floor.

As to whether John would have felt any pain, Barnard added:

> It may be quick. We do not know as none has survived to vouch for it. We make the assumption that the *danse*

> *macabre* is but a reflection of a disconnected nervous system ... and the massive trauma of the neck tissues and spinal column does not register in that area of the human psyche where horror dwells.

In keeping with the custom of the Pretoria gallows John was left to hang for fifteen minutes. In the corner of the gallows chamber was a concrete staircase leading to a high-ceilinged room below. Set into its floor was a 'blood pit' about eighteen inches deep, lined with coloured tiles, a plug hole in the middle. To one side was a huge low wooden trolley, big enough to wheel over the whole pit. The doctor stood on it after John had been stripped to certify his death. Then his body was lowered onto the trolley and washed off with a hose, the water draining into the 'blood pit'. A warder put a rope around John's body which, with a pulley, was then lifted to allow the noose to be taken off. He was then lowered onto a metal stretcher and placed directly into his coffin.

Adelaine Hain had woken unusually early at dawn, waiting still and silent. At 5.30 a.m. the family phone rang and she picked it up, recognising the familiar voice of a security police officer who said scornfully, 'Your John is dead.'

1

Soldier

Although the name *Hain* means 'small wood' in German, Walter was from Scottish stock in Glasgow. Yet – even from a city renowned for its socialist activism – little in his background hinted at his later political radicalism.

His grandfather William, a toolmaker, hailed from the Fife town of Auchtermuchty. His father Walter (Senior) and mother Mary were brought up on opposite sides of the main park in their working-class Glasgow neighbourhood of Tollcross. They remained there when they married, living with his parents in a 'wally close' – an apartment with a tiled entrance leading off a communal staircase in a tenement block. The ceramic tiles were a distinctive pale cream with a raised ornamental band of green above denoting marginal superiority in a deprived community of similar apartment blocks typical of the city. (The Scots word 'wally' means pale ceramic.)

But after the 1914–18 World War, Walter Snr, a newly qualified structural engineer, could not find a job and, unwilling to accept his lot, they joined many others in similar predicaments and emigrated in 1920 to Natal, South Africa, his parents joining them as they made a new life. Walter Snr got a job at a steel construction firm in Durban, designing bridges, but for Grandfather William it was a sad move as he could not find work to continue in his proud role as an engineering toolmaker.

Walter was born on 29 December 1924 in Northdene, a satellite suburb to the north west of the Natal city of Durban, in a house that his father and grandfather had helped build. It was in Parkers Hill, a street located between the main railway line and (now) the M5 north to Pretoria. There were few houses nearby and the children had open fields in which to play, across which were Indian families who grew vegetables and fruit which they sold to the Hain family and other white households. His mother used to make sandwiches for lunch at school, containing special Virol malt extract, which he was told was very good for him. But he habitually swapped them with local black workers for the traditional fare of Zulu labourers, *stave pap* or *putu* – made from maize.

He had a carefree young life with his two elder brothers Bill and Tom, playing, swimming, fishing in local streams and enjoying sport, and was especially close to his grandfather, who spent time talking to the young boy. But then came a family crisis. In the great slump of 1929 his dad lost his job and, desperate to work, travelled back, first to Britain then to Canada, moving between various short-term jobs, none utilising his structural engineering skills. The global depression continuing, his dad eventually found work in Kenya with the Vacuum Oil Company and six-year-old Walter recalled being frightened that the passenger ship transporting the family to Kenya's Mombasa port might sink.

After a year living in Mombasa, they moved back into their house in Northdene, his father rejoining his previous engineering employer in Durban, which now had a job available. Walter was then of school age and did well at Escombe Primary School in a settlement a few miles away, to which he walked daily. It was the only time he wore shoes – at home he and his older brothers were usually barefoot in the typical way of South African youngsters. Once, walking to school with white friends, he recalled coming up behind a group of Indian boys on their way to their school: 'Get out of our way!' the young whites shouted merrily at the young Indians; Walter and his mates were the masters. Except for the open-air South African lifestyle and the Indians with whom he came into contact, it was a very British colonial upbringing; most Northdene families had also recently emigrated from Britain.

It was not until his family (with grandparents) moved to Pretoria in 1935 that Walter encountered Afrikaans-speaking whites. He attended Arcadia Primary School and later, with his older brothers Bill and Tom, Pretoria Boys High, probably the best state school in the city, where everyone played rugby in winter and cricket in summer. (He had actually begun high school at another renowned state school, Parktown, when his parents moved briefly to Johannesburg in 1937–8.) Though an enthusiastic cricketer, he did not reach the standard of brother Bill, who had previously captained the first team at Boys High.

Walter was brought up with traditional manners and courtesies, his father strict and his teachers even more so, as he absorbed the prevailing family values of discipline, hard work, honesty and decency. At the same time he was instilled with a spirit of questioning everything, soon developing a vigorously anti-establishment temperament. Perhaps this – together with an instinctive and unusual empathy for the Africans he encountered – was the genesis of what much later became his anti-apartheid activism.

Yet his parents never discussed politics with him. Despite the fact that they had both been Labour Party members in their youth in Glasgow, they shunned the politics of their adoptive country. Like most British immigrants they turned a blind eye to the racism entrenched around them and went along with the status quo. Indeed, of working-class stock and therefore subordinate in Britain, they rather enjoyed being 'superior' in South Africa. Whether they knew or acknowledged this, they were an integral part of the institutionalised racism of South Africa, and their views were broadly part of a British colonial view of the world at the time, which even the British Labour Party, despite its emancipatory tradition, was affected by. Therefore, in common with his white school friends, the young Walter took it for granted that blacks were a servant class, both to white families like his and the white society in which they lived cordoned off from areas where blacks resided. Propitiously, however, he was brought up to treat black people with some civility and respect, unhappily not the norm among many whites.

Walter was just fourteen when Germany invaded Poland in 1939, triggering the outbreak of the Second World War. His father and two older brothers quickly enlisted and were involved in the military campaign to drive Hitler's allies the Italians from Abyssinia (Ethiopia) in 1940–41. Meanwhile, with his mother Walter had moved back to Pretoria and to Boys High.

English-speaking teenage boys like him were keen as mustard to join up. However, unlike in Britain, there was no conscription as the South African Parliament had decided only narrowly (by thirteen votes) to support the Allies rather than the Nazis. The Second World War had divided South Africa's white population, English descendants backing the Allies, Afrikaners siding heavily with the Nazis. Some of their leaders, including a future Prime Minister, John Vorster, were interned for pro-Nazi activity including sabotage of Allied troop trains. Ben Schoeman, later a Cabinet minister for twenty-six years, had said in 1940: 'The whole future of Afrikanerdom is dependent on a German victory.' A German U-boat submarine abortively landed a former Afrikaner South African boxing champion on the west coast, having trained him in sabotage – he was arrested and jailed.

But his dad insisted Walter continue with his studies and wouldn't allow him to enlist until he turned eighteen at the end of 1942. He matriculated with a First Class Secondary School Certificate at the end of 1941, including a Distinction in art. His dad, struck by his artistic ability, had already encouraged him to train as an architect and Walter went from school to work as an architectural assistant for Pretoria municipality during the day, studying in the evening for the five-year degree in architecture for which he had been accepted at Johannesburg's Witwatersrand University.

A year later, now aged eighteen and enjoying his work and studying, he was still determined to serve in the war. Eager to realise his dream of becoming a fighter pilot, he went early in 1943 to Waterkloof military airfield outside Pretoria. The normal tests began encouragingly well. Then, abruptly, his dream was shattered. A test found him unable to distinguish some colours – a form of colour blindness – which barred him from being a pilot. It was a savage blow – made worse since it was so unexpected. He hadn't been aware of his impairment before. Bafflingly, he was an excellent artist and nobody else had ever noticed it either. Utterly bereft, he didn't wait for a bus and walked ten miserable miles home, feeling it was the end of his world.

His father, however, who had enlisted at the start of the war and was now a captain in the Engineers at Sonderwater east of Pretoria, said there was a shortage of signallers and suggested he should join the Signal Corps. So he went to the recruiting office, meeting up there with an old school friend, Brian Blignaut, who also decided to become a signaller. Brian was six feet four inches tall and Walter ended up referring to him as 'Loftus', later to become his army nickname.

After eventually being accepted into the army aged eighteen at the beginning of 1943, Walter received basic training at Potchefstroom and then at various locations in Natal, with his friends Loftus and Pete de Klerk. Then they left Durban docks on a troop ship, the converted French luxury liner *Ile de France,* on 30 April 1943, arriving in Egypt at Suez a fortnight later. Serious overcrowding on board meant that, once the ship started rolling in heavy seas, the rail was lined with men throwing up over the side. Serried ranks also about to throw up stood a few paces behind; as soon as convulsions seized one of the latter he would shout a warning, and someone bending over the rail would step aside as he flung himself forward to puke.

When they landed, an overnight troop train infested with bugs carried them to Cairo where Walter was excited to see the pyramids towering outside the city. Still aged only eighteen, it seemed like a real adventure as his train journey continued south along the river Nile to Khatatba in the desert outside Helwan. Here he was to be trained as a radio operator in the 14th South African Signals Brigade. After he and his friends had completed their training they were posted to the Royal Natal Carbineers (RNC), in C Company.

Army life, especially in a north African Arab country, was an eye-opener for the teenager, innocent in many ways and even unworldly. Walter's was very much a *boy's* upbringing – girls were almost a foreign species, to be respected but not touched. Unlike his friends he was also teetotal and did not smoke.

They were able to visit Cairo quite often, including its ancient wonders, and were intrigued by the soldiers' frequent haunt, the local brothel, 'Sister Street'. They hadn't been inside one before and decided to investigate why it had a reputation for being notorious, discovering a walkway in front of a line of prostitutes' rooms, with women sitting outside dressed only in panties, as customers circulated to make their choices and be taken inside. Walter certainly wasn't intending *that*, but as the friends walked along, one of the women reached out and snatched off his army cap. She quickly turned to take it inside but he grabbed it back and they made a hasty retreat – a narrow escape, his relief palpable.

More appropriately, his older brothers Bill and Tom had been to Alexandria for a weekend where they had met some British army girls and taken them to the beach for a swim. They gave the girls' names to Walter and he and Loftus and Pete did the same, enjoying the platonic outing. Walter's other strong memory from the resort was encountering a mystery fitting in the bathrooms at their small hotel; they had not the faintest idea what a bidet was for.

His training and preparation over, he was ready and excited about the prospect of action: *this* was what he had come for. His unit left Port Said on 12 April 1944 on the ship *Ascania*, landing at Taranto on the southern tip of Italy on 21 April and proceeding to Gravina. A week later they left for Boiano, south east of the raging battle at Cassino, arriving there on 1 May. The Allied advance had been halted there for four months of carnage and his battalion moved into a holding position, relieving a Canadian division just outside the town on 4 May.

Cassino mountain towered above them, commanding the town at its foot and providing observations of the country for some ten miles around. A famous Benedictine monastery, the Abbey of Monte Cassino, crowned the peak like a sheer rock outcrop. German forces were entrenched all the way up the steep mountain sides and in the town itself, mercilessly pounding Allied forces.

On 11 May the final assault on Cassino began in

earnest. Now nineteen, Walter joined his unit in the Allied line on 15 May. On the night before the foremost infantry units filtered silently back to a safety line and from 8.30 on the morning of the 15 May, Allied bombing of the town, mountain and monastery began – by noon, when it ceased, some 500 aircraft had dropped more than 1,000 tons of bombs. Only then did the Allies begin advancing into the town and up the mountain, in the face of still very determined resistance from enemy machine gunners and snipers, rain after dusk washing some of the blood away. All hell had broken loose.

Although still high on the adrenalin of innocence, and based in a holding position back from the front, young Walter was astounded by the scale of the action to the fore, planes continuously overhead, the thumping of bombs and the billowing smoke. Exhilarated in anticipation of his first experience of action, his nervousness was dulled by the proverbial predicament of the army private – lots of hanging around and little information. Long, long hours dragged by.

But the rebellious streak which always lurked underneath his polite, respectful exterior prevailed as it invariably did. In contravention of army regulations – which forbade keeping a diary as a potential source of intelligence if captured – he maintained a detailed, well-written one, made more captivating by his beautiful pencil sketches of places, people and incidents. His handwriting was painstakingly clear and neat, often in pencil (he always kept one on his person). 'I went up and joined our troops in the line. We were in prepared positions which Allied troops had occupied for months, there was a lot of rubbish and debris around, no showers or latrines and the place smelt.' He was on the reverse slope of a hill and incoming shells 'ripped over us'.

By 18 May both Cassino town and mountain had been taken, the medieval monastery destroyed, and the successful Allied advance towards Rome began – but at an appalling cost to the Allies. In this battle for Cassino about 200,000 Allied men – including British, Americans, New Zealanders, French, Poles, Indians and Gurkhas – were either killed or wounded. (German fatalities were around 25,000.) It was certainly the most brutal single conflict in the entire war.

A week later he was withdrawn to Fernelli and 'had porridge with milk for the first time for a week'. Thankful he had not been advanced enough for the four months of slaughter which finally pushed the Germans out of Cassino, Walter was now in the RNC Support Company's Bren gun carrier platoon. The lightly-armoured carriers, used mainly for reconnaissance, were small, roofless, tracked vehicles, driver and Bren gunner in the front and one seat on each side of the engine in the back. As a radio operator, Walter travelled with his Number 22 set in the back of the platoon commander's carrier.

The roadsides had been strewn with mines by the retreating enemy and he was shocked that the towns they entered were so battered as to be scarcely habitable. On 3 June they parked next to an artillery battery and incoming German shells blew up one of their parked carriers, fortunately empty. Next day, the Americans took Rome, and on 6 June – 'D Day' of the Allied Normandy beach landings – Walter's carrier moved through Rome, the 'populace lining roads and cheering, a very clean, fine city with very good-looking women'. Rome, he noted, was known as the 'Open City' because its irreplaceable historic heritage encouraged an agreement between the Allies and Germans not to fight in it.

They moved thirty miles north on the Via Flaminia to Civita Castellana, the first of series of walled towns on hills, surrounded by lush ravines. The main road through, he noted, consisted of 'old, rendered, colour-washed buildings with curved tiles on the roofs, balconies and flower boxes everywhere'. Then they came upon Viterbo, its medieval centre preserved within a stone wall, sitting astride a hill with long views of the plains and lakes around.

No engagement yet with the Germans retreating along towards Florence. But on the twisty road down from Montefiascone, another typical hilltop town, was Lake Bolsena, ringed by hills, a cacophony of croaking frogs and 'knocked out Panther and Tiger tanks that lined the road on the west side of the lake'.

Continuing north through sunken, leafy lanes, they

were now on the tail of the Germans, in a 'Bren gun carrier probing gingerly forward to make contact with the enemy'. In the rolling country near Belvedere, they stopped up some little tracks to replenish energy in a splendid captured farmhouse which he sketched. Afterwards they drove past the position where 'a Spandau scythed down seven comrades from D Company' who had taken some prisoners in the engagement. They slept nearby and he recorded: 'Dead Jerry aged 18 lying in the trees. Two German prisoners buried him. Grave too short so they jumped on his ankles until these broke then stuffed his feet in. His cross said "Died for Greater Germany".'

The weather was warm and fair throughout his period of action in Italy over the summer and into the autumn. But despite his keen eye for the greens of all shades in the sweep of hills and the kaleidoscope of colour – red poppies in field after field, bright flowers and bushes – the tempo of action left him little time to enjoy the beautiful countryside. Stunning Tuscany largely passed him by, the breathtaking Apennines with their little villages tucked away hardly registered.

On through twenty miles of twisting roads, action all around: one 'lot got mucked up', and he 'watched Jerries shelling a road and saw a despatch rider go for a loop' (crash and die). Nervous but pent up as they passed the hill-top town of Cetona, he 'sketched from atop the carrier' its distinctive town tower. In these comfortable little Umbrian towns life had been flowing gently by – as it had done for generations and would do again after the war – but now on 26 June in Chiusi there were 'shattered houses with outside walls blown away, bedding hanging out forlornly and personal possessions strewn obscenely around'. More action: 'Roy and Mac wounded.' But then an opportunity in the little town: 'Got some good books. (Also the diary in which am writing).' Two days later having left Chiusi, A Company 'had good show, killed 8 and took 11 prisoners, lost 2 killed'. Despite the ferocity and killing around him, these diary entries were factual, rarely revealing Walter's emotions: that was not what traditionally brought-up boys like him *did*. But the customary neat writing, flowing prose and regular, conscientious entries revealed a characteristic orderliness, an organised mind.

Pushing forward in pursuit of fleeing German forces, he called by regional headquarters, pleased to see his brothers Tom and Bill (signallers with an artillery unit). Then on 3 July he was transferred from the Bren gun carriers to C Company signals team with his new signals partner, Letsie. However, that partnership was sadly all too brief. On 9 July, Letsie 'copped it'. But fate had been on Walter's side as it was to remain throughout the weeks ahead.

> Letsie and I went to have a bath at a little village, Rapale. Letsie washed. When he'd finished I took the bath round the corner to fill it at the well. As I was pumping the first shell landed – didn't hear the explosion as much as the shrapnel whistling everywhere. I dived next to the wall. Masonry tumbled down

> just behind me. When all quiet I shot round the corner to find Letsie being attended to by a medical orderly – a shell had sliced off one leg above the shin and he was in a lot of pain. There were two men unconscious in the rubble – heard later they had died. Slept in the rain. Jerry shelled us at about 2 in the morning.

In action, Walter's company consisted of three platoons (8, 9 and 10) – the soldiers who actually did the fighting – and a headquarters section (HQ). This had a commander (a major), an intelligence officer (Stan Jones) who carried the maps and orders for attacks and a two-man signals team, Walter and Loftus (who had now taken Letsie's place), to keep the major in touch both with battalion HQ and with his platoons through Lanky. In normal action the HQ section was out of sight of the enemy and did not receive small arms fire, though it did receive shell and mortar fire. The signals team radio came in two sections which had to be connected up, together with a heavy car-sized battery, headphones, microphone and tubular steel aerials. When it was being taken into action, Loftus carried the larger section on his back and Walter the smaller one, with the battery, other bits and his rifle in his hands. When not being carried this radio set was in the major's Jeep as were Loftus and Walter. Lanky's set was a one-piece, smaller and carried on his back.

In the days that followed the loss of Letsie, Walter travelled in the major's Jeep with his radio, repeatedly recording '*deadly*', with colleagues killed or wounded. The

Germans were still being pushed back, but were resisting all the way. Most of the time he wasn't sure what was happening. He was carrying on, doing his duty. But there was danger around every corner, up every rise, down every valley. At Panzano, in slitties they had dug next to the Jeep: 'Tanks above road. Bazooka & spandau on corner. Shelling quite close. Spent chunk hit my book about 6 inches from Lanky's face, another ricocheted off left front wheel past my face into ground beside Lanky.' Still more fighting and horror as the days in late July flew by. 'Smith hit, Corbett and McMorran badly … Next day [26th] quiet – Sonny got hit … 27th Benny wounded, Johnny and Red badly wounded, Pete Beaton killed outright.'

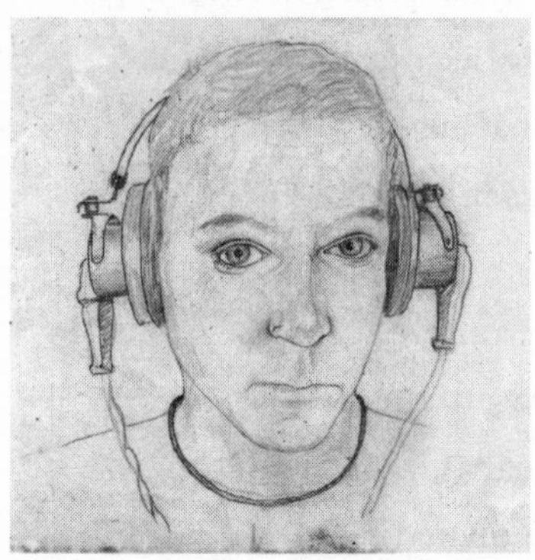

Self-portrait aged nineteen as radio operator, 18 July 1944.

Then – some relief, and also a delight: '4 Aug: climbed on top of pt.350 and had first look at Florence.' It had been a place of awe from his art courses at school. Three days later, three weeks' rest: visiting Siena, another captivating place for the young soldier. Afterwards 'lazed around and cleaned and serviced truck. Got pinched by the RP Sgt for firing shots from captured Mauser without permission. The RSM just warned us. Got two letters from Mom – a treat.'

On leave he was thrilled to visit Rome.

> Went up to the Sistine Chapel and saw Michelangelo's wonderful frescoes on the ceiling. They seem to stand out in a 3 dimensional way, heaps better than the reproductions one sees … went to see the Colosseum and clambered all over it. It was very interesting and jolly impressive. In the afternoon saw 'A Canterbury Tale', excellent film. Went to see *Aida* at Opera that night but didn't enjoy it much as all dialogue was in Italian.

Back on duty on 24 August, they 'took over from the Yanks' and based themselves at Podere Campolivo, a farmhouse near 'Caruso's Castle'. This was a palatial building once owned by the world-famous Italian tenor Enrico Caruso, and C Company's 10 Platoon was based there. When a company was stationary for some time (as was C in this position), battalion HQ signallers would lay telephone cables along the ground to company HQ whose signallers did the same to their platoons, with communication by telephone rather than radio. Thus at Campolivo Walter's and Lanky's time was taken up with laying telephone lines to the platoons, then going out to repair the many breaks in these caused by what seemed like constant attacks from shells. There were casualties and deaths on both sides: 'We had to "keep our head and eyes moving" – as it's quite scary.'

Moving on, they waded across the river Arno and on 2 September found 'good grapes and some lovely pears'. Then, on the way up past Empoli and on to Vinci, they took over a house 'where a girl in white raincoat was. She had many admirers but unfortunately she left.' Next day, 8 September, they occupied another house. 'Went for a walk that evening. Country very hilly and looked beautiful in the afternoon sunlight.' Five days later, well north of Pistoia, 'had a lot of trouble laying a line to 8 platoon when a spandau fired. We got down quickly, then a burst of fire "rrr…rip" then "clack-ack-ack-ack" as Lanky accelerated. We did not linger.'

Amid the gruelling action, their lines constantly shelled and needing incessant repairs and re-laying, he was allowed a day off in Florence on 23 September. 'Saw the cathedral. Stood on the bank of the Arno near Ponte Vecchio, bridges on either side blown.[‡] Man in a skiff sculled gracefully along amid all the shambles.'

‡ The medieval Ponte Vecchio, originating from Roman times, was not destroyed by Germans during their retreat of 4 August 1944, unlike all other bridges in Florence, allegedly because of an express order by Hitler.

But, within a month, the almost-charmed life Walter seemed to have lived amid all the death and injury swirling around him very nearly came to an end.

On 2 October 1944 'moved up at about 5 in the morning through the small village of Castiglione dei Pepoli', passing the gentle glade in which, forty years later, he would discover an immaculate South African cemetery had been erected to house so many of the army comrades now with him.

On Monte Stanco death nearly got him. But, before that, they had come upon a church standing proud on its own in Vigo, on the way 'cleaning up' some Germans. In the tiny rural church, he 'got some big candles' and saw 'two SS officers, one very haughty though shot through the shoulder. The other shot through the cheeks with great gobs of blood and spit on his chest, moaning in a bewildered, animal-like way.'

They moved towards the small Stanco mountain on 10 October, only too aware that a German SS infantry battalion was holding it. An Indian regiment had tried and failed to capture the stronghold. Now it was C Company's turn. One of their platoons was ahead on top of Stanco and

> chowed [killed] spans of SS who they said came walking towards them saying 'Surrender Tommies. Hitler will treat you well'. Thought they were drugged. We went up and parked until our other platoons had gone into a casa (at the foot of Stanco). Mortars came over all

> the time and fell quite close. As we came up the slope towards the casa through the vines, a Spandau opened up on Lanky and Loftus and I. We all fell flat and tried to go straight down into the earth (Loftus had the 22 set strapped to his back, I had the 22 power pack and was carrying the battery and aerial tubes, Lanky had his 21 set strapped to his back). Lanky said he was hit then said 'No', and got up and jolled [jogged] for the casa and got there OK. Then Loftus hopped up. They gave him a burst and a wine wire caught under the 22 radio on his back and whipped him to the ground. I thought he'd been chowed but they missed him. He hopped up again and ran for the casa. I got up and hammed and they gave me a burst – I felt something slam me and the other shots from the burst seemed to press past me.

The sheer impact of the bullet knocked him to the ground. Confusion – but all too quick to be terrified, or to understand.

> I yelled to Lanky I'd been tonked and he came running back to help me but I found I was OK and told him just to show me a clear space through the wire. Then I got up and jolled, zigzagging along and they left me alone. I climbed through a window into a bedroom in the casa, a wounded German on the bed in a bad state and one of ours also wounded on the floor.

Then – an explanation for his narrow escape: 'I found the Spandau bullet in my emergency bully beef tin in my Tommy pouch (over my heart), with the tip of the bullet bent'. Although its force had tumbled him over, the bullet had been blocked in the corned beef tin, miraculously saving his life.

Action at Monte Stanco.

No time to reflect or to worry, because their advance platoon had been 'shoved off Stanco' and they were told to pull out. But a German sniper was firing at the only door they could get out of.

> We called for a tonk on our casa then closed up shop. Cellier the Bren gunner fired some bursts and we went out one by one and gathered behind the casa, where we were hidden from the Germans on the hill. They took a shot at me as I rushed out and it went past my head. Then we all started to joll back and they were shooting at us. I could see little wavy blue smoke lines in the grass in front of me where the bullets were hitting. It was really quite amusing (the whole mob careering across this field, discarding bits of equipment – Brens, Tommies, small packs etc – as they ran). Lanky took a mad tumble and I thought he'd been tonked but he'd only tripped and hopped up again. I was bloody tired with the 22 power pack, battery, aerials and telephones. We ran past a dead Indian, struggled up over the road til we got behind a rise then up over a little gnoll. Then something burst about 1 yard ahead of me on the path. I just saw a flurry in the sand then a hole appeared. It blew the aerials out of my hand, missed Lanky ahead of me and a flat piece bounced off Loftus's neck cutting it a bit (probably a rifle grenade). We dug in for that night.

Three days later on 13 October two other South African regiments acting together finally pushed the enemy off Stanco and it was taken, despite a lone Spandau still firing. 'The field we'd run over looked like a real battleground with equipment strewn everywhere.' A few days later, on the road to the village of Grizzana Morandi, he was 'molto paura' (very scared) by dozens of phosphorus shells and 17 October was

> a lousy day. Luckily had slitties dug for us. There were shells coming in like an express train. You'd hear them coming, reach their highest altitude then descend near us with a terrific rush and one killed Sgt Taffy – a good bloke. I was shit scared as you could hear the Spandaus going and mortars arriving – I was very pleased I was a radio operator and not an infantryman.

In slit trench, reporting over radio the Germans shelling Grizzana.

Now came the fateful day on 21 October 1944 at point 806 on Monte Pezza. 'At 0400 hrs we moved past D Company and took over. The slitties were delightful. Loftus and Lanky were on the sets so I laid a line back. Then Lanky and I (who were sharing a wide slittie) started improving our one.' They settled down to sleep. Suddenly 'at about 12 o'clock a piece of shell tonked me in the leg (having come through the access opening in the roof near our feet). The wound was in the right groin. I took my shell dressing and put it on my leg.' Lanky was screaming. 'I pulled him back into the slittie. Couldn't see any blood or anything on Lanky but he was moaning. Tried propping him up this way and that but all ways hurt. Then James and Dutch arrived and gave him morphia but made no difference.' Stretcher-bearers took Lanky away and Walter limped painfully to the medical centre at Casa Ruzzone. 'Passed stretcher-bearers having a breather and they said Lanky was dead.'

The blunt way they told him did not make it any easier to absorb. Why Lanky? There, right next to him in the slittie? The deaths and injuries to comrades in action swirling around him over the last weeks seemed to have escalated. Shells and machine gun fire had brushed by him. A bullet aiming at his heart had lodged millimetres away in the corned beef tin. Uncannily, he always seemed to have been in just about the right place at the right time to miss injury or death. But now he had been wounded and, appallingly, his mate killed. Of course he knew when he enlisted that war was dangerous. But he never really thought it would happen to him.

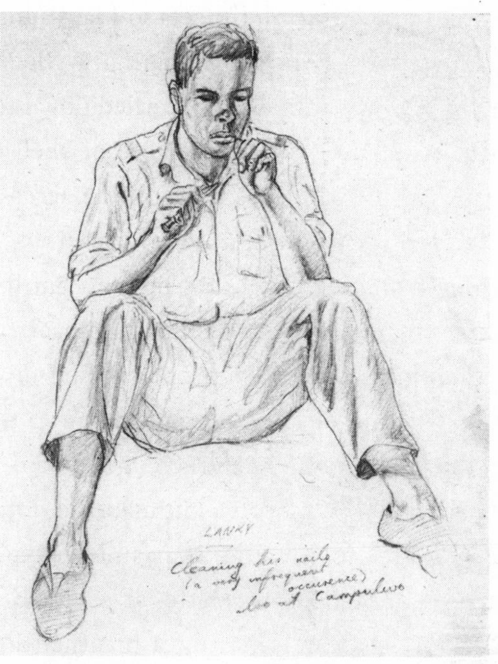

Lanky Brasler, later killed next to Walter.

Shivering, dazed and in a state of shock, at the medical centre he was given a new dressing and some hot tea. Then he was directed into an ambulance bound first for Grizzana. The intelligence officer Stan Jones had been very badly wounded and was in the same ambulance but died before they reached the hospital, just seeming to drift away on the journey – a second, terrible shock for Walter. Then he was transferred to a second ambulance to Castiglione and a third – 'tried to swass [urinate] in the ambulance but it hurt' – to the South African General Hospital at Florence. 'They put me into bed. Tried to swass again as I was full but hurt myself and yelled so a nurse came and gave me an injection.' He was desperately anxious: how badly was he injured? 'At about 0400 hrs on 22nd I went into theatre (operated on – they put a catheter through my belly into my bladder – the quack [doctor] called it my "super pubic" – with the other end into a bottle to relieve me).'

Eventually, after being moved by ambulance first to Arezzo then to Rome, respite at last:

> Went to theatre twice, bottle removed and started walking. (The piece of shrapnel had entered in my groin and penetrated into the pelvis, missing everything important on the way. The surgeon decided it would do no harm leaving it where it was rather than trying to remove it.)[‡]

After time first in a convalescent depot, a transit camp outside Rome (where he was able to enjoy evenings and afternoons in the city), then at Santa Barbara with the Reserves and again the 13th Brigade signals squadron

‡ Fifty-seven years later, Walter felt an uncomfortable lump protruding from the skin near his back passage, and a British surgeon discovered and removed the shrapnel: apparently it had travelled right down from his pelvis.

about ten miles outside Florence, Walter was assigned to the Natal Mounted Rifles (a tank regiment turned into infantry) at Bagnolo. His friends Loftus and Pete visited him there and he went on two manoeuvres.

Infantry going in on tank.

Now, however, severe winter months had halted the Allied advance in the Apennines south of Bologna. He was billeted outside Florence in a large house owned by a wealthy family. It was snowing and he drew their tanks parked up and covered in white. With other troops, Walter was sleeping on the first floor and, to avoid the chore of finding a toilet, they urinated out of the window leaving little steaming holes in the snow lying on the ground, years later the source of one of his many army sayings: 'like piss holes in the snow'.

Afterwards the advance began again and he moved up towards Gardaletta where he saw Allied planes bombing the enemy. Accelerating northward, destruction was everywhere. 'Every house along the road to Bologna had been attended to by Yank bombers and all the fields were pitted with craters – they simply saturated the whole countryside.' North of the city, they parked up for the night:

> Either side of the road in beautiful fields in bright moonlight. Convoys were coming down the road with lights on, suddenly the rip of a Spandau burst. Lights out, screaming of tyres as brakes hastily applied. Had a couple of Jerry planes messing around all night. I was very jittery – heard a plane coming down towards us so got out of bed and sauntered towards a dyke, ostensibly to have a swass. Suddenly plane was on top of us, so I ran through pool and crouched against dyke wall. As the machine passed over me at about 50 feet it opened up with cannon firing over us at the road – I almost went into the dyke like a mole from fright.

They crossed the river Po and pushed on, racing forward with the German forces fleeing rather than fighting. Through flat country divided by small canals with trees planted along them, they pushed towards Venice, and 'peasants lined roads, cheered and dished out eggs like good things'.

Infantry moving up front.

No longer the deadening apprehension of conflict, in the days that followed there was time for a quick enjoyable look at Venice – another icon from his school studies – and later a trip round Lake Como.

On 'the night of 8 May 1945, Victory in Europe Day, there were celebratory tracers going up into the sky' and they left that night for Monza in a very slow, nose-to-tail convoy. Walter 'drove all night and at about 0300 fell asleep and hit a tree. If I hadn't hit the tree we would have gone over the edge into a huge ditch about 10ft deep which ran beside the road.' Fortunately nobody was hurt: 'the only damage was a bust spring'.

Then, 'the Monza Victory Parade – I wasn't on it', and a stay at Monte Grappa military barracks in Turin where he was delighted to be reunited again with friends Loftus and Pete.

The war over, they waited to go home, frequently visiting the seaside resort of Rapallo, once for a week's leave in a rest hotel, the Albergo Grande Italia.

> Had wonderful 3-tonner rides down as the drivers used to give it big stick. The truck would be going flat out at about 60 when one of the blokes in the back would lean forward and shout through to the driver, 'what's the matter, is the petrol stuck?' The cry was always 'Faster!'

In Rapallo his friends persuaded him to try some alcohol for the first time in his life; it wasn't too bad, he thought. They also 'met fine mob of girls' from well-off families, one with a holiday home in the resort. His Italian improved rapidly and he was introduced to some of their parents, one an Englishwoman. When they called at her summer house in Rapallo Walter danced (for the very first time) with the girls and they all swam together in the warm Mediterranean Sea, having great fun in a platonic, innocent way. He had never had much contact with girls before. Their strict upper-middle-class parents would never normally have permitted their daughters to consort with Italian soldiers ranked as mere privates. But when they discovered Walter had embarked upon an architectural degree and his friend Pete de Klerk was a teacher, that professional standing made them 'suitable company' for their girls.

Assigned to guard duty for two weeks in Rapallo, he 'had good fun as the girls used to come and visit us at the door to Divisional HQ. (Once I gave Mara my rifle to hold for a few moments, to the consternation of everyone in sight!)' Finally, on hearing they were leaving for home, 'kissed the girls goodbye – the first time we'd kissed them!'

He had carried a rifle throughout the war, having been trained in the desert, but never fired a shot in anger. Leaving by train down Italy to Taranto,

> crossed the Med on *Medina Victory* – Yank ship, fine grub, fine conditions. Landed Port Said where Wogs (Egyptians) talked to us in Italian. Helwan for a month (over Christmas and my twenty-first birthday). Then to Cairo West and home by Dak (Dakota aircraft) stopping overnight at Kampala and landing at Waterkloof airfield north of Pretoria. Mom and Dad and Auntie Alice were there to meet me.

There 'Italy Diary 1944/45 – W. V. Hain' ends. And with it his great and searing adventure – the war that so nearly cost him the life that it cost many of his soldier comrades. But also the war that was a profoundly formative experience for the now 21-year-old man, both changing him and enlarging his perspective on life to one so much broader than that of a home-grown, young, white South African.

In 1996, again retracing his route to Point 806 where Lanky had died and he was wounded, he looked out eastward towards the A1 Florence–Bologna *autostrada* over foothills basking in the late afternoon sun. It was about the same time of day as he had 'limped down towards the road, passing fresh troops coming through to take the next peak Pt 826, looking over hills and valleys reverberating to the crash of explosions and seeing the smoke rising from the shellbursts'.

Would he have done it again? His reply was immediate and unequivocal: 'When there is such a war, then you have to be involved. It's your *duty*. Yes, I wouldn't have missed it.'

Downtime.

2

Settler

There were only slightest flickers in her upbringing to suggest Adelaine Stocks would become in her thirties the principal target for Pretoria's apartheid security police.

Her maternal great-great-grandfather came from Ireland – John Duffy of Dublin. Her great-great-grandmother came from England as one of the 1820 settlers who had left for a 'better life' which they had been told awaited them in the Eastern Cape. In fact, they were settled on land from which 20,000 Xhosa people were driven by the British army – a ruthless and brutal exercise by the British which has been described as 'the first great "removal" in South African history'. The settlers were meant to act as a kind of buffer against still independent local chiefdoms and the colonists in the expanding Cape Colony.

Adelaine's forebears among the '1820 settlers' landed at Port Arthur, later to become Port Alfred. They were a hardy group with a pioneering spirit, surviving first the long crossing by ship and then the hazard and toil of making a new life in harsh surroundings.

Nearly two centuries before, the first permanent Dutch settlers from Europe had landed at what became Cape Town in 1652. They rapidly adopted the nomadic farming methods of the locals and had moved 600 miles along the south east coastline of Africa by the time the British arrived. As British settlement increased after Britain annexed the Cape in 1806, conflicts over land, resources and power intensified – both with African communities and with the Afrikaans-speaking whites. Afrikaners – descendants of the earlier Dutch, German and French Huguenot settlers – began 'the great *trek*' north from the Cape into the Orange Free State and the Transvaal. Known as the *Voortrekkers* (fore-marchers), they drove with their livestock into the heart of South Africa in search of more land and independence, in turn displacing and violently subjugating African communities.

Conflicts with the British spawned a fierce Afrikaner nationalism with a deep and enduring resentment of their English-speaking compatriots. Two bloody Anglo-Boer Wars occurred in 1880–81 and 1899–1902, during which 26,000 Afrikaner women and children died in British concentration camps. Eventually, to end the civil war within the white population and to ensure control, both over the African populations and the fabulous diamond and gold reserves which had meanwhile been discovered in the Highveld areas, South Africa was granted self-government under British rule in 1910.

After the 1820 settlers had established themselves, Adelaine's paternal grandfather, Richard Stocks, arrived with his two brothers from the Devizes area of Wiltshire and settled in Grahamstown, a frontier trading and market community inland from Port Alfred, founded in 1812.

It was named after a British colonel, John Graham, who had 'cleared' the area of the Xhosa with methods which were efficient, but savage. The locals were shot on sight. 'This is detestable work ... we are forced to hunt them like wild beasts,' Graham noted. With broad tree-lined streets and a Memorial Tower commemorating the 1820 settlers, Grahamstown had, and still does have, a very English feel. Unlike in England, where most towns have a Victorian 'High Street', Grahamstown's is the only traditional 'High' in South Africa. Its elegant nineteenth- and early twentieth-century Pre-Renaissance shop facades have canopies and cast-iron supports. In the town stands South Africa's oldest official letter box, painted the traditional British Post Office red, a make of pillar box manufactured in the late 1850s.

Richard Stocks eventually started his own large department store in the town. He married Agnes Stirk, whose family were also 1820 settlers and had a large hardware store in the same street, and they had a son, Adelaine's father Gerald. After his schooling, Gerald travelled to London to train as a draper and when Adelaine was young he told her stories of the store, explaining that the women assistants came from England where they had trained in the trade, their dresses graceful with sweeping trains.

Having met in Grahamstown, Adelaine's mother Edith and Gerald got married in Cape Town where they began life together. He was serving in the First World War and they moved home periodically, settling first in Grahamstown and then finally over thirty miles down a steep winding road to the coast at Port Alfred. The small seaside town had been first established in the early 1820s by British settlers moved into the area by the Governor of the Cape Colony, Lord Charles Somerset. It was later named after Queen Victoria's son Prince Alfred.

Adelaine's father was farming there when she was born on 16 February 1927 in a little nursing home, the sixth of seven children. Afterwards he became a building contractor and the family moved to a small house he later extended called Mentone, on the banks of the Kowie River upstream outside Port Alfred.

Living in Mentone until aged nineteen, she had a happy childhood, centred on the river. At a very early age her mother taught both Adelaine and sister Josephine (Jo), eighteen months younger, to swim by holding them under their chins. Soon they were squelching their way through the muddy riverbank below their home and into the water all on their own. They quickly learnt to dive off the wooden landing which jutted out from their front lawn, or climb from it into boats tethered at the end. And later they joined their older brothers and sister swimming, boating, canoeing and adventuring in the Kowie. Their brothers built rough canoes from a corrugated iron sheet, folding it around half-circular wooden blocks at both ends and nailing it on; the girls shrieked delightedly as they paddled into the fast-flowing river, constantly bailing out water leaking in. Once, her father laboriously reeled in what seemed like an enormous catch until out of the water emerged one of these sunken canoes with a catfish on the end of the line trapped inside. Both parents took part in many of their activities, her father Gerald teaching cricket to other older children who came to play with her brothers after school.

He became affectionately known as a local character. When fishing at night in winter he used to cast out a line and then insert his fishing rod through the living room window, put the ratchet on and lean it against the window sill so he could sit in the warmth around the fire with his family; when he felt a bite he would go outside, retrieve the rod and reel in a fish. Unlike Adelaine's mother Edith, a strict Christian Scientist, Gerald was more free spirited, smoked Springbok cigarettes and liked the odd drink, his favourite a brandy.

Their home was close to those of Coloured families. These were the pre-apartheid days of the 1930s: there was certainly a deep and historic racial divide with whites very much in charge, but it was not as rigid or harsh as later under apartheid. Coloured children even attended Adelaine's school, Queen Alexandra Secondary School, which took in ages seven to sixteen. Up the hill near Mentone she remembered a Coloured woman lived with her white husband.

All her dad's workers – bricklayers, plumbers and carpenters – were Coloured. So it was natural to be mixing with them, including playing together with their children. Xhosa-speaking Africans walked on the road passing their house en route to the small seaside town, their singing very distinctive and melodic to the fascinated and growing Adelaine. From the African location across the river, she would also hear their singing carrying across the water. She grew up very aware of the different cultures of her country and had no instinct for the racial superiority gaining ground among fellow whites.

Although no academic high-flyer, she was bright at school and, for some reason, quite independently minded. Moving to the very English Victoria Girls High School in Grahamstown to take higher school qualifications, she and her younger sister Jo were boarders. When she was a school senior she was elected prefect and head of her school house, Barnard. Always thought to be a bit of a rebel, it was a family joke that she won a 'deportment girdle' for 'good general behaviour and good deportment'.

Two of her school teachers made a formative impression on the young Adelaine, each communicating in different ways to her that everyone should be treated equally. Mrs Powell, the school music and singing teacher at Queen Alexandra, was a plump, large woman who habitually wore a long cardigan with pockets stretching down past her hips. When she was aged about eight Adelaine first heard a gramophone recording of Paul Robeson, the black American singer-actor, played to her class by Mrs Powell, who deliberately asked the children to say who they thought he was. When nobody knew, she said that he was 'a native', meaning he was black, and that he was also a film star from America: a subtle message to her pupils that blacks could be more than equal to whites. This made a huge impression on the young Adelaine: she thought the singing was beautiful, such a warm and deep voice.

Later when she was at Victoria Girls High in Grahamstown, she heard that the film *Sanders of the River* starring Paul Robeson was showing in Port Alfred's cinema. Because she was away with no access to a telephone, Adelaine wrote urging her mother Edith to see it for her. Her mother at first said she wouldn't feel comfortable seeing a black man singing on the screen. But when Adelaine replied firmly and quoted her mother's religious belief as an intense Christian Scientist that 'all of us are children of God', her mother was persuaded to see the film. Edith was quietly impressed and they talked about it when Adelaine came home during the subsequent school holiday. What a lovely voice and smile Robeson had, her mother said, admitting how glad she was to have seen it.

A second influential teacher was Miss Druce, whom Adelaine remembered as having 'communist leanings'. Jewish, plain and stout, she used to invite senior boarder girls to listen to classical music in her sitting room/study and, while telling them about the music, quietly spoke about her belief in racial equality. This again made a lasting impression on teenage Adelaine, who was also intrigued that a couple of girls in her group proudly stated they were from 'left-wing' families, explaining to her what they thought that meant.

She soon found herself having arguments with other school friends about whether blacks should be treated properly. Taking a literal interpretation of the Bible in line with her Christian Science upbringing, she challenged her classmates: 'Why shouldn't people be treated equally? Why can't everyone go to the same cinemas?'

'But they *smell!*' her classmates retorted.

'So would *you* if you had to live in dreadful conditions without facilities to wash like *they* are forced to!' she replied sharply.

Her father Gerald was by then prominent in the Port Alfred district of the Eastern Cape branch of the mainly English-speaking United Party. It had dominated South African politics for a generation and was led by the wartime hero and Prime Minister, Jan Smuts. Although in opposition to the National Party, it was built on similar white supremacist foundations, and its paternalistic policies never envisaged black South Africans getting the vote.

Adelaine gained a feel for politics by sometimes accompanying her dad to public meetings, on one occasion startling everyone by challenging the visiting United Party MP, Tom Bowker, from the meeting floor about a statement he had made suggesting 'we should do what Smuts says', feeling that this was not very democratic. Afterwards, when Bowker returned to spend the night at their home, she continued a lively discussion over dinner. Her father was taken aback, but never forgot – indeed rather admired – his teenage daughter's spark.

Her first job after leaving school was working for the town's community news-sheet (to which her dad, active on local issues, contributed), staffing the tiny office, and learning and acquiring basic secretarial skills. She typed the newsletter on wax sheets and printed it off on a small duplicating machine. Adelaine also wrote news snippets of town events told through the eyes of two fictional local boys – her stories gaining a popular following, readers even enquiring where the boys lived. She was therefore the more politically aware with some of the basic arts of political organising when, aged twenty-one, she married Walter, two years older, in Pretoria on 1 September 1948.

Wartime acquaintances brought them together. Adelaine became friendly with a young man called Gordon

Boyack. He had spent some years in a German prisoner of war camp and, with his friend, Walter's brother Tom, visited Port Alfred on holiday. Tom had served with her brothers in Abyssinia (Ethiopia) during the Second World War and, with Gordon, met Adelaine's father in the Port Alfred Golf Club. They were invited to the Stocks family home where they ended up spending much of their holiday, and Adelaine and Boyack became interested in each other.

He lived in Pretoria and she went on holiday later in the year to meet his family. The long journey up to the big city was her first ever away from her upbringing in the Eastern Cape. However, it didn't work out. She felt gauche, a small town girl who didn't fit into his family circle, and decided Gordon was not the person for her. But office skills gained working on the Kowie newsletter helped her get a job in the local United Building Society through her brothers, Hugh and Mike, who also lived in Pretoria.

Walter was in Gordon and Tom's circle, having returned from Italy early in 1946 to resume studies for his architectural degree at Witwatersrand University in Johannesburg, living there during the week and returning home to his parents in Pretoria at weekends.

Like his fellow ex-servicemen Gordon and his wartime comrade Loftus, also studying architecture, Walter was in receipt of an ex-soldier loan to cover their degree course fees and living costs. Living quarters had been provided for the students by transforming a temporary wartime hospital at Cottesloe, not too far from their university. Walter and Loftus travelled to Pretoria and back in Gordon's car, and spent the time there crammed into it with others, going to the cinema and various leisure pursuits, including dances.

He and nineteen-year-old Adelaine met when he accompanied his friends on a horse-riding outing. At first they were simply part of the group, squeezed into the car on trips around Pretoria. Soon they became great friends, though there was no visible sense of romance. But once, the car had to stop for Walter to get out and Adelaine was sitting next to him. 'Give him a kiss, Ad!' one of their friends urged. She did and rather enjoyed it – so did he.

Soon they realised that theirs was a much closer relationship. With the help of Wal's mother Mary, who found it, Ad moved to a room across the road from the Hain family home and was always popping in. Mary loved seeing her as she had never had a daughter of her own. Ad and Wal were growing much closer, enjoying each other's company. In 1947, Ad's holiday from the building society coincided with Wal's university vacation and they travelled down by train to Port Alfred – in different compartments for the 700-mile overnight journey, and in different bedrooms at her parental home. He was introduced to her parents. Wal played golf with her dad and teased her mother Edith a great deal – including about her strict Christian Science beliefs – which she rose to, loving his banter. There was a glut of guava fruit at the time and Edith made them stewed guavas, which to her delight Wal was always ready to eat at any time.

There was the occasional comical adventure too. Her dad's pre-war Morris car was prone to crises. Wal was at the wheel on the way to the beach with Ad in the front and her sister Jo in the back when he suddenly noticed one of its wheels rolling slowly past him. Apparently it had come loose – not to worry, his future father-in-law said, that happened from time to time. On another drive, coming down the slope into the small town, they heard a loud clanking. They stopped and found one of the front wheels was no longer connected to the steering rod – her dad's repair with a wire coat hanger had failed. Wal twisted the wire back into place and they limped back. Just routine for her dad: he airily tied it up with his handkerchief, pending something permanent.

But a year later their holiday periods clashed because Wal was working, and Ad travelled down on her own. Wal discovered he missed her desperately and wrote a series of letters in which he explained his feelings of emptiness and loss. The letters arrived one after the other, impressing her parents and her sister Jo.

On her return Wal picked her up at Pretoria station in his dad's car and told her he simply couldn't live without her. They had to get married – and right away. Ad had thought they might get engaged first, but Wal wasn't interested 'in all that palaver'. He had made up his mind. Marriage it was, and now.

'But we can't, we have nowhere to live!' Ad replied.

'Then we'll find somewhere,' he insisted.

They searched around and eventually found a place – though they had to occupy it without delay or lose the opportunity. So they applied for a special licence to get married at once. It cost £5 – a great deal of money in those days.

Although the registry office venue conformed with Wal's strong atheism, Ad didn't mind, despite remaining a regular at the local Christian Science church, with her mother Edith, brothers and elder sister especially devout.

But the attitude of Wal's mother Mary changed abruptly at the news. Her disapproval was transparent, apparently just as it had been when his eldest brother Bill got married. Ad was no longer the favoured surrogate daughter, but was taking her son away. It upset Ad greatly and she found it awkward to adjust, especially when Mary wouldn't even talk to her anymore when Ad and Wal called by; she didn't know quite how to handle it, comforted only that his mother's perverse reaction made Wal even more entrenched and determined to proceed.

When Mary discovered it wouldn't be a church marriage, she told her son: 'I won't come then.'

'In that case, don't,' Wal replied, ever stubbornly

strong-willed. (She did come but still wouldn't acknowledge or speak to them.)

When Ad confided to her own mother how difficult it had become, Edith was sympathetic but advised: 'Just keep trying and it will probably work out because remember, we all love Walter and she's his mother.'

His brother Tom, previously part of their close circle of friends, sided with his mother and suddenly would not talk to them either. Once he drove Ad and Wal to the local cinema, they all watched a film together and he drove them back without saying a single word, even getting lost on the way because he couldn't bring himself to ask for directions.

If 1948 when they were married proved a turning point in their lives, so too it was for the country of their birth after the general election that year. Segregation and white domination – which had come to influence every aspect of life in South Africa – soon became institutionalised in the hated system of *apartheid* (meaning 'separation') after the Afrikaner National Party won the election, ushering in probably the worst racist tyranny the world has ever witnessed.

Ad and Wal had both voted for the United Party of Jan Smuts – which amounted to choosing one set of racial supremacists sympathetic to Britain and its empire over another who were anti-British and more outspoken in their racism. The so-called 'Nats' would eventually lead South Africa out of the Commonwealth, and the newly-weds discovered that they both shared an instinctive distaste for the crude racism and brutal policies of the new rulers.

They had got married during Wal's 'practical year' as a university architectural student, while he was working in Pretoria at an architectural practice, and moved in together at a local boarding house. Their bedroom had a basin, but bathrooms and toilets were communal as were all meals.

However, when he returned to Johannesburg for his final year of studies, they moved into Cottesloe, the accommodation provided for ex-servicemen at 'Wits' University in which he had previously lived. Rooms had been converted off a long corridor with married quarters in the old staff residence, all meals again provided in a communal area. They lived there rent free as Wal had done as part of a loan which, with degree fees, needed to be repaid over a working life.

By now Ad had fallen pregnant and felt nauseous as she walked past the kitchen to their rooms. They were both excited and also nervous at the prospect of their first baby, though they hadn't made a conscious decision to have one: it was just the normal thing that happened to young wives in those days.

After his final year studying architecture in 1949, Wal searched for his first job. But South Africa was experiencing a building slump and he found the only one available was in Nairobi, Kenya – arranged for him by a partner in the firm in Pretoria for whom he had worked during his practical year.

Flying up there was familiar to Wal from his war service but a novelty to his young wife Ad, who had never left her homeland. Although she was eager to see what the rest of Africa might be like, air travel in those days was very basic and, nearly eight months pregnant, she found the bumpy flight uncomfortable. There was no toilet and she was sick, the air hostess fortunately understanding. She felt queasy when they came down on an airstrip for a toilet stop, walking across to basic toilets without running water, in shacks on the edge of the field. The journey from Johannesburg took two days and stopped overnight in Southern Rhodesia (Zimbabwe) at the capital, Salisbury (Harare), where there was an eye-opener: for the first time they saw black people sitting with friends in the lounge of the hotel where they stayed.

Settling in Kenya, then a British colony with a white ruling elite owning farms and other land expropriated long before from indigenous Africans, they discovered a society with racial divisions much less formalised and extreme than South Africa's – which again made a positive impression on them both, though the Mau Mau uprisings and a tough struggle for independence against fierce British resistance lay just ahead.

On 16 February 1950 – also Ad's birthday – Peter, the first of their four children, was born. It was a straightforward birth in Nairobi's Maia Carberry nursing home, white nurses delivering the baby with black assistants who tended to Ad, brought her food and cleaned her room. Husbands were strictly forbidden from being present for the birth.

Ad and Wal were both thrilled at their new arrival, discovering the delights – and the challenges, especially being isolated away from relatives – of youthful parenthood. She was then aged twenty-three and he twenty-five. Twenty-first-century parents living in modern societies would be horrified with what Ad had to put up with as normal: linen nappies which had to be hand washed, no wipes, none of the mod cons and no mother nearby to advise and help.

At Ngong, just outside Nairobi, they shared a number of *rondavels* (thatched, circular hut-houses) with Jock Barnes (a fellow South African who had been recruited like Wal to the same architectural firm), his wife Nicky and young son. They shared communal facilities for eating so they got to mix more than would otherwise have been the case, and got on very well. With what, in hindsight, may seem to have been uncanny prescience, Jock regularly told Wal: 'Hain, you are a friend of all the world.'

An Englishman called Smirthwaite, also living in their small community, struck up a bond and invited Ad and Wal to visit a settlement of *bandas* (*rondavels* with thatched roofs that extended outward to form circular verandas) belonging to the Kenyan Masai chiefdom.

Nomadic, thin and tall, the Masai were an enigma to so many whites. But Ad and Wal were intrigued, taking their six-week-old baby with them as Smirthwaite gave instructions. When the white visitors arrived, the Masai were intensely curious at their rarity, and captivated by the new baby. Suddenly Ad was confused: it seemed to be raining but the sky was bright and clear. Then Smirthwaite explained: the Masai were anointing the tiny baby in their traditional custom of spitting. Ad and Wal were exhilarated at this show of respect and intimacy.

It was pleasant enough living at Ngong, though Ad was horrified at the behaviour of a neighbour, a white Kenyan, when a black man knocked at their doors selling *mealies* (maize). The woman tried to beat the price down, exclaiming: 'After all *you* didn't grow the mealies, *God* did!' Ad and Wal were increasingly realising that they seemed to have different attitudes from other whites in Africa, as, they realised to their relief, did their friends Jock and Nicky Barnes.

'Kenya should learn from South Africa how to manage its natives,' one of the partners in the Kenya architectural practice where Wal worked told him at a staff party. An Englishman from India, the man had opposed Indian independence in 1947 and decided to relocate to Nairobi for his preference: still a British-controlled colony. They had a fierce argument over the man's offensive remark.

Wal also had little in common with him architecturally, finding both him and the firm as a whole far too old-fashioned in its approach to building design. Wal had formed fixed views that design should make use of modern methods and technology, not try to recreate old colonial structures. Partly because of this, Ad and Wal decided to return home to South Africa, and Wal arranged to rejoin the firm where he had worked during his university practical year and where there was now a post available.

However, because the young parents had no experience of the African countries between Kenya and theirs – Uganda, Belgian Congo (DRC), Northern Rhodesia (Zambia) and Southern Rhodesia (Zimbabwe) – Ad and Wal thought driving home would be a wonderful way of seeing them. They had bought a car – a 1936 Lancia Aprilia – which, although old, had an advanced design which he admired. The entire space between its front and rear seats was packed with all their possessions up to the rear level of the front seats, with baby Peter inhabiting the top; seat belts, let alone baby seats, were unheard of in those days.

The Aprilia had already been used for Wal's daily trips from their home to work in Nairobi city centre, and also for a trip to Arusha to see the majestic Kilimanjaro mountain, and there had been no warnings of problems to come on the arduous trip to South Africa.

On April Fools' Day 1951, with Peter just over a year old, they left Nairobi in the fifteen-year-old car on a daring drive several thousand miles down the African continent. Some might say it was foolhardy and, expecting strong disapproval, they hadn't informed their own parents – or anybody else except Ad's younger sister Jo, who felt burdened with apprehension. They were young, adventurous and hopeful that, as all the countries they would pass through were still white colonies, there would be other English-speaking whites like them for help or advice. Fortunately they were to find warmth and friendship all the way down – also from all the Africans with whom they came into contact.

❦

Just as well, because only thirteen miles from the start they encountered the first of countless calamities: a puncture, Wal changing the tyre as he was to do on numerous other occasions along the rutted, mostly sandy roads.

Another of his meticulous diaries in trademark clear handwriting – this time of the whole five-week journey – excitedly recorded seeing Mount Kenya and Lake Nakuru ablaze with pink flamingos. Then, soon after Solik,

> thought we'd taken a wrong turning, backed into a bank, disturbed ignition timing, blocked exhaust pipe and blew exhaust manifold to pipe gasket. Went back to Solik, truck came along – were on right road after all. Car misfiring badly. At 0300 stopped and slept in car.

All this on the first day.

'Next morning, local white farmer came past, stopped, towed us to his house (about one and a half miles), gave us breakfast and reset engine timing.' They set off again to a terrible noise from the exhaust and low power, just managing to limp to Lambwe near Kisi where Ad's uncle, Blythe Duffy, lived. Fortunately, he was able to replace the gasket and repair the punctured tyre and they stayed with him for a couple of days.

It was a pleasant interlude, marred only by an 'argument about Belgian attitude towards blacks in Congo, when he said they had the right idea in allowing blacks to do any sort of job, but not allowing them to vote'. As it happened in South Africa, blacks could do neither, but Wal thought Blythe's 'concession' was totally inadequate – the first of what were to be many such arguments with their relatives.

Unusually for whites in Africa at that time, both Ad and Wal automatically treated Africans as normal human beings – but they had yet to realise the political implications of such an attitude, which seemed to come naturally to them. To the extent that such a consideration even crossed their minds, they would never then have seen themselves as having 'political' views.

A few miles after waving goodbye to Uncle Blythe on the morning of 5 April, they ran out of petrol, saved only by being able to buy a gallon from an Indian lady. Filling up again in Kisi, they drove on but later were hit by another emergency. About ten miles short of Kakamega, 'water pump packed in. Limped into Kakamega and slept night in car in police station.'

There an 'Indian garage fixed water pump pulley (twenty-five shillings) and we bought lovely cheddar and biscuits. Left 10.30 and just outside throttle linkage came loose – fixed it with wire ... On to Jinja but puncture in same tyre as before, changed wheel.' They passed into Uganda at Tororo and finally arrived at the capital, Kampala, relieved to be able to sleep the night in a hotel.

Then onward, 'car going like a bird', and an unexpected night in a guest house at Fort Portal, the owner taking pity on them when they asked for directions on the main road, followed by another night sleeping in the car in the yard of a police station, slumped on the front seats. Baby Peter slept on the back seat, soon reluctant to leave the car since it had become 'home'. Heading south for Kisoro on the Ugandan border with the Congo, 'misty, lovely country like Zululand, climbing, twisting and turning through Kanaba Gap 7,820 feet, view of three volcanic-looking mountains'.

At the Belgian Congo border post of Ruhengeri, they were confronted with a demand for a deposit on their car: 'We had no money so customs official lent it to us, saying we could return it when we left Belgian Congo at Elizabethville (when deposit would be returned to us!). He said he had done this a week ago to a South African so was sure we would be OK!'

Although aware the Belgian Congo had an appalling

record of violent colonial rule, Ad and Wal were struck by the decency, almost innocent goodwill and absence of corruption on this occasion, as for the rest of their trip. Despite the often brutal oppression of its indigenous peoples by European powers, colonial Africa still had some attractive values that Ad and Wal admired: trust, honesty, mutual support and care from both whites and blacks.

On the road again, about ten miles short of Kisenyi, 'there was a sharp crack and the rear torsion bar snapped (the car was overloaded). Drove on to Kisenyi with car rear bottoming over rough sections.' They were unable to get the broken torsion bar fixed there, and hobbled on through the town of Goma, exhilarated by the breathtaking scenery of extinct volcanoes with hardened molten lava, then Lake Kivu, deep valleys and steep hills.

But...

> Car not pulling well and at about 2000hrs stuck on steep hill. Two young Belgians coming past in truck towed us up to the top. On again ... but tired (about 0200) pulled off road and slept. Woke at 0400 and went on, stuck on small hill, thought no petrol (gauge not working); couldn't check tank as lock was stuck. Sawed it off with hacksaw and found petrol was OK. Found petrol pump connection leaking, fitted washer, went on. Soon stuck again, cleaned connections, went on, stuck again. Young Belgian stopped and helped me clean connections, drove on, stuck again. Took

> carburettor apart, cleaned jets, off again, roads slippery, car sliding and wheels spinning. Blow out in right front tyre. Changed wheel, into Costermansville. Had expected to find South African bank there where we could get money but the nearest one was in Ndola in Northern Rhodesia which said it would send money but would only get here on 14 April (four days later). Hotel Minerva kindly made a 'room' for us at the end of a corridor by putting a curtain across and a bed inside.

Over the next days: 'Waiting for money to arrive so could only manage proper food for Pete (14 months) and bread rolls for us (plus anything he couldn't finish).' As if that wasn't enough the money did not arrive on time. They were penniless. But, again, generosity and trust in the heart of Africa came to their aid: 'Cashier in bank lent me 500 francs to last until Monday, on no security though hadn't seen me before! Had terrific dinner tonight. Pete walking at slightest opportunity.' Baby Peter taking his first steps delighted them both.

Finally, on Tuesday 17 April – after a full week's wait – the money came through and they set off for Albertville on Lake Tanganyika. Ignoring advice to park up for a month because of heavy rains, they ploughed on in the small, fragile car through one drift. Just short of the next one,

> stopped short, then car wouldn't start, no run so cranked, backfiring – approach of another black (it

> was dark) with spear, but he seemed frightened and backed away. Crank took at last, mad revs and crossed. Next drift, stopped back enough to get a run, recede, ran down but engine didn't take and car stopped dead in 'gue' [mud] about 10 feet from bank, with aqua just below floor level. Cranked then stalled on a hump. Tried starter, worked, away. Last gue piece of old hat. Struck mud and hills, machine pulling well, passed stranded trucks, car sliding and swaying madly. Last hill, steep gradient, almost at top stuck, usual ropey loose stony surface and bends. Couldn't get away, slept there.

Next morning, 18 April, they woke wondering how on earth they would manage to drive off. Fortunately, a group of African road workers arrived and willingly pushed them up the hill – they were mercifully off and away. At the top they marvelled at the 'wonderful view down over the hills to Lake Tanganyika sparkling in the sun, villages and happy people'. But then the familiar:

> Hit something, handbrake cables broke and wrapped around prop shaft. Took them off so no handbrake now … went on and stuck on steepest hill – usual surface. Nobody about, then road gang arrived, pushed like hell, got away. Got water from stream – then down, wonderful view over range of hills then undulating level country through bush. Villagers good.

Yet another blown tyre and they parked up for the night 'on swampy stuff'. They had no water and awoke 'irritable, thirsty. Pete very thirsty, performing, parched, but Jeep stopped just outside Albertville and gave us bottle of water which we finished off in no time.'

The following days were the usual mixture of crises – getting stuck, getting a push from helpful Africans, breaking down, repairing a broken pump and other vehicle parts, sleeping in the car. They went to the toilet in the bush, Ad always feeling uncomfortable because Africans would appear out of nowhere, not at all threatening but instead inquisitive at these exotic white interlopers.

Once when Wal was changing a punctured tyre, she had just pulled down her panties when she spotted a large black column of giant 'soldier ants' marching stentorian-like towards her: she leapt up hastily out of their way. They had a reputation for devouring almost anything in their path.

'20 April: decided to sleep on road, lovely moonlight, moths, jungle drums. 21 April: fixed tyre to audience of natives who almost drove us crazy.' Most of the time they were short of water and hungry, with baby Peter 'behaving wonderfully' – except when 'slept on road around 3 a.m. Pete had motion all over car – not popular with parents'. Throughout the journey they continued to enjoy warmth and hospitality from total strangers especially at Kolwezi – a bath here, a meal there – interspersed with the relief of the odd hotel stay to recuperate: what luxury! Ad always grabbed these rare opportunities to wash nappies, dry and clean.

Eventually they arrived at Elizabethville near the border with Northern Rhodesia on 24 April. Here Wal tried unsuccessfully to get money from the consulate, who instead filled up their petrol tank. Then it was on, first to Congo customs at Sakania and then Rhodesian customs at Ndola where they slept the night.

The car continued to plague them – flat tyres, broken fan belt, engine failures, towed to garages for repairs – the breakdowns seemed endless. On down to Livingstone, 'the bonnet suddenly reared up and disappeared over our heads. Put back on – no one behind luckily.'

On 30 April they arrived to enjoy seeing the magnificent Victoria Falls. Soon afterwards, filling up with petrol, another car driver looked hard at Ad and said: 'You must be a Stocks from Port Alfred!' Although her home town was 1,500 miles to the south, they felt they were almost there.

Journeying through Southern Rhodesia, still plagued with car problems, they arrived at Bulawayo. Then it was on to the South African border crossing, Beit Bridge, where customs officers demanded £10. They only had £5, which fortunately was accepted. Driving into their homeland was such a relief after all their travails. However, they now had no cash left and, to compound their predicament, it was a public holiday when they arrived on a Sunday morning at Messina. When they tried the local Barclays Bank on the off-chance, they discovered the manager was working overtime. Even more fortunately, he had known Walter's army comrade Pete de Klerk and so gave them the cash they required and accepted their camera as a deposit, to be posted on when the money was repaid.

Finally, on 4 May 1951, over a month after they had left Nairobi, the battered old car limped into Pretoria and to Wal's parents' house, having called in on the way to a farm where Tom was staying. There was a huge pot of mealie-meal (maize porridge) on the stove and Tom, astonished to greet them, was enthralled as his tiny new nephew happily polished off one bowl of porridge and then another.

Home – and utter relief – but exhilaration too at a sense of achievement on their voyage of discovery. They remained transfixed at the wonder of Africa: its beauty, the vast distances and the constantly changing terrain – mighty mountains, deep valleys, wide-open spaces, muddy rivers, parched bush, the awe-inspiring Victoria Falls – and also the special light, somehow brighter, bigger and wider. Above all, they were entranced by the warmth and friendliness of its people.

Although journeying thousands of miles over five weeks in an old and faulty vehicle on rutted, bumpy roads had turned out to be an on-going trial, Ad and Wal had no regrets. Their children and grandchildren couldn't imagine how they had coped, why they never despaired or gave up. 'Once we had started, there was never any question of turning back. We had no option but to plough on,' they explained. 'Yes, we had some bad times, but we also had lots of good times. It was an unforgettable experience.'

Despite many opportunities to do so, nobody ever took advantage of them; in fact most people went out of their way to help, as Ad and Wal would have done too, having been brought up that way in that more trusting, mutually supportive era – albeit for most whites it was strictly only for other whites.

And baby Peter showed no ill effects as he munched happily through his food, oblivious that his parents had sometimes run out of money to feed themselves properly out on their own in the middle of Africa – and in their hunger, wryly envious. Born a British subject, Peter was to remain so; Ad and Wal never got around to paying the charge necessary to acquire his South African citizenship…

Wal's new job was in the Eastern Cape 600 miles away, to which they were travelling by train. Fortunately, they were able to park their battered old Aprilia in the yard of some friends of his parents in Pretoria, for him to return and collect when he was able to.

He was posted to Port Elizabeth, the main city and port in the Eastern Cape, known as the 'Windy City', with long stretches of white beach. Near to Ad's parental home in Port Alfred, she and Peter first stayed there for a few weeks while Wal worked in the city and searched for somewhere for the family to live. It was the first time they had been separated since their marriage and she found that jolting. Ad had not realised why tiny Peter was sleeping so badly until her mom said: 'He's missing his dad.' And so it proved, because when Wal returned for the weekend the tiny child took his dad's face in his both his hands and crooned 'Ooh, ooh' over and over. After that, though Wal had to go off again back to work, Peter was never so upset.

Following a spell living just outside Port Elizabeth, Wal was asked by his firm to move offices. First they lived in Pietermaritzburg, founded by the *Voortrekkers* after the defeat of the Zulu king, Dingane, at the Battle of Blood River in 1838. It was the capital of the short-lived Boer republic, known as Natalia. When the British seized control of Pietermaritzburg from the Afrikaners in 1843, they established it as the administrative capital of the new Natal Colony.

The small city had an English feel to it and Ad and Wal also discovered that it was famous for an incident early in the life of the Indian independence leader Mahatma Gandhi. In 1893, while Gandhi was travelling in a train to Pretoria, a white man objected to his presence in a first-class carriage. He was ordered to move to the luggage section at the end of the train. Gandhi, who had a first-class ticket, refused, and was thrown off the train at Pietermaritzburg. Shivering through the winter night in the waiting room of the station, Gandhi made the momentous decision to stay on in South Africa and fight racial discrimination against Indians there. During that struggle he developed his own vision of non-violent direct action, known as *Satyagraha*, which he was later to apply in his homeland in the campaign to end British colonial rule.

They rented a one-bedroom flat with its own kitchen and dining room but shared bathroom and toilet. Peter, they noticed, was fascinated by cars and had soon developed an expertise enabling him to distinguish between different models of the same car better than they were able to do themselves. Ad was also amused to notice how he used to wander out from the flat and sit with black labourers as they munched their food during a lunch break, offering him tit-bits after he had shared his own tit-bits.

Their accommodation in Pietermaritzburg included a yard with space for the Aprilia, and on a weekend when a friend was driving to Pretoria, Wal got a lift, collected the car and set off home. On the way he came upon a car parked at the side of the main road, with a family standing alongside and looking distraught. Wal wondered if they might need help and drew up, noticing as he did so that they were South African Indians, probably, he thought, from the next town, Newcastle, a mining town with a large community of Indian miners. It transpired that the father was a miner, needed to be at work the next day and was stranded, his car broken down. Wal immediately offered them a lift. Although it was highly unusual for any white to offer assistance in this way across racial lines, it didn't occur to Wal to do anything else.

They arrived with night falling at Newcastle's Indian Quarter, still some distance to Pietermaritzburg. So when he was invited to share a curry meal and stay the night, he gratefully accepted, blithely ignoring the conventions of apartheid and the white culture which had reared him, both rigidly resistant even to the very thought of such intermixing. Next day he arrived home to his own family with Ad relieved and Peter delighted to see him, as they hadn't known when he would arrive because they didn't have a phone; Ad was anxious as the car was not in a good state. (The Aprilia was later sold to someone who wanted it for driving in veteran sports car races.)

She was now expecting another child, and soon Wal's work took them to Ladysmith to establish the firm's office there. It was a pleasant town with an even more English culture, on the main road north from Durban to Johannesburg and Pretoria. Also a former Afrikaner (Boer) stronghold until taken over by the British in 1850, Ladysmith was named after the wife of Sir Harry Smith, then Governor of the Cape Colony. It was the first time Ad and Wal had experienced a subtropical highland climate of hot, rainy summers and cool, dry winters. They rented their first house in the town, modest and basic but – as was the norm for whites – set on its own in ample grounds. A black maid lived separately in a room with toilet and shower next to the garage – the usual servant's accommodation.

There was much excitement in the young Hain household when their second boy, Tom, was born on 9 May 1952 in a nursing home run by a midwife known as 'Sister Sandals'. The birth was easy and Wal arrived soon afterwards with Peter to inspect the contented baby. To avoid jealousy, Sister Sandals had her own routine for small siblings: they had to give her a sixpence and be taken in to 'buy' the baby. Tom was having his nappy changed and two-year-old Peter was thrilled, returning to tell his parents excitedly: 'The baby done a poo!'

Their lifestyle, at least to begin with, was a conventional one in the 1950s and 1960s for a white family of moderate means. Wal worked, Ad ran the home. They were not well off, but were able to live comfortably; there was never a shortage of Africans knocking at whites' doors desperate for house maid or male gardener jobs. Their social circle was typical. They would visit relatives and friends and invite them back. Their children had a happy, carefree and secure childhood, with the weather and the space for outdoor activities.

3

Political Awakening

Like the vast majority of white South Africans, Ad and Wal continued to enjoy a life of comfort and pleasure. Whites benefited from the good fortune apartheid conferred upon them, yet were curiously insulated from its unjust and oppressive consequences. Only a very few were at all interested in the conditions affecting their servants and it would never have occurred to them to visit the poverty-stricken black townships separated off from their towns and city suburbs. Although aware Africans lived an infinitely inferior life, they chose not to go there, not to subject their consciences to the realities of dusty or muddy tracks between rows of shacks where over 80 per cent of South Africans lived.

Current affairs was not taught in schools, the dominant media were government compliant and the South African Broadcasting Corporation (SABC) gave no airtime to opposition views. So the young Ad and Wal had little knowledge of the mesh of repressive laws that increasingly stultified black life as apartheid intensified. They were barely aware of the African National Congress (ANC), nor of its new emerging leaders in the late 1940s, including of course Nelson Mandela.

At the time of their adventurous trip through Africa, neither had thought politically about the predicament of Africans, any more than most of their fellow whites had done. 'We had both grown up in South Africa and like most people in most countries assumed ours to be the norm for how countries were run,' Wal later explained.

But, unusually, neither had grown up with the derogatory attitude most whites in Africa held towards Africans. Neither of their parents had treated their black servants in that demeaning way. Ad had been brought up with black families living nearby. She had also developed a fledgling interest in politics, though this had rather faded with the demands of motherhood. Wal's youth was in the country, and he was familiar with Indians coming to their door from the sugar cane plantations on which they worked, with fruit and vegetables carried in baskets at each end of long bamboo poles resting upon their shoulders. Moreover, the nearest shop for general household provisions was two miles away and run by Indians. Wal also recalled a dairy farm near their house to which he used to walk and he had fond memories of the 'head boy' on the farm, a Zulu man called Robert, who took him milking and gave him drinks of frothy fresh milk from the pails. Robert even let the young boy take a baby calf home for a few days.

Always keen on and excellent at art, he developed a love for sketching at high school in Johannesburg in 1940, and began visiting the city's Africana Museum. There, he discovered a range of memorabilia on his country's past. He became fascinated by ancient Bushmen (Khoisan) paintings, and African artefacts of war: knobkerries (sticks with deadly round ends), assegais (spears) and shields. He was also captivated by a full-size and realistically coloured cast of a Khoi man. Becoming increasingly intrigued by his country's ethnological history, his art drawings now tended to be of Africans and their habitats. None of his white classmates had the same interest in or empathy for their African compatriots.

Back in Pretoria in 1941 and at Boys High, his art teacher was Walter Battiss – a prominent South African artist who was writing a book on Bushmen rock paintings. When Wal asked Battiss if it was 'alright to draw natives', the response was immediate: most unusually, his pupil would be given access to a series of fascinating monographs by the Pretoria Reference Library. From these he drew African warriors, spellbound at their proud bearing, the only white boy in his art class to show the slightest interest in black South African life.

Another experience stuck with Walter. Before he enlisted with the army, he was required to do a theodolite survey of a site outside Pretoria. Three African assistants – Andries, Welly and Andrew – carried all the equipment and during sandwich breaks for lunch,

Walter recalled asking each where they came from and to which chiefdom they belonged. 'We got on great,' he remembered.

There was another formative influence. The Second World War did have a radicalising impact on young, especially English-speaking, South African soldiers. Like Wal, their eyes were opened to the wider world of Europe and – on their way up to fight and then before returning home – north Africa. Serving in the anti-Nazi cause, they became much more aware of its democratic values and of racial discrimination – in that case against Jews. Afterwards, the commanding officer of the South African Army Education Service, and subsequently a South African Liberal Party founding member, Leo Marquard, reported: 'Many young South Africans came to think seriously about their country's racial problems for the first time during the war,' with 'corps of over 200 young men and women [who] in lectures and discussions thrashed out the country's social and economic problems'.[‡] He added that some had been moved 'by the stirring claims to freedom in speeches of Churchill and Roosevelt'. Another founding member of the Liberal Party, Terence Beard, began thinking seriously about race in South Africa after serving with black troops who were not permitted to bear arms – confined instead to stretcher-bearer and ancillary duties. In May

‡ Leo Marquard, *Liberalism in South Africa* (Johannesburg: South African Institute of Race Relations, 1965).

1945 on Victory-in-Europe Day, Beard was struck by an Afrikaner soldier calling for blacks to be treated better after witnessing the bravery of black stretcher-bearers at the battle of Monte Stanco (where Walter had nearly been killed): 'He had seen them tear off their Red Cross armbands, seize the rifles of dead white comrades and help turn defeat into victory.'[‡]

Ad and Wal had also been impressed by the more relaxed racial structure they found in Kenya. For instance, Indians living in Kenya – originally brought in by the British to construct the railway line from Mombasa to Nairobi – had their own businesses and did not face the discrimination prevalent in South Africa. When Wal inspected a building designed by his firm, he was struck that the contractor was an Indian, as were all the skilled craftsmen – bricklayers, carpenters and plasterers: something out of the question back at home. Similarly, Africans were much better treated – he noted for instance that the telephonist taking all incoming calls at his office was an African. And on their eventful drive down the continent in 1951, Ad and Wal warmed to the friendly, welcoming faces of the Africans they encountered and were interested in their different chiefdoms.

‡ Randolph Vigne, *Liberals Against Apartheid: A History of the Liberal Party of South Africa 1953–68* (Basingstoke: Macmillan, 1997), pp. 5–6.

That meant they were open to an invitation late in 1953 from Jock Barnes, the South African friend who had worked alongside Wal in Nairobi and who was a neighbour of theirs where they lived outside the city. Barnes recommended to those then forming the new non-racial Liberal Party that they should be invited to join. Ad and Wal were both keen, as the idea of a more liberal, respectful attitude to their black countrymen and women appealed. They were also intrigued, though a trifle concerned, at the strange novelty of joining a political party, wondering what membership might mean.

Then living in Ladysmith, Wal had opened an office there for his firm. An architectural student, Annette Cockburn, had come home during her university holiday to gain experience working in the office and had recently joined the Liberal Party, offering further encouragement. She recalled:

> Walter was engaged (among other things) in the very unglamorous job of redesigning the sewerage system of Ladysmith as it was changing over to waterborne sewerage. I had to hold up the pole on site while he did the surveying and I worried about what I must look like upside down. I was delighted to meet fellow Liberals. I thought Walter and Adelaine were exceptional and had never met anyone like them before. They were so full of life and fun. In their house they kept their possessions in fruit boxes adapted for the purpose while their small boy [Peter] with bright fair

> curls whizzed around on his tricycle in the garden. I thought it was all wonderful.

But for Ad and Wal to join meant forming a new local branch in Ladysmith and at the national party's request they helped plan the inaugural meeting with Annette. There was nowhere else to hold it except in their modest, rented house. Party officers helped with organisation and recruitment. Annette persuaded her father to lend them some chairs and stools which he brought over and everyone crammed into their sparsely furnished living room.

The party's national president, Alan Paton, and chairman, Peter Brown, arrived early and introduced themselves. Paton, the more senior, was author of the renowned novel *Cry, the Beloved Country*, which Ad and Wal had recently read and were moved by. It told the story of an African parson's search for his delinquent son in Johannesburg, highlighting the outrageous treatment of the black majority and concluding with the prophetic: 'I have one great fear in my heart, that one day when they turn to loving, they will find we are turned to hating.' Peter Brown, Wal's age, became a good friend and, it turned out, had also served with South African forces in Italy. (Indeed, they later realised, he had also been a signalman and, a few days after Wal's company had been forced to retreat from Monte Stanco, Brown's company moved up and took it – something he never failed to pull Wal's leg about.)

Strangers soon began to arrive, Ad and Wal most taken with a black man who had a wispy moustache, an engaging manner and an infectious smile. He was Elliot Mngadi, later to become national treasurer of the party, who, as he arrived, delightedly told his welcoming hosts something that was to make a lasting impact on them: 'This is the first time I've ever come through the front door of a white man's house!' (Black servants or tradespeople would always come in the back door, which, in colonial style, was invariably connected to the kitchen.)

Nearly twenty Africans, Indians and whites squeezed into the meeting. There was a buzz as first Alan Paton and then Peter Brown spoke, the rest like Ad and Wal rather in awe of these top party figures. But soon the pair were organising other meetings and leafleting sessions, word spread and membership began to grow among blacks recruited mainly by Mngadi; no other whites joined, however.

They were therefore delighted that, after discussing the reasons for signing up with Ad's younger sister Jo when she paid them a family visit, Jo herself joined too. She resigned as secretary of her local United Party branch, causing consternation among its officers, one of whom was despatched from the nearest city, Port Elizabeth, to try to persuade her to stay on – instead the attempt reinforced her decision to join the Liberals. Jo became active in her local branch in Grahamstown, which, with Rhodes University situated there, had some leading party lights.

Yet Ad and Wal had no inkling to where this idealistic, innocent acceptance of participation in the party might lead them and their young family. They both felt they must do something – it just seemed to them the right thing to do at the time. Had they known then that their decision to join the Liberals would be the first momentous step on a road to restriction, stress and then exile, who knows what they might have done? So often, seemingly small life decisions can lead to big life changes.

At this time Wal was still driving his firm's car, but they wanted one of their own. When he heard about a new, exciting, small, rear-engine 750cc Renault, he was enthused and arranged to purchase one in Johannesburg. He got a lift with friends, taking four-year-old Peter with him and spending the night with Jock and Nicky Barnes. Next morning he bought the car and drove it home, Peter sitting elated in the front seat next to him chatting away, not a seat belt in sight.

However, within a year they were getting eager to return to Pretoria to be nearer to friends and close relatives. One of his firm's partners was keen to move to Ladysmith and Wal was able to get a job with another firm in Pretoria, attracted by the fact it was run by a man of his own age, Chips Sive, more receptive to Wal's more progressive ideas on architectural design.

In July 1954, Ad drove their boys the 250-mile trip to Pretoria in the Renault, Wal driving a loaned van full of their effects. Instead of their comfortable Ladysmith house, they moved to a small flat in the suburb of Sunnyside, the boys sleeping in the single bedroom, themselves in the living room. Several months later, in another straightforward birth, a new child was born on 11 October 1954. Thrilled at their first girl after two boys, they named her Jo-anne, after Jo, whose full name was Josephine Anne. Excited and absorbed by the new baby, Peter and Tom kept stroking her feet, amazed at how tiny they seemed.

The political culture in Pretoria was deeply conservative, dominated by pro-apartheid Afrikaners, with English speakers indifferent to the remorseless advance of new apartheid laws and restrictions.

No local Liberal Party branch existed then, and their political participation temporarily ended. Yet they remained members, noting with dismay that apartheid was marching on, step by step intruding into every facet of life, with the government recently having enforced racial segregation in all schools.

The Minister for Education, the apartheid fundamentalist Hendrik Verwoerd, complained that the pre-apartheid system of schooling – including Christian mission schools – had misled blacks by showing them 'the green pastures of white society in which they are not allowed to graze'. The 1953 Bantu Education Act, Verwoerd said, was to train blacks for their station in life: 'What is the use of teaching a *Bantu* [African] child mathematics when it cannot use it in practice?' Apartheid in schools became the norm, later to be followed by an end to the few black students allowed at the main white universities and the removal of the independence of Nelson Mandela's old academy, Fort Hare. Mandela and most of his generation of ANC leaders had indeed been 'allowed to graze' at such pastures; their successors would no longer.

The perverse grand design of apartheid was enshrined in the 1950 Population Registration Act, legislation which defined the four different racial groups[‡] by statutorily defining 'whiteness' in terms which for Ad and Wal perfectly captured the Orwellian absurdity of apartheid:

> A white person means a person who –
>
> (a) in appearance is obviously a white person and who is not generally accepted as a Coloured person; or
>
> (b) is generally accepted as a white person and is not in appearance obviously not a white person.

Ancestral inter-breeding inevitably spawned unexpected and fraught family crises. One conventional white Afrikaner couple – supporters of the ruling National

‡ Whites, Africans (blacks), Coloureds (mixed-race) and Asians (including Chinese).

Party – discovered that their new baby girl, Sandra Laing, was of a more dusky appearance. They thought little of it as they brought her up with love and pride. But, when she went to school, other children and parents complained that – unlike her elder brother – she was not white. There was an official investigation and the small girl was declared Coloured. She was forced to leave the school and to separate from her family – apartheid required that she could no longer live with her parents: it literally wrenched them, emotionally distraught, apart.‡

Alban Thumbran, a Coloured who was later to become a good friend, once told Ad and Wal that there were a number of people living in Pretoria's Cape Reserve (designated for Coloureds) who were similarly born into white families but prevented from living with them. He added that there were also occasional Coloureds who could pass for whites and lived in white areas – their Coloured relatives never visiting because that would have 'shopped' them.

By 1954 Verwoerd was preparing a much more ambitious programme of 'grand apartheid'. He was a visionary, convinced of the moral rightness of his plan to completely separate blacks and whites, which could only be achieved by drastic social engineering and mass removals of blacks living near to white areas; only the Soviet Union's leader Stalin had implemented anything

‡ See *Skin* (2008), a moving film on the turmoil which engulfed Sandra Laing and her family.

like this, though Verwoerd invoked Christianity in support of his eccentrically oppressive ideology.

This forced removal policy came to a head at the unique multi-racial township of Sophiatown four miles from white Johannesburg's centre. Originally intended as a white development, its location next to a rubbish dump put off many whites and the developer was forced to sell to anybody of any race who could be found. Sophiatown had become an overcrowded slum, one of South Africa's most cosmopolitan areas, and the only part of the city where blacks could own freehold property. But apartheid dictated that black residents were to be forced to leave their homes for Soweto, many miles away, and given puny compensation.

There was uproar locally and, for the ANC, this was a serious trial of strength. A major campaign against the removal was organised. It was supported by Father Trevor Huddleston, an English priest who presided over the Church of Christ the King there, and wrote *Naught for Your Comfort*, an important book that stirred an international conscience. But the authorities were not to be deflected and, early on the morning of 9 February 1954, thousands of police and soldiers cordoned off the township and ordered the dismantling of houses, and heavy trucks arrived to take out the tenants and their furniture.

As Nelson Mandela recalled, by then it had become

> a crime to walk through a Whites-only door, a crime to ride a Whites-only bus, a crime to walk on a

> Whites-only beach, a crime to be on the streets after 11 p.m., a crime not to have the right pass book and a crime to have the wrong signature on that book, a crime to be unemployed and a crime to be employed in the wrong place, a crime to live in certain places and a crime to have no place to live.

It was, in short, a crime to be born with a black skin, indeed to be an African.

Going with this was the Immorality Act, outlawing sexual intercourse between whites and members of any other racial group, following reports of liaisons between blacks and whites which both repulsed apartheid purists and also embarrassed them, especially when Afrikaner men were involved: the purity of the 'master race' had to be protected at all costs.

Though aghast and feeling powerless at these developments, Ad and Wal were meanwhile pre-occupied with their young family, enjoying both reading and talking to Peter and Tom, who were growing fast, as tiny Jo-anne gurgled away, a source of fascination to the boys. Although Wal enjoyed working in Chip Sive's architectural office with its young staff, they were still both free spirited and healthy, and wanted to see more of the world. Ad argued they had better do so before their three children were old enough to incur substantial travel costs. Her sister Jo, single and keen on travel, was working in London and living in a bedsit at the time, and in her holidays hitchhiking around Europe. One of Wal's work colleagues had just returned from employment in London and, with his help, Wal arranged for a job there with Easton and Robertson, a known UK architectural practice from pre-war days.

The small family car was sold to pay for the ocean liner fare – the most economic and convenient mode of travel – and the family caught a train down to Port Alfred for a two-week break before they boarded another train for Cape Town. It ran right up to the quayside from where they embarked at the beginning of 1956.

They enjoyed both the journey and the excitement of their arrival at Southampton, from where they caught the 'boat train' to Waterloo. Ad's sister Jo was there to meet them. When she had first come to London she had stayed while looking for a place to live with Harry and Marjorie Bull. An RAF officer during the war, Harry had become friendly with Ad's family when working at an RAF aircrew training facility at an aerodrome outside their home town, Port Alfred, and both Ad and Jo had kept in touch when he returned to London. Now the Bull family welcomed the Hains to stay temporarily at their house in Staines while they searched for somewhere of their own. It was a bitterly cold winter and Ad was open-mouthed as her washing froze when she put it out on the line. Once, she looked out of the window and wasn't sure what she was seeing – there were a few flakes like she had seen in films at the cinema – but then Harry confirmed it was snowing.

Eventually, with Jo's help, they found a rented first-floor flat in a house in the west London suburb of Ealing. But they had to search hard for one suitable because few landlords liked so many children. Jo found one flat but when she asked the landlord why there was no bathroom, he pointed to public baths down the road; they were astonished at the very idea of not having access to a bathroom. Their choice was also limited because Wal's salary was meagre and the rent levels seemed very high.

London then remained in hangover from the war, with bomb sites still being rebuilt. There was thick smog in winter from coal fires which provided the bulk of home heating. It sometimes got dark in the middle of the day and Jo was startled to arrive at work in the City with smuts on her face. Ad, pregnant again and at home with three small children aged six, four and two, found it cold and so starkly different from the open, warm South African lifestyle with a servant to assist with the drudgery of cleaning – especially washing, which she had to do by hand since there was no washing machine or even spinner. Most difficult, she found, was where to hang the washing, as she had no access to a garden and in any case the weather was at best unpredictable.

They had no fridge at the beginning in the Ealing flat, but if a visitor brought ice cream she would put it on the window sill outside the kitchen to keep cold. Milk was delivered every day, which was a relief. They were so broke that she could only afford to buy a shin of beef and make a stew, cutting the best bits out and keeping the rest for a main meal of soup the following day, but cuts of meat were different from back home in South Africa and she found it difficult to get her purchases right. On another day she would do the same thing with lamb. She always bought the cheapest cuts of meat and often had cottage pie with mince.

Knowing that their marriage was very close gave Ad strength, helping her cope with the long weekdays until Wal came home from work to offer relief. However, they had great help from Jo, who would babysit to allow them to catch the underground to central London to a classical concert, ballet, opera or play, which she always booked for them – though the children would report: 'Jo is very strict.' In good weather at weekends, Ad would cook a roast and pack a picnic into a box and they would drive off, with Jo giving directions to somewhere interesting. The family had acquired a battered old car/van to much excitement from the children. But it was all they could afford and always seemed to break down.

Ad and Wal were firm, instilling in their children the fundamentals of good manners and good behaviour, and making sure they got to bed on time. Family meals were around the table, cutlery held properly, the children told off if they didn't put knives and forks down in between mouthfuls or spoke with food in their mouths. Honesty, morals, discipline – these were the values they tried to instil in their children. If one of them was especially naughty they would get a light smack on the bottom, but never a beating. Usually, just a sharp stern word from their dad would be sufficient: away at work during the day, he didn't have to cope with the constant pressures faced by Ad and his authority was instantly respected by all his offspring. They worshipped him, but if they stepped out of line he could be very severe.

However, Ad and Wal brought up a family with love, not fear. Easily young enough to play actively with their children, Wal was soon teaching his sons to play cricket and football – rugby would come later. With Jo he took the boys to Putney to see the Cambridge–Oxford boat race, choosing different sides to support, while Ad stayed at home with Jo-anne and watched it on a friend's television.

Wal was also passionate about cars and especially motor sport. A highlight of his stay in England was going to the British Grand Prix at the old wartime airfield race track of Silverstone. There he saw the greats of that era – the master, Juan Manuel Fangio, the star British drivers Stirling Moss, Mike Hawthorne and Peter Collins – and he came home to thrill his young sons with his experience and show them his grainy black and white photos, the cars mere specks in the middle.

Ad and Wal kept their chins up even though little went smoothly. Six-year-old Peter began his schooling at a primary school in Ealing, interrupted with an acute ear infection and visits to hospital. Jo-anne was bitten on her cheek by a dog from downstairs and Ad had to rush her off to hospital.

Then, both because the rent was much less and Ad was expecting another baby which might have been frowned upon by their landlord, they moved to a tiny cowman's cottage on a farm in Ruckinge, overlooking Romney Marsh in Kent; they had heard of it from a friend they met on the boat over from Cape Town, whose sister was the farmer's wife.

Legend had it that a lantern in one of the cottage windows was used to alert smugglers in the old days. Driving down from London in their old brown vehicle Ad was at her wits' end because she was very heavily pregnant and every bump on the rickety suspension seemed to tear right through her. Then it broke down on the way and they were forced to get a local taxi for the rest of the journey; the vehicle was got rid of soon afterwards.

Their last child, Sally, was born on Christmas Day 1956. Ad, feeling uncomfortable the night before and worrying the birth might be imminent, got up early and set the table with Weetabix and small presents first thing in the morning. She then started cooking the Christmas chicken (the small oven wasn't big enough to take a turkey). Leaving it rather too late because she wanted to finish the Christmas lunch preparations, she struggled up to the farm to ask if she could use the phone, saying: 'It's going to be a Christmas baby.' The local hospital matron answered and sent an ambulance as Ad left Jo in charge of the excited youngsters.

Wal went with her to the local hospital, as she panicked all the way that her baby was about to pop out. Yet on arrival the sister instructed her firmly: 'Please take your place and wait.'

'No, this is my fourth baby; I *know* it is coming now!'

'Calm down, calm down,' the sister instructed.

'No, I can feel it coming!' She lifted her skirt to reveal that she'd had a 'show' of blood.

'Oh,' said the startled sister, and took her immediately to the labour ward. She was rushed in, the midwives asking if they had time for a coffee break. 'No!' she again insisted, now desperate.

Baby Sally burst out just after she had changed and got into bed, her picture in the local paper as the first to be born on Christmas Day. Ad had learnt to have no food beforehand because, in her earlier births, she had been so advised and also to go to the toilet, so the birth wasn't too messy. But she was ravenous afterwards and gulped down a full Christmas dinner to the utter astonishment of other mothers and the nurses.

In those days birth was strictly a women-only business, and Wal had hardly arrived before being told: 'Kiss your wife goodbye.' He was quickly hustled away carrying Ad's suitcase and clothes because the hospital wouldn't allow her to keep them. However, nobody had told Wal that there was no bus back on Christmas Day – and it was a tiring three-hour walk carrying his load nine miles home for dinner. It was only when he had returned to the farm and asked to use their phone that he discovered they had a second girl.

Meanwhile, Ad was finding the whole experience very old-fashioned and unsettling compared with her first three children. She was used to getting out of bed, going to the toilet and washing properly in a bathroom. Instead she had a bed pan, was not allowed to get out of bed and was supposed to lie there having her abdominals washed by nurses with a curtain pulled around. But knowing full well that she could easily do so, she stood up when the nurses were absent, pulled the curtains around herself and strip-washed standing in her bowl. Despite feeling fine after another uncomplicated birth and baby Sally being healthy, she was also amazed to be confined to bed for ten days in the very old-fashioned hospital, as was the rule in those days. She couldn't wait to get home; her births in Africa had seemed so much more modern. She found the nurses warm and supportive but the procedures suffocating. It was a tremendous relief when she was finally released, the three children thrilled to see their brand new sister.

The ancient cottage was minute: just two rooms up and two down with steep, creaking, narrow stairs and bare floorboards upstairs through which light from downstairs could be seen. The end of the kitchen was partitioned off with a wooden strip for a bathroom with toilet. The children would all bath together because keeping water heated was difficult: the hot water tank was in a cupboard at the end of Ad and Wal's small bedroom. But it had no insulation so Wal lined it with some soft board, which made a real difference. Sally slept on the pram mattress in a suitcase at the foot of Ad and Wal's bed. Adjoining theirs was a slightly larger bedroom in which the children slept; it had a wardrobe curtained across one corner as was common at the time; Jo squeezed into the children's room to sleep when she visited at weekends.

The electric cooker was a tiny Baby Belling. The coal-fired stove for heating water and occasionally food only worked properly when the wind was in a certain direction – Ad would get the sign by spotting where the chimney cowl was positioned.

Life wasn't easy for her, especially having again to wash everything by hand – the drudgery made worse by having baby Sally amid the wet winter weather. Yet she never really complained because 'it was only to be expected' – life was like that for the great majority in England in those days: 'You just got on with it. I didn't have any time to think "what on earth are we doing?" Life was just about survival,' Ad was later to reminisce.

But it was a real boon having a garden again. Ad could hang out her washing and make jam from local plum trees and blackberry bushes.

There were other advantages. Country life in England at the time had a strong sense of community which she had certainly never experienced as an incomer to anonymous London. The local health visitor and district nurse called by and everything was delivered – including milk and fresh vegetables from Stanger's local village grocery store, a post office behind it within walking distance. Mr Stanger gave Wal a lift in his car to catch the train when he later returned to South Africa. Mrs Stanger took down her own washing line for Ad and sold it to her, saying she could easily replace it. A local baker called with fresh bread; so did the butcher and fishmonger (who Ad thought had 'fish eyes'). The postman would also collect mail for posting.

The boys went by school bus to a local school at nearby Orlestone and the children played happily on the farm, seeing cows milked and calves born and being chased by fearsome, yapping geese. Wal, cycling through the farm to work and back, had to hoist his feet in the air off the pedals and coast along to avoid being bitten by the geese. When Jo came to visit she arrived by train five miles away at Ham Street and Wal gave her a lift on the bike bar to the cottage, threading his way through the geese, Jo lifting her legs too.

Five-year-old Tom was in his element, herding the cows and helping the farmer. Tom loved being with the cows except when he was wearing a red jersey and was chased by a small bullock. Come summer the boys helped with the haymaking amid the excitement of combine harvesters and tractors. In one spell of very hot weather, the family took their bedding and slept out on the front lawn – a real adventure for the children, especially when the milk woman surprised them in the early morning.

❦

Soon after they had arrived in London, Ad and Wal discovered the liberal newspapers, *The Guardian* and *The Observer*, through which they gained a much better understanding of world affairs than was possible from the parochial and conservative South African media.

Great events occurred in the year they came to London, 1956: Suez, when the British, French and Israelis attacked Egypt, and the Soviet invasion of Hungary. These made a big impact upon them both and they began to discuss the implications – a radicalising experience, as their eyes were opened more widely even than by their reaction to apartheid. They identified with progressive British opinion in strongly opposing both the British government on Suez and the Soviets on Hungary.

They also read of tumult in their home country. In August 1956 10,000 women of all races gathered at the seat of government, the Union Buildings in Pretoria, in protest against the extension to women of the hated pass laws, which controlled every movement of African men. That December, 156 people – including Nelson Mandela and the entire leadership of the ANC – were arrested for high treason. The following 'Treason Trial' lasted several years before they were finally acquitted – the state responding with a violent clamp-down, as apartheid laws provoked increasing protests and boycotts by black South Africans.

Following all these events closely from England, Ad and Wal became increasingly concerned and restive. Additionally, Wal was becoming tired of the long daily journey to his workplace in London, which meant he had to leave home early and get back late – sometimes missing seeing his children in the evening. So he resigned from his London firm and began working for Kent County Council's architectural department in Maidstone, half the distance to London. But then he found that, instead of a short bicycle ride to the nearest minor station, he was obliged to use a major station – Ashford – which was several miles longer a ride.

But they didn't have the means to return home. Wal's salary was low and they never really thought they could suddenly up and go. So when Chips Sive of his previous architectural firm in Pretoria telephoned and asked him to return late in 1957, they decided to do so. Because he was required as soon as possible, he flew out alone early in December (the firm loaning money for the flight back).

Wal went with considerable misgivings: he hated leaving his wife, baby and three children in the Kent countryside and then to make their way back alone to South Africa. When Wal left, Ad remembered Peter – nearly eight years old – saying: 'Well, I had better cut the bread then.'

Wal also felt guilty as Ad had no car and she was left with the stress of packing up and travelling with four small children. But what else was she supposed to do? Once more, she just got on with it. A few weeks later the local farmer was kind enough to drive them to the nearest station from where they caught a train up to London. There they stayed overnight in a guest house and then took the regular 'boat train' to Southampton – Ad extremely tired and greatly relieved to board the ocean liner, where there was a nursery where the children could play during the day. Staff also listened out for the children back in the cabin when adults were served dinner. It was Ad's first real break for a long time.

Although she enjoyed what amounted to a holiday with all meals served on board, she had her hands full because the children were over-excited. She was also prone to sea-sickness. Sally turned one on Christmas Day and the captain presented her with a special cake and a bendy toy. Finally, after a fortnight's journey, there was a hum of eager anticipation as the ship pulled into Port Elizabeth docks in the hot summer sunshine. On the quay below, Wal, whom she had not seen for six long weeks, waited with both sets of grandparents. Holding onto the railings, three-year-old Jo-anne spotted the group way down below and sang over and over again a little song, 'Hello, My Daddy'. She hadn't slept properly since her dad had left.

4

Into Activism

Returning to the city where they had fallen in love was uplifting. Pretoria had been founded in 1855 by Marthinus Pretorius, a Voortrekker leader. Its wide streets were lined with over 50,000 jacaranda trees, majestically purple when in flower; it was also known as the 'Jacaranda City', the first jacaranda trees imported from Rio de Janeiro in 1888 by a Pretoria resident. Whites-only parks – blacks could only enter if they were gardeners or acting nanny for white children – gave the city lungs. It wasn't too big and bustling like Johannesburg and whites like them enjoyed living there in suburbs with detached homes and gardens neatly manicured by black gardeners.

At the same time the old capital of Afrikanerdom was a bastion of apartheid. Where cosmopolitan Johannesburg attracted a mix of activists – from communists to liberals – parochial Pretoria had few progressive instincts. Yet a branch of the Liberal Party had become active by the time they arrived there early in 1958, and Ad and Wal keenly sought it out and rejoined.

Their introduction was dramatic. A peaceful women's demonstration against being forced to carry passes in the nearby township of Lady Selborne was broken up by baton-wielding police. Many were injured and, when their men folk returned from work, feelings ran high. The township was soon in uproar. The local Liberal Party chairman, John Brink, whom they had got to know, had driven in to try to restrain the police. When he failed to return, a small search party of Liberals set off to look for him: Wal, Colyn van Reenen and Johann van den Berg, in Colyn's car.

Ad and the children worriedly awaited Wal's return. To their relief, he came back soon – but only because they had met Brink returning from the township, bloodied, in a windowless car which had been stoned by residents venting their fury at a white intruder, not knowing he was on their side. Brink – mild, with twinkling eyes and a short, white beard – had just managed to escape after the local ANC organiser, Peter Magano, recognised him and jumped onto the car bonnet to urge the ugly crowd back. The shattered glass all over his car was a grim reminder that he could easily have been killed – and maybe Wal, Colyn and Johann too, trying to rescue him.

The incident was a salutary lesson on the implications of their increasing involvement in the Pretoria Liberal Party. And it was not about to get any better: in fact, the very reverse, as Wal soon had his first brush with the fast-developing police state. As a favour, he had agreed to allow a black boy called Tatius, in his early teens, to stay with his mother in the servant's quarters behind the rented family home in Hilda Street, in the Pretoria suburb of Arcadia. Tatius, minding his own business and walking innocently along the pavement, was set upon by two white men. It seemed they took exception to him penny-whistling, and beat him up 'to teach him a lesson'. He arrived home crying, bloody gashes and bruises on his face, his legs and arms raw. It was all too sadly typical of the random, savage cruelty blacks might face. Outraged, Wal protested to the local police station. But the response was only smirking contempt, and so he angrily wrote a letter to the *Pretoria News*. On publication, his name was duly noted by the Special Branch as somebody new to keep an eye on.

Many whites in Pretoria remained bitterly opposed to the very existence of the Liberal Party, seeing it as, in some respects, even worse than the ANC because it contained whites like them. Students at Pretoria University, an Afrikaans-speaking institution, were militantly pro-apartheid and extremely conservative and would line up outside party meetings, shouting slogans and abuse. This happened once when the Hain family attended the home of John Brink and his wife Meg for a members' party. There was multi-racial dancing together on the lawn: a serious provocation to the students who barracked in noisy intimidation outside, frightening the children, who wondered if the students might burst in at any moment – until they finally went away.

Nevertheless, the Pretoria Liberal Party branch unusually gained some support in 1958 from a small number of the students, notably Maritz van den Berg, his younger brothers Johann and Sammy, Colyn van Reenen, Micky Mikilades and Aubrey Davies. There was such vehement hostility to even the term 'liberal' on the university campus, that it showed enormous courage for them to declare their allegiance.

Such was the culture in which Ad and Wal tried to do their bit for change. Daunting though it was – and depressing to be confronted with such a citadel of bigotry and hatred – they still felt they had a duty to do something against an apartheid system so evil and so wrong. Now they had got involved, they were enthusiastically committed – there was no turning back.

Lady Selborne outside Pretoria was unusual, for townships were normally separated from the white towns they served by open country and enclosed, with entry through a supervised check point. It had an old British colonial heritage, named after the wife of Lord Selborne, an English diplomat, and was cheek by jowl on one side with a white suburb, without restrictions on access for anybody.

During the day Ad visited, regularly accompanied

by her youngest child, Sally, who was under school age, usually leaving Sally in the local English mission, called Tumelong, as she went about her party business – for instance collecting names for a petition or taking food to prisoners' wives. Her little daughter meanwhile did the unthinkable for a white child and played happily in the mission's crèche for black kids.

The women running the mission, Hannah Stanton and Cecily Paget, were Liberal Party members. Both were 'posh and very English', Ad thought, Hannah tall and almost regal, Cecily small and sprightly, each down to earth in manner and with a good sense of humour. Cecily fiercely defended the principle of one-person one-vote to some Liberals who remained sceptical and in disagreement with their party's policy, reminding them that women had only won the vote in Britain comparatively recently through the struggle of suffragettes. 'People used to say in England that if you give women the vote they will only support good-looking men. Tosh of course,' Cecily would remonstrate scathingly with sceptics. A few years later, Hannah was jailed during the state of emergency and then deported by the security police, her vital mission work far too much of a threat to be tolerated by the apartheid state.

At weekends all four of their children – too young to be left alone at home – occasionally went along to Lady Selborne and Tumelong mission too. Initially it was a novel experience as they peered out of the car at the houses, some ramshackle, others more solid. All were starkly different from the comfortable white communities in which they and their schoolmates lived. African women hung out clothing to dry, pristine despite the primitive conditions for washing. African men, many unemployed, sat about wherever they could – by the roadside, at their front doors, on the grass – watching the world go by. Children wearing rag clothes ran around kicking decrepit old balls and peering curiously at the incomers.

Once, in a township shop collecting names for a petition to oppose the removal of Lady Selborne, Ad was shocked when, waiting to get the signature of the shopkeeper, she saw a child purchasing a single slice of bread to take home. Watching the shopkeeper fold it carefully into a piece of paper, she was struck at just how poor these people were: 'I have never seen anything like that before. Does this often happen?' she asked. 'Yes – all the time,' he replied.

Later when their maid Eva Matjeka used to go home on Saturdays, Wal would drive her to catch her train, stopping on the way at Hatfield bakery to buy her two loaves of hot bread. She explained how the children would wait at the township station to meet her because it was a real treat for them to have fresh bread. One day the bread was late coming out of the oven and she had to leave without it to be in time for the train, Wal apologising. 'Don't worry – it can't be Christmas every week,' Eva replied.

Although witnessing such conditions spurred Ad and

Wal on, they fell into what later became their leading roles in Pretoria, rather than setting out with that intention. Indeed they had no 'game plan' as such. Starting by showing a willingness to do the necessary chores in a small, beleaguered, voluntary organisation, Ad and Wal were both soon on the Pretoria Liberals' Committee, recalling: 'Once we had got involved, one thing led to another. There was always some injustice to be tackled so you got stuck in. People asked you to do things and so you did.'

In 1960 Ad became branch secretary, a position she held until she was banned from doing so in 1963. In between caring for her four children, she worked away at home typing up party documents and organising activities and drove around the city on party business. She quickly became a leading activist and – with Wal busy at work earning their keep – she became the more prominent of the two. Wal would often write elegantly forceful letters to the paper protesting or answering critics and she would type and sign them: they would be printed above her name '(Mrs) Adelaine Hain, Pretoria'.

The couple were very close, their love obvious to all. Although he was the male 'head of the house' Wal never thought of it that way. He might pull her leg – telling his children stories as they grew up, some pure fiction such as 'cleaning the dung from between her toes' in a humorous reference to her country background as he introduced her to life in the 'big city' when they first got together. But she didn't mind, feigning resentment, because his respect for her was total.

Wal was simultaneously a conventional man, a product of his era, and yet different from his circle of young men. Unusually for young married males, and despite being urged by friends and his brother Tom to go after work to a local golf club for a drink, he always drove straight home to be with his family. He was a home boy, and one of the few times outside his work that he left Ad on her own was to go with friends to watch the Springboks play rugby – a game he loved. He enjoyed an occasional beer, but only had too much to drink on very isolated occasions – one of these over Christmas in Nairobi, when Ad shoved him firmly into baby Peter's playpen to sleep it off. Decades later, if he was getting boisterous at family meals and occasions, Ad would remind children, grandchildren and even great-grandchildren of his errant behaviour. Needless to say they loved this story – and many others which revealed a person at once radical and very traditional.

Notwithstanding his devotion to Ad, care for his offspring and his refusal to 'go along with the boys', nobody could accuse Wal of being a 'new man'. An example was his fund of army tales, songs and sayings with which he would also occasionally delight family occasions. A favourite was: 'Drink, drink, the glasses clink, making lovely music till the dawn is breaking. / Bang, bang who gives a damn when we're out upon a spree! / Over the teeth behind the gums, look out stomach here she comes! / Have another drink with me – ee, ee!' The impression created was of a boozer, yet he was anything but – he liked a drink but was disciplined about his drinking.

To peals of laughter, his grandchildren learnt to recite a staccato chant of his: '"What was that that you said?" I said: "Who said?" He said: "You said," I said: "Me?" He said: "Yes you," I said: "Not me," He said: "I've got a damn good mind to hit you," I said: "Hit me?" He said: "Hit you," I said: "Not me," He said: "Yes, you," I said: "I'm off."'

They also enjoyed: 'Ain't she sweet, just-a-walking down the street ... and I ask you very confidentially – ain't she sweet? Ain't she nice, look her over once or twice ... and I ask you very confidentially – ain't she nice?'

Even more daring, and decidedly questionable, was: 'Take it off, take it off, the boys all shout, and the band plays the polka while she strips,' always adding a 'da da, da da da', to finish it off. Interesting, that one; although he shunned the strip clubs frequented by army mates before or after the war, he had evidently imbibed their culture.

Another politically *very* incorrect gem was: 'It must jelly because jam don't shake like that (da da, da da da). Mamma, she's so big and fat (da da, da da da).' To which Ad would always shout in protest: 'Wal – *don't sing that*.'

Wal's sayings were also renowned in the family, not least because they shone a light on an era long gone.

If he thought food or something else was wonderful he would say it was 'just-a-like-a-million sardines' or 'vintage', as in 'This is a vintage roast, Ad.' If he was uncertain about an item of food, it had 'a touch of the old Bombay duck'. If doing something was easy, then it was 'a piece of old hat'.

But he was careful about swearing. 'Ruddy' – like 'ruddy awful' – was about as 'rude' as he got – very much an exclamation of its time. There was seldom 'bloody' – *that* was a bit too far. And certainly never 'fuck': *that* was completely beyond the pale, though 'Jeesa-mah-Christ' was a regular.

Bringing up a close-knit family, somehow Ad and Wal managed to be caring parents amid all the increasing trauma of their participation in the resistance to apartheid. The children experienced a blend of normality and abnormality in their day-to-day lives, a mixture of excitement, stress, shock and yet plenty of family fun and togetherness too.

The boys – and sometimes the girls too – were also taken regularly to one of Wal's favourite hobbies: watching motor racing, first at Grand Central and then at the newer Kyalami circuit some thirty miles away on the road to Johannesburg. To get a good view they would typically perch on the roof of the family Volkswagen minibus parked up at Kyalami's Clubhouse corner. The nine-hour, all-night race was a special treat, with the boys' favourite, the British driver David Piper, seemingly winning every time in his green Ferrari.

Wal had schooled his boys in his love of the Italian marques with stories of the great post-Second World War Formula One cars and their drivers. Apart from Ferrari, the other Italian racing cars – Alfa Romeo, Maserati and Lancia – were Wal's favourites. His all-time great was the Argentinian genius Juan Manuel Fangio, whom he had seen win the British Grand Prix during their stay in England. He also subscribed to the monthly *Motor Sport*, which used to arrive after a delay from Britain, with its distinctive green cover, and the weekly *Autocar*, which had road tests on the latest road car models.

Wal took time to teach his boys about cricket, to come and watch them play in school teams and take them to club football matches. He made space to help with Peter's homework and to discuss his emerging interest in what his parents were doing in politics. Amid all the persistent political pressure and crises she faced, Ad by hook or by crook managed always to be there for her four children. She was the fulcrum of both their political activism and family life, somehow balancing both. None of their children complained that their activism came ahead of parental love and care. However, there were inevitable stresses, strains and fears, especially for the younger children.

Early in 1960, aged nine and seven, the boys woke before dawn, shivering in shock to discover strangers in their bedroom. Who were they? What on earth were they doing? Were they stealing? Would anyone get hurt? When Ad and Wal realised their boys were awake, they came over and gave them a hug in bed, explaining the strangers were security policemen and not to worry.

But the episode soon turned more incongruous than threatening. Taking after his dad, Peter was keen on cars and motor sport, and the men were peering at his scrapbooks culled from Wal's weekly car magazine *Autocar.* They searched in vain for 'incriminating evidence' they obviously felt might be secreted there. Then, further embarrassing the officers, Jo-anne and Sally (aged five and three) called out from bed next door that the cupboard drawer for their panties was being searched. The children were very upset when the officers knocked over the cage of a pet white mouse which escaped only to be pounced on and killed by the family cat.

Despite the continuous and increasing buzz of political activity, they were enthusiastic and devoted parents, their relative youth encouraging them to join in their children's outdoor pursuits and games, Peter and Tom's school friends thinking they were wonderful when they came around to play. Pretoria in those balmy days of the late fifties and early sixties was easy-going. Ad and Wal allowed their boys to roam without restriction with their friends, on bicycles and also in soapbox carts the boys had built themselves from wood and pram wheels. Once, they went to support their boys and Peter's best friend, Dave Geffen, in a great box cart race down a steep hill behind the Voortrekker Monument. The boys entered their two 'Team Gefhain' carts, which they had to have checked at the Pretoria Roadworthy Centre first to ensure that they were safe.

When Peter and Tom were aged between eight and twelve they organised bicycle races around the house and through the garden of 1127 Arcadia Street, out via the garage gate onto the pavement, then back in through the front gate. These sometimes went on for several hours with school friends teaming up in pairs and sharing the cycling as Ad and Wal acted as race controllers, their two small girls and school friends cheering the boys on. During a night bike race the girls held torches to light up particularly dangerous spots. Once, they invited spectators from the school and charged an entrance fee to raise money for the black caretaker when he retired and their children discovered he had no pension, Dave's mother Gladys and Ad providing refreshments for sale towards the collection. In his early teens Peter with Dave Geffen organised bicycle rallies in local roads, competing with their schoolmates, Ad and Wal acting as timekeeping marshals along the route.

To his children Wal seemed something of a Renaissance man. From motor racing, rugby, football and cricket, to art, science, literature, history and politics, he seemed to know enough about most things to give an opinion or at least some guidance. Dave Geffen remembered him with great fondness, impressed that 'he was practical; could adjust a bike's wheel bearings for instance'. He was equally fond of Ad: 'She baked the best rock cakes. Both were always there for us (I include myself, as I felt like another son).'

Every December, the two rear bench seats of the family's Volkswagen minibus were turned into a bed for the 700-mile overnight trip to Ad's parents' home on the banks of the Kowie River at Port Alfred. There they spent Christmas holidays, the boys fishing off the jetty, the girls excitedly playing, the family spending long lazy days on the broad sandy beaches and swimming freely in the warm waters of the Indian Ocean.

In one sense Ad and Wal were a remarkably conventional, almost traditional, couple. She cooked and supervised the maid doing the washing and cleaning. He didn't do any cooking at all. She put up with the kids during the day, he would enjoy them after work and at weekends. In short, a 'normal' white couple for those times – and not simply in South Africa.

But in another key sense they were completely abnormal and unconventional. The rented family houses in Pretoria, first at 2 Hilda Street and then nearby at 1127 Arcadia Street, saw regular visitors and callers from Liberal members and others, not just white but – *scandalously* – black as well. And blacks entered through the *front* door. They even partied together with whites. Neighbours were quite taken aback: they had never encountered anything quite like it. At Hilda Street, when two African women knocked on the back door, little Jo-anne and Sally opened it and called to their mother: 'There are two ladies to see you.' There were giggles from the women: they had never been called 'ladies' by two little whites – more used to the casual description, 'girls'.

Initially Ad's mother Edith found it difficult to come to terms with the fact they had close black friends, and Ad and Jo used to have fascinating discussions with her.

'How can they be friends like the rest of us?' Edith asked.

'But Christian Scientists believe we are all God's children, we are all the same in the reflection of God. How because some people have a different skin colour can they stop being God's children?' Ad and Jo replied.

Their mother pondered hard. She knew that in America there were black members of the Christian Science Church. The conundrum was discomforting. Her daughters had a case which her religious beliefs found hard to fault. Eventually, when she was seventy, she joined a demonstration in Grahamstown by the Black Sash (white women standing silently to bear witness to an apartheid injustice) – ending up proud of both Jo and the by now notorious Ad, just as her two daughters were proud of her.

In August 1958, Ad and Wal first met and talked to the charismatic Nelson Mandela, his close comrade Walter Sisulu and other defendants during what became known as the 'Treason Trial'. Held in the Old Synagogue courtroom in Pretoria, many of the accused went outside during the lunch break for food provided in turn by the local Indian community, Liberals and other sympathisers. Helping out with these lunches, Ad and Wal remembered Mandela as 'a large, imposing, smiling man', impressed that both he and Sisulu were so friendly and keen to talk to them. Increasingly their activities crossed over with Mandela's African National Congress (ANC), whose Pretoria leader, Peter Magano, became a friend and key contact. The Liberal Party's national annual conference held in October 1958 in Pietermaritzburg was addressed by the ANC president, Albert Luthuli, who got a standing ovation from the 400 delegates present.

Meanwhile, Hendrik Verwoerd had taken over as Prime Minister on 2 September 1958, after the death of his predecessor, J. G. Strijdom. A more intellectual leader than his predecessors, he maintained a total belief in the ideology of apartheid. That same year the Liberal Party stepped up its activities, launching a news and comment magazine, *Contact*, covering the anti-apartheid struggle. Ad and Wal subscribed, and she later became its Pretoria correspondent. Telling her children – then ranging from age two to eight – to 'keep quiet and go and play', she would clatter away on her small Olivetti typewriter, covering the Treason Trial and later Nelson Mandela's own trial as well as others in Pretoria. She was a self-trained 'journalist' – but, unlike Wal, not university educated, having gone to work for her father's town newsletter straight from school.

At this time in her early thirties, dark haired and pretty in an unaffected way, she increasingly cut a diminutive dash as she scurried about, organising and harrying the authorities. Barely five feet in height, she spent very little time on make-up, dressing neatly but simply. Because she was a woman in a very male-dominated, traditional culture, the officials she encountered and often confronted weren't always quite sure how to handle her.

Much of her activity was directed at courts and police stations, trying to find black prisoners whose families could not locate them. She became known in Pretoria as the person for non-whites to contact whenever anyone fell foul of the police. Sometimes this was made even more difficult by prisoners being identified by number only. It was time-consuming but she became indispensable.

Ad explained: 'I didn't start off thinking I must go and help out around the courts. I got asked to help and then word spread. I quickly found I was the main contact in Pretoria for parents and relatives desperate for information on loved ones.' The authorities became increasingly aware and frustrated at the hours she was spending haunting the courts – sometimes dashing from one building to another when 'grapevine' information told of yet another group of black detainees. She would find out their names, inform the parents and get legal representation if necessary.

Often the phone would ring at home with a caller unknown to her but desperate for help in search of a husband or son who had simply disappeared into the clutches of the security police. Many had been assaulted and tortured. Once, when she was alerted to an arrest, she rushed to the police station where its officers were flabbergasted that she had arrived so soon. Another time she helped bail a group of eight women from Soweto, including Alice Sisulu, elderly mother of Walter Sisulu. Ad took them back to the Hain house for tea and sandwiches and, when Wal returned from work, he drove them home fifty miles to Soweto.

On another occasion a group of black teenage boys were arrested at their school. Ad knew one of the mothers from Lady Selborne and was deeply upset at a rumour that her son was going to give state evidence. As it transpired, the boy couldn't confirm in court the evidence the prosecutors demanded from him and so they were all released. In another case Ad noticed a young teenager, his gangling arms and legs protruding from clothes he had long outgrown, standing morosely with his parents, looking painfully sad: he was going to be a state witness, but she was impressed that the mothers of his young comrades being prosecuted weren't at all hostile to him or his family, as if they all understood the desperation of his predicament.

Although she got hardened to being emotionally strung out by the cases she dealt with, some still left her shaken. During a trial of young Pan Africanist

Congress (PAC) activists from its underground *Poqo* wing, a young man she tried to help had been so badly beaten about the head and ears and subjected to electric shock treatment that he couldn't hear properly and appeared to be in a permanent trance, perhaps one of forced insanity. To try and take up the case, Ad asked a local black priest, Father Tsebe, to take her to see his mother in Atteridgeville township where she asked if her other son, who had also been arrested but then released, could somehow help his brother. There was a pause as her question was translated by Father Tsebe to the mother, who spoke no English. When her response came it was firm: 'No, I have got two sons and I want to keep one safe.' Ad felt almost ashamed to have asked it of her.

On another occasion, young PAC activists involved in *Poqo* were on trial for capital offences of plotting to 'overthrow the state' – by marching unarmed on Pretoria. Jimmy Makojaene, one of Ad and Wal's PAC friends who had attended Liberal meetings, was involved in the same group but had not been caught. So, in a carefully rehearsed routine, all the defendants blamed him, and were convicted for lesser offences.

Once as she waited outside the Pretoria court, one of the township women whom she knew from Tumelong mission asked Ad to get permission for her to see her husband, who was on trial, so that she could tell him their young son had died. Ad was determined to get news to the father before the child's funeral but nobody in the court, despite being well aware of the exact circumstances, would give the required permission. Finally, exasperated at her unwillingness to accept a 'No', court bureaucrats directed Ad to the Pretoria chief of prisons and she left the court immediately for his office, insisting to reluctant subordinates that she must see him. She was marched along what seemed like an endless corridor in the old colonial-style building. Stocky and intimidating, he looked up from his desk and shouted impatiently: 'Yes?'

He prevaricated until Ad told him firmly: 'It wouldn't look good, would it, if the press found out that his little son had died and the funeral had happened without his wife being able to visit and tell him?' By now infuriated that he had been cornered, the prison chief reluctantly replied: 'I will see to it then.' Permission was later granted.

One young PAC activist whom Ad helped at his trial in Pretoria symbolised the remarkable story of South Africa's transformation. Interviewed for this book in October 2012, Dikgang Moseneke recalled:

> During or about July 1963, at the age of fifteen, I was arraigned before the Supreme Court, Pretoria, with fifteen other accused who were charged with a variety of non-violent activities relating to the Pan Africanist Congress. All the accused were either teachers or students from a residential township known as Atteridgeville in Pretoria. In essence, we

were accused of holding meetings and stating that apartheid should be overthrown. That was said to amount to conspiracy to overthrow the state. The trial was before Justice Cillie and was held in a court house which was generally known as the Synagogue. The building was seemingly a synagogue that was no longer used for worship.

The trial lasted for approximately four weeks during mid-winter. All of the accused were held in detention as bail had been refused. Mrs Hain, who none of the accused knew before then, attended our trial virtually every day. Most mornings she brought along a large pot of hot soup and bread rolls as well as other food for our lunchtime serving. Mrs Hain came to know that one of my childhood loves was chocolate. She made sure that she brought a bar of whole nut chocolate every day of our trial. That little mercy saw me through a very difficult time. She was deeply empathetic and expressed concern that we were likely to be sentenced to long terms in jail despite our young ages and our right to express our displeasure of apartheid repression.

At first we couldn't understand why as a white person she was supporting us. We had never experienced that before: whites were always either the oppressors or couldn't care about us yet she was there every day. We were unaware of her political or activist profile. At the time, it will be remembered, apartheid orthodoxy was alive and well. It had created a considerable racial and social distance which made it unimaginable that she would have at all been concerned about our fate. Moreover, her support for 'terrorists and communists' was unlikely to endear her to the security police, who often stared at her with obvious disapproval, if not hatred. It was also difficult to understand why a white lady of such a tiny frame would want to invite the wrath of that hideous system on herself and family.

I remember quite clearly seeing her tiny frame waving at us shortly after Justice Cillie had imposed sentences ranging from life to five years' imprisonment. For my part, I picked up a ten-year imprisonment term. I gathered while on Robben Island that she had been exiled to the United Kingdom. As I waited for the verdict I was very stressed and started sweating profusely, so much that the chocolate she had given me and which was in my pocket began to melt. She was an inspiration to all of us. She was amazing and I am eternally grateful and she did much to form my own notions of a non-racial South Africa because suddenly she criss-crossed, she cut across lines that we thought were eternal.

Besides when we met at the courthouse, my deep regret is that I never thereafter had the opportunity to express my gratitude for the courage of principle she displayed in very dire circumstances. Much has happened since then and I am now privileged to serve as Deputy Chief Justice of our democratic country in

> the highest court of our land, South Africa's Supreme Court.

Other political organisations at the time represented the different racial groups – Mandela's ANC for example was mainly for Africans, and the Congress of Democrats (a surrogate for the Communist Party, banned in 1950) mainly for whites. The Liberal Party's appeal was based on membership open to all racial groups on an equal basis. Committed to universal franchise, it contained a range of political opinion from socialists to free market liberals as well as a minority who believed in a property-based qualified franchise, which was the stance of Helen Suzman's Progressive Party. But the Liberal Party's unity and its radicalism sprang from an uncompromising support for human rights and a fierce anti-racism, the principles which, above all, inspired Ad and Wal and were adopted by their children.

The appeal of the party was well articulated by Eddie Daniels, a black Liberal Party activist imprisoned upon Robben Island in 1964 where Nelson Mandela took him under his wing despite him not being a member of the ANC. He described why he had joined in Cape Town in 1959:

> Here was an organisation that tickled my fancy; it satisfied the criteria that I was seeking, being both

> anti-government and non-racial … there I met some of the nicest and bravest people dedicated to the principles of non-racialism and justice.‡

Ad and Wal allied themselves with the younger more radical leaders such as Ernie Wentzel, a lawyer who became chairman of the 1961 Transvaal Provincial Congress and a close friend. This radical wing of the Liberals favoured working with anyone who opposed apartheid and Ad and Wal also supported the party's new commitment to extra-parliamentary protest – the latter causing some members to leave in 1959. Ad and Wal backed Liberal leaders such as Jordan Ngubane, national vice-president, who saw this commitment as 'clearing the way for supporting non-white campaigns, not all of which were strictly constitutional'. They also favoured the joint statement on 20 February 1960 by ANC president Albert Luthuli and Liberal chairman Peter Brown advocating an overseas boycott of South African products, which, it stated, was 'yet another phase in our struggle to liberate non-whites from the intolerable bondage of apartheid and to create in South Africa a non-racial democratic state'.

‡ Eddie Daniels, *There and Back: Robben Island 1964–1979* (Cape Town: Mayibuye, 1998), p. 93.

Meanwhile, Ad and Wal had become close friends with many Africans, David Rathswaffo a particular family favourite who would call by and take time to swap greetings and stories. Known for one-liners where syntax and grammar got mangled to hilarity all round, he would say 'Can I see you *in camera*' if he had some confidential information. And he never quite came to terms with telephone-tapping. One day, needing to give Ad an urgent message about helping a black comrade who had escaped from the court, David lowered his voice and whispered: 'Please come, Jimmy has escaped' – as if the whisper might fool those listening in.

He always called her Ad, except when he disapproved of something she had done or said, in which case he would call her 'Mrs Secretary'. David never took a taxi – he always 'boarded a cab'. When he got frustrated in meetings trying to describe something, out would pop to no particular purpose a series of 'fucks'. Others in the meeting would reprimand him with a '*David*!' 'What have I said?' he would reply, startled, until the next meeting when the same rigmarole would be repeated.

Another close friend with a penchant for an eccentric phrase was Poen Ah Dong, a Chinese South African, and the party's accountant. Poen was once arrested and taken to a police station and interrogated. Recounting the incident to Ad and Wal he said: 'They dressed me naked, but I wouldn't tell them anything.'

David had been a clerk at the Supreme Court in Pretoria, where all the major political trials took place.

Until, that was, in 1959 when the government decided that blacks should not carry out such 'responsible tasks', from then on reserved for whites. David was made redundant and replaced by a white man – whom he had to train for the job. (Ad and Wal persuaded colleagues in the Transvaal provincial executive to find the funds to take him on later as a fulltime Pretoria party organiser so that he had an income.) Incidents and events like this were the staple diet of Ad and Wal's daily lives, and Wal used to spend time explaining some of the absurdities of apartheid to their children: that black decorators could paint the undercoat but not the final coat, that they could pass bricks to white builders but not lay these themselves. All a product of 'job reservation' laws designed to ensure blacks remained a servant class.

In 1959 a prominent Pretoria Liberal and local doctor, Colin Lang, contested the Pretoria East by-election to the provincial council as the Nationalists' only opponent (the main opposition United Party declined to compete in what was a safe National Party seat). Ad and Wal's family home became the campaign headquarters and, with volunteers calling in almost continuously, it buzzed with activity. They also had their first experience of electioneering and canvassing – a tough exercise for a non-racial party among the overwhelmingly pro-apartheid white electorate in the capital city. One woman moved quickly to slam her front door on Ad, pausing only to summon in her friendly little dog as if it too risked contamination.

Wal drove campaigners around to leaflet the tree-lined suburbs, including Peter and Tom, aged nine and seven, who had enormous fun pushing the leaflets through letter boxes. Party members came across from Johannesburg to help. One, Ernie Wentzel, relished addressing open-air public meetings from the back of a flat-bed lorry, silencing the bitterly hostile audience's shouts of 'Would you like your sister to marry a Kaffir?' with the response (in a heavy Afrikaans accent): 'Christ man, you should see my sister!'

To Ad and Wal's astonishment, the Liberals achieved a creditable 24 per cent of the vote, saving their deposit, the by-election raising the profile of the Pretoria branch. However, it also brought Ad and Wal and other key activists even greater attention from the authorities. Now aged thirty-three and thirty-five they soon got more and more involved, helping to produce a monthly newsletter called *Libertas*. It was typed by Ad and printed on a noisy and dilapidated old Gestetner duplicator which stood in a corner of the dining room, its black ink frequently dripping where it shouldn't, and its wax stencils hung up for reuse if needed. The children would get roped in to collate the sheets for stapling and Peter and Tom helped push it through doors as it was distributed by a team transported in their blue Volkswagen minibus, now a familiar vehicle to party members. Ad once got bitten by a dog trying to deliver *Libertas* but fortunately was wearing new thick jeans and the teeth did not pierce her skin. Eva's predecessor as their maid was Rahap, a Sotho, who used to help with translation of newsletters into her language – until she left to have a baby.

In 1960 the annual party conference was held in Cape Town and Wal loaded up their minibus's front and two back seats with black, Coloured, Asian and white members, driving them the 900-mile journey there and back. En route, while he was filling up with petrol and the passengers were relieving themselves in the toilets, a white hitchhiker asked him for a lift. There was one spare seat left and Wal offered it to him – just as the man saw the blacks and Coloureds returning to get in, and had second thoughts. However, having unsuccessfully sought a lift from other white drivers, the hitchhiker got in anyway. When Wal looked back later, he was fast asleep – leaning on an African shoulder.

In February 1960, the British Prime Minister, Harold Macmillan, addressed the South African Parliament, speaking of the 'winds of change' blowing through the African continent, and greatly embarrassing the apartheid government, who had good reason to expect the usual platitudes of complicity from Britain which Ad and Wal had now become resigned to expect. They were delighted at this international shot-in-the-arm for anti-apartheid forces, who felt increasingly alone and besieged in what was by now a full-blown police state.

The speech engendered hope among black activists burdened by anger, poverty and frustration, and the ANC called for an economic boycott in protest against the 'passes' Africans had to carry on their persons at all times. These identity documents were designed to restrict and control the movement of blacks about the country and, if a black person was outside a designated rural area, they had to be in order and signed by a white employer.

On one occasion Ad illicitly signed passes for men fearing arrest in Lady Selborne. She had heard on the grapevine of trouble in the township with police engaged in sweeping up men for intimidating checks and quickly drove in with Colyn van Reenen to warn people and then observe. They drove first to her PAC activist friend Jimmy Makojaene and found him at home in his room. Ten minutes later Ad remembered something else she should have told him and they turned back, astonished to find his door padlocked as if nobody had been there for ages. Ad had never been close up to police with drawn submachine guns marching threateningly, half a dozen in each line down one of the main streets. But local men recognised her and sidled up asking surreptitiously if she would sign their pass books – which she did, even though she was thereby committing a crime.

Then on 21 March 1960, at Sharpeville township south of Johannesburg, policemen sitting in armoured vehicles suddenly opened fire on people protesting peacefully against the pass laws. Using over 700 rounds they killed sixty-nine men, women and children and wounded over 180 others. Most were shot in the back while running away, captured in media photographs appalling the world. To apartheid's rulers and their police force, black lives were expendable and the name Sharpeville became synonymous with the terror that was apartheid, Ad and Wal receiving the news with grim foreboding.

For days afterwards the police laid siege to Sharpeville: food was running short and, explaining the horror of the massacre to her children, Ad said she had to go and help. The children were worried something might happen to her – maybe the police might open fire on her too? So it was a relief when she returned, buoyed up, explaining that, after filling up the minibus with provisions donated through the Liberals, and accompanied by Pretoria student Aubrey Davies, she had stopped for petrol at a service station and asked for the tyre pressures to be checked, explaining: 'We are heavily loaded with food for Sharpeville.' The van was instantly surrounded by the black attendants, checking the tyres, cleaning the windscreen and then escorting the vehicle onto the highway, with encouraging shouts and whistles.

A state of emergency was declared as riots and strikes swept the country in protest, the police response to which was brutal. In black townships outside Cape Town police went on the rampage, kicking in doors and randomly assaulting anyone in their way:

Hammington Majija, the local Liberal Party leader in Guguletu, had both his arms broken. When he went to the police station to lay a charge against the officers he was prevented from doing so under threat of a repeat attack. For ten days strikes paralysed Cape Town, closing factories and even the docks, local Liberals raising money to support the strikers – until mass detentions ended the 'stay away'.

Meanwhile, the Treason Trial was proceeding in Pretoria and, while giving evidence, the ANC president, Chief Albert Luthuli, was staying at the house of the Pretoria Liberal chairman, John Brink. Luthuli publicly burnt his pass on 26 March 1960 and called on others to follow suit – his defiance, together with global condemnation of the appalling killing of innocent women and children at Sharpeville, shook the government. It seemed momentarily uncertain and suspended the pass laws, Ad and Wal hearing this with great excitement – and also pride, because many black activist friends were burning their passes too.

But Luthuli was arrested, tried and later fined, Ad having what she regarded as the privilege of being asked to pay the fine and drive him back to the Brinks' home. Ad was so in awe of Luthuli, a grandfatherly figure with silver grey hair and an austere but friendly manner, that she hardly knew what to say to him during the short car journey. However, he was smiling and friendly to her children when they were later introduced to him when the family visited the Brinks again.

The temporary relaxation of the pass laws had given false hope that they were to be abolished, although police vehicles still patrolled potential trouble spots. Excited but tense, Ad and Wal drove into Lady Selborne to spread the word about the good news; one of their contacts, Bob Leshai, a township head teacher, was interested but responded: 'I will believe *that* when it happens.' For a short period there was a feeling throughout the country that apartheid was teetering. Ever a hard-nosed realist, Wal felt it was a mistake to raise expectations. He was proved right: hardly a week had passed and the pass laws were reinstated on 7 April 1960.

Two days later came the astounding – but also exhilarating in a way that made them feel slightly guilty – news that the Godfather of apartheid, Prime Minister Verwoerd, had been shot. He had just opened an agricultural fair to mark the jubilee of the Union of South Africa when one of the VIP guests, a 52-year-old farmer, David Pratt, walked up to him and fired two shots from a .22 automatic pistol at virtually point-blank range, one into Dr Verwoerd's right cheek, a second into his right ear. 'Someone had to do it,' said Pratt, 'so it better bloody be me.' In the panic that followed as Verwoerd fought for his life in hospital, the edifice of white power swayed uncertainly and there was even a hope that some concessions might follow to create stability.

Then grip was restored and, miraculously, Verwoerd returned to public life on 29 May, less than two months after the shooting. By a hair's breadth, the bullets had avoided damaging key areas. Verwoerd's would-be assassin Pratt claimed he had been shooting 'the epitome of apartheid', and was eventually declared 'mentally disordered and epileptic'. On 26 September 1960, he was committed to Pretoria Central Prison and a year later he hanged himself in a mental hospital.

Meanwhile, on 10 April the ANC and its break-away, the PAC, had been banned as unlawful organisations. This was a heavy blow, particularly to the ANC, which for nearly half a century had struggled peacefully against harsh discriminatory laws that in Europe would long before have led to bloody insurrection. Mandela and his colleagues decided they had no alternative but to reorganise the ANC to enable it to function underground, and the PAC adopted the same course.

In March 1960 the Treason Trial had ended with the acquittal of all defendants and the ANC president, Oliver Tambo, immediately left the country to ensure that the organisation survived outside South Africa. Nelson Mandela went underground before he could be rearrested, and became leader of the ANC armed wing, *Umkhonto we Sizwe* (Spear of the Nation), which he said would perform sabotage with strict instructions not to kill.

Wal was always fundamentally opposed to violence. But he did not attack the ANC; indeed he sympathised with Mandela's decision because he understood the ANC had been so badly repressed, and it had little option. He and Ad acknowledged to their elder son

Peter and others that the longer apartheid continued the more violence there would inevitably be. That was why apartheid's rulers had to be persuaded to change before it was too late. Instead the state moved remorselessly on with more and more repression.

This period in 1960 was a tense time for family Hain. Along with some 2,000 anti-apartheid activists, many prominent Liberals, including John Brink and Colin Lang, were detained and it was chilling that they included many whom Ad and Wal knew on first-name terms and who had visited their home. Soon there was a serious shift in their family's situation. For the first time their phone was tapped, mail intercepted and the house regularly observed by the security police. The children also learnt that even everyday phone calls to friends were no longer private.

As tension rose and night-time police raids increased Ad and Wal were worried and so slept away from home on a number of occasions in Wal's parents' tiny studio flat nearby in Pretoria, restless and uncomfortable on the floor with only a blanket; a trusted party friend, Ansie Preller, moved in to be with the children. (Ansie was an extraordinary woman, an Afrikaner from a fiercely pro-apartheid family who nevertheless concluded while at university that she could not countenance racial oppression. This caused a painful breach with her family, especially as her father was a member of the Broederbond, an exclusive apartheid sect with a shadowy but powerful presence in the top National Party echelons. She became a senior librarian, once tipping off Ad and Wal that the English children's classic about a horse, *Black Beauty*, had been banned by South African censors.)

Then in June 1960 Ad was advised that her name had been seen on a list of people to be arrested, that she should leave immediately, and meanwhile go quickly to the home of friends unconnected with the Liberals. The children arrived home from school to be told they were going on holiday right away. Although it was a nice surprise, when Peter (as the oldest) was told the real reason, he was frightened that they might be caught. Then aged ten, he had to ensure clothes and toys were properly packed – though Ad later opened her case to find far too many underclothes and very little else of any use.

Wal came home from work and they all loaded the vehicle, checking no Special Branch were around before driving quickly to collect Ad. She took the wheel and they waved Wal goodbye for the fourteen-hour overnight drive to her parents' home in Port Alfred, repeatedly looking back at the road behind and relieved to see that they were not being followed.

But Ad was worried throughout the journey that she would be stopped. Early on, nearing a bridge, she was terrified to see police ahead stopping and searching vehicles. Her heart was thumping: what should she do? But before she had time to think she was upon the bridge and then across: the police were clearly on the lookout for someone or something else, not a mother driving her children.

Her relief was tempered by lacking confidence in driving that distance because her sense of direction was never good. At home, Wal worried continuously, feeling helpless that there was nothing he could do to protect or support her and the children. They had always driven the long journey to the Eastern Cape seashore together, even managing to relieve each other by exchanging the wheel across the bench front seat while the car ploughed on. He would have worried himself silly had he been aware that Ad nearly fell asleep at the wheel driving throughout the night, and pulled off under a tree by the side of the open road and locked the doors for a snooze.

In the Orange Free State she turned up at the house of a Liberal Party member whom she knew previously from Pretoria. He was shocked to see her, filling the car up with petrol at the garage he owned. Ad and Wal discovered much later that he was a Special Branch informant but he obviously hadn't informed on her this time because she went safely on her way, the tension receding as the miles swept by under the high African sky, through wide plains, steep passes and majestic mountains.

The VW minibus, powered by only a small 1,200cc engine, took ages to traverse long hills and passes along the single carriageways which spanned the entire 800-mile route. It became foggy during the latter part of the journey in the Eastern Cape and she had been forced to slow as she peered through the front window searching for the white lines to guide her. By the time she was nearing Grahamstown just an hour short of Port Alfred it was pitch dark and she didn't want to surprise her parents, who had no idea she was coming (any phone call was too risky). So she knocked on Jo's door in Grahamstown and they all stayed overnight, squeezing into her small bedsit.

But on arrival at Mentone they were welcomed by her startled parents, and quickly settled into the familiar routine of a break by the seaside, albeit (unlike their normal sun-baked holidays) this time in the middle of the South African winter. Wal, missing them anxiously, had been designing Ad's brother Hugh's house to be built next to Mentone and needed to inspect the site. To his relief he was later given a lift down in Hugh's private plane to join his family (Hugh had been a bomber pilot in the Second World War).

It was a criminal offence under the state of emergency to divulge information on detainees and there was difficulty communicating between areas because of tapped phones and opened mail, so Wal had been asked to check on the state of the party in the Eastern Cape Province and Natal by visiting key figures. They set off on the long circular drive east before returning to Pretoria and called in at Alan Paton's house, The Long View, high up overlooking the hills north of Durban. They remained slightly in trepidation of the internationally renowned author and party president, who could seem severe. But he quickly put them and their four children at their ease as he sought a report back on the Pretoria Liberals' predicament and in turn updated them on the general position across the country.

Returning home from their unscheduled break after the countrywide state of emergency was lifted at the end of August 1960, they learnt that the remaining detainees had been released. But soon afterwards their home was raided by the security police and statements by people wounded at Sharpeville the day after the shootings were seized, never to be seen again. Ad and Wal were frustrated with anger at the loss of this precious evidence but could do nothing about it. Only because they spoke Afrikaans, and therefore seemed respectable to security guards, had Pretoria University Liberals Johann van den Berg and Mickey Mikilades been allowed into Baragwaneth Hospital outside Johannesburg secretly to take down these statements.

From then on, their servant Eva Matjeka always took a suitcase overnight to her quarters with any sensitive papers they had in the house. But on one occasion, as she had been out late, this routine was suspended and Eva was shocked to arrive from her quarters to find security police in the house. Realising that Ad had secreted the case away in a slot between a kitchen cupboard and the cooker, she opened the cupboard door and searched in it for an inordinate time, deliberately screening the case from the prying officers.

Once, Eva called from a phone box to say she couldn't come to work because – without giving any advance notice whatsoever – the authorities had ordered workers to take the roof off her house in Lady Selborne, forcing her and all other Africans to move out to make space for whites. Eva had three children and they had nowhere else to live. As the workers moved in to kick her out, she was officiously informed she had to go on a list to find a house in Atteridgeville township, miles away. Although Ad and Wal had been campaigning against such forced removals from Lady Selborne, it had suddenly become personal. Eva had to take her furniture and search for somewhere to live, staying temporarily with friends.

Ad later asked what was happening. 'I don't go past my old house anymore because it makes me sore to the heart. It is still there, empty – they haven't even taken off the roof yet. They just wanted to get rid of me.' Eventually, when she did get a place in Atteridgeville, she was in luck – because it had a surfaced floor. Most newly removed residents had no such luxury, merely bare earth.

With the ANC and PAC now illegal, black membership in the Pretoria branch of the Liberal Party – by this time the only legal anti-apartheid group in the city – grew. There seemed a constant flow of people in and out of the Hain house. Branch meetings were held in their living room with Wal and others collecting African and

Asian members from their segregated townships and driving them home afterwards.

Whites in the local Liberal Party contributed food parcels for the families of ANC or PAC detainees and the children sometimes accompanied Ad and Wal, as they delivered these in their minibus to Pretoria's townships of Lady Selborne, Atteridgeville and Eastwood.

In October 1960, Prime Minister Verwoerd called a whites-only referendum to decide whether South Africa should become a republic. The Liberal Party called for a 'NO' vote, not because it opposed a republican state but because it saw this as heralding further apartheid restrictions, not least since posters for the government-supported 'YES' campaign stated bluntly: 'Vote Yes to Keep South Africa White'.

Ad and Wal helped put up large 'NO' posters after dark and surreptitiously pulled down 'YES' posters from telegraph poles and other vantage points whenever they could safely to do so, replacing them with their own 'NO' ones, which Maritz van den Bergh had illicitly printed in the office of the Transvaal Works Department. Although not illegal, the clandestine poster activity would have invited restriction by the Special Branch, but they and other Liberal activists gave that no serious thought: they simply had to do what they had to do.

Gratifyingly, the result was quite close: 850,000 voted Yes (overwhelmingly Afrikaners) with 776,000 No and so, after 150 years, the country's links with the British Crown came to an end. On 31 May 1961 South Africa officially became a republic and was excluded from the Commonwealth – making anti-apartheid activists like Ad and Wal feel even more isolated: whatever they did, the apartheid juggernaut just seemed to roll remorselessly on.

5

Prisoners

Nelson Mandela was still underground and being hunted by the security police when he called for black workers to adopt a three day 'stay-at-home' at the end of May 1961 to protest against all racial laws. A great success on the first day, the stay-at-home soon fizzled out after massive police intimidation and raids (some 10,000 were detained). It proved to be the last disciplined, mass, non-violent demonstration to be held in the old South Africa until resistance flared up again in the 1980s.

When Mandela first made his call, Ad and Wal responded enthusiastically and decided to distribute stay-at-home leaflets and put up posters in the Lady Selborne township. With Colyn van Reenen, they drove there at night to put up a few initial posters and make plans for full-scale leafleting the next day (because their phones were tapped these plans had to be discussed in person). Fellow Liberal Party activist Maritz van den

Berg was nervous about participating, but needed a lift to his parents' home and joined them to wait in the car while they jumped out to put up the posters, which were rather bland.

They had hardly arrived when a car drew up behind theirs. Two Special Branch officers, Viktor and van Zyl (familiar to them), stepped menacingly out. Although stunned, Ad didn't panic, quickly chewing up and spitting out the draft of the incriminating next-day leaflet she wanted to discuss with the others. She jumped from the car with the posters and ran off to a nearby shop which she knew had a back entrance through which she might get away.

But, to her dismay, the shop was locked up for the night: now she was cornered, the officer Viktor pounding up to grab her. Wal, confronted by van Zyl, responded cheekily (as he was prone to on occasion) and demanded to see his police identity card: provocative and a big mistake.

Van Zyl exploded: 'Mr Hain, you *know me*!'

But when Wal persisted, van Zyl angrily retorted in Afrikaans: '*Now* we're going to take you in.'[‡]

They were driven off to the nearest police station, arrested and told they would be held without trial. Colyn managed to phone his mother, Nan van Reenen. A kindly, middle-aged, English-speaking woman, she

‡ Ironically, some months later, Wal and van Zyl found themselves in a waiting room together as blood donors, formally acknowledging each other without any conversation.

was also a determined Liberal Party member, frequently giving the Special Branch a piece of her mind. When she arrived at the police station Ad and Wal could hear her angrily denouncing duty officers for holding them. But she got nowhere and, worried about their children, Ad and Wal asked her to go around to their house.

They had previously warned Peter, now aged eleven, that such was the security clampdown they could be detained at any time, making contingency plans for Wal's mother Mary (who lived nearby with his dad) and their maid Eva to look after the children. Peter was used to taking responsibility and to looking after his younger brother Tom, then aged nine, and two small sisters Jo-anne and Sally, aged six and four.

It was around midnight when Nan van Reenen, anxious in the gloom, bent over the sleeping Peter and gently shook him awake. 'Your parents have been put in jail,' she said, holding his hand.

He was drowsy and confused. Although he seemed calm, she could sense his worry, explaining what she understood had happened. Then together they checked that the others were still sleeping; she tucked up on the living room sofa and sent Peter back to bed.

In the morning, before she handed over to Eva and spoke to their grandmother Mary, Nan told the children what had happened. The girls were wide-eyed and Tom very quiet. They did not cry but Nan could see that tears were being held back.

Their gran soon came over and moved in – though not

Grandad, who took the view that his son and daughter-in-law had been reckless and disapproved of the extent of their activism. Eva quietly took charge and ensured everything went as smoothly as possible, and an activist friend, Anita Cohen, brought a huge meringue cake round to cheer up the children.

Although worried and missing their parents, they were not traumatised. The family had become used to their telephone being tapped, to Special Branch surveillance of their house in the Pretoria suburb of Hatfield, to police suddenly raiding and searching the house, and to being told that friends had been imprisoned. That this had now happened to their parents seemed almost normal.

As was the practice in most countries, the police were entitled to hold suspects before charging them, in South Africa's case for two days. But a new law had just been brought in allowing for twelve days' detention without charge and, after their two days were up, Ad and Wal were taken to court and then to serve their twelve days in prison, the first people to be detained under this new law aimed at curbing rising political dissent. But not before the magistrate – in front of a crowded press gallery – insisted upon a copy of the new law being brought in for him to see first. There was none available and he proclaimed to the state prosecutor: 'If I don't receive a copy before the court closes at five o'clock I will have no alternative but to release them.' A frisson ran round the courtroom, Ad and Wal sitting in the dock together with Colyn and Maritz wondering what might happen, their spirits rising as they viewed the unexpected panic among prosecutors and police with some amusement.

But, with minutes to go to the deadline, a uniformed despatch rider came sprinting in and handed the magistrate the required document. As the men were led separately away, Ad quickly hugged Wal, feeling apprehensive as nothing like this had happened to her before. She had to climb into a large police bus, the only woman on board, African prisoners separate in the back. Several white males who had been sentenced for conventional crimes were with her in front, one of them having a last cigarette.

She was the first to be dropped off at the women's prison.

'What are you in for?' a belligerent white woman warder asked.

'Political,' Ad replied.

As they decided what to do with her, Ad winced in disgust as she witnessed black women prisoners being deliberately humiliated by being forced to strip, the warders leering at a pregnant woman. In the days that followed she became increasingly angry at the gratuitous nastiness of prison staff to black women prisoners.

Ad and Wal knew their children would be cared for by their gran and the ever-reliable Eva and were relieved to learn later that very little was made of their arrests by the children's teachers or friends. But that didn't stop them worrying continuously. Would the children be up and to school on time? Were they being fed properly? Peter, they thought, would be OK as the eldest of the four. But what about Tom – and especially the girls, who were still so young? The long dragging hours inside prison with nothing to do left more than enough time for Ad to lose sleep as she agonised. Although thrilled to get a letter from Peter, she cried as it brought home their predicament. 'Gran and Eva are looking after us well but we are missing you a lot,' it said in clear, careful writing.

Her mood swung between guilt at how she had abandoned her children, to determination that she would not be cowed by her imprisonment. She had no doubt it had been the right thing to help after Mandela's call, but her detention sharpened the tension between her responsibilities as a mother and her duties as a human rights activist.

After the two initial days in a police station, Ad was locked up alone in a large echoing hall in Pretoria Central Prison in which white women detainees had been held during the 1960 emergency. With nobody to share and talk to, she fought against being enveloped by despair, her isolation seeming to compound her predicament from one almost expected – she and Wal had discussed the likelihood of detention and resolved not to be deflected – into one of desperation.

Reverberating up the stairwell, she could hear the haunting screams of African women prisoners being assaulted, reinforcing both her misery and her position of relative privilege. She found the wardresses flesh-creeping and intimidating, especially when they deliberately came to watch her having a bath; so much so that she decided to forgo the pleasures of a relaxing bath and instead wash in a hand basin where it was more private.

Meanwhile, Wal and his two male comrades, Colyn and Maritz, were taken off to share a cell in Pretoria Local Prison where conditions were not bad. At least the men had their friendship to share and support each other, whereas Ad was alone. Nevertheless, he also slept badly throughout, worrying not just about his kids but mainly about her. Because his mother Mary and Nan van Reenen always visited the men first, he got no news about Ad until the two women came round again for their next permitted visit several days later.

What made it worse was they had absolutely no contact until they were finally released. He had no real idea whether she was in good health or how she was coping. Determined and phlegmatic a character though he was – and hardened from his war days to coping in adversity – that did not prevent him worrying continuously about her. They were inseparable then and would be for the rest of their lives – now they were separated.

His anxiety was increased almost immediately by receiving a letter in prison from his municipal employer sacking him. With no job to go back to, how would he support his family? He was the only breadwinner. Finding out the news, having visited Wal first, his mother Mary then visited Ad and told her thoughtlessly, using a

Scottish phrase of the time: 'Wal's been put off his work.' It was said as if it was only to be expected – jolting Ad.

She used to keep herself occupied on her own in the huge hall, by timing herself in a hop-skip exercise, setting herself a target and trying to stick to it. Although she received newspapers as a detainee awaiting trial, the time dragged interminably. Completely alone, she wondered at one point whether she should continue being active – then quickly dismissed the thought as a moment of weakness.

Meanwhile, the police searched in vain for evidence to bring charges. And because Ad had chewed up the one serious piece of incriminating evidence that could have led to charges – the draft leaflet urging people to go on strike and stay at home in breach of the law – much as they tried, the Special Branch could not find anything to bring a prosecution because the posters were innocuous. After fourteen seemingly endless days they were suddenly told they would be released immediately – to the obvious deep frustration of the Special Branch.

Ad saw Wal for the first time in court immediately before they were let out, hugging emotionally. Unlike Wal, detained with colleagues, Ad's isolation in a different prison for women meant she felt extremely disorientated, flat and empty. They were all driven home by Nan van Reenen and four-year-old Sally leapt into Ad's arms in sheer joy, though a little frightened when she first saw her dad because he had grown an unfamiliar beard in prison. Peter, Tom and Jo-anne, walking home from school, were surprised but delighted to see their dad strolling along to meet them with little sister Sally in her favourite perch on his shoulders. Jo-anne, especially close to her father, looked up from chatting to a school friend, had a rush of happiness and ran across the road to be scooped up for a huge hug.

To their immense relief, the children seemed to have survived their absence in good spirits. There were no clinging aftermaths. Peter and Tom seemed to have borne the experience cheerfully. But Ad was concerned that six-year-old Jo-anne seemed to have been desperately wanting to feel her mother near her when she modified a petticoat she had always loved her mom wearing. It had layers of stiff net which made her skirts stick out, rather like a modern-day crinoline. There was a thin nylon section from waist to hip before the netting and Jo-anne cut holes in this, so that she could wear the petticoat with her arms through the holes.

The joy of family reunion was tempered by Wal losing his job. For two long months – the only time in his working life – he was unemployed: deeply unsettling and trying for him – and a big financial blow. Somehow they struggled through with the help of a donation from an anonymous Liberal Party member, surviving on account and relying on the understanding of local shopkeepers as Ad, Wal and Peter signed for essential items in the chemist or grocery store.

Then after two months Wal was offered a temporary post by Leslie Cooper, a party member in Johannesburg. Although he was relieved, having to travel the hour there and back every day ate away at time with his family and for his party activities. So when a Pretoria architectural firm offered him a post, he happily accepted, finding the office a very good one in which to work, designing hospitals, which he particularly enjoyed. But Wal was contemptuous of having to design entirely separate facilities for blacks in one remote rural hospital. 'It's also a chronic waste of public money,' he came home to tell Ad in disgust.

Government attacks on the Liberal Party were now plentiful. Leading Liberals Jordan Ngubane, Bill Bhengu and Julius Malie were arrested, charged and found guilty of 'furthering the aims of communism' by working with and assisting ANC members – though they were finally acquitted on appeal. The 1961 law, introduced to enable detention without trial for twelve days, was subsequently extended to ninety days, then 180 days and finally an indefinite period. The 1962 Sabotage Act was designed to catch even those anti-apartheid activists who were engaging in non-violent direct action; it defined sabotage in such broad terms that a strike by railway workers could be construed as 'sabotage'.

During the second reading of the Sabotage Bill, the minister Blaar Coetzee spelt out why the Liberals were being attacked – because of their support for universal suffrage. The legislation, he said, was partly designed 'to get at another group and that group comprises, wittingly or unwittingly, the agents of communism in South Africa [who want] to force the policy of one-man one-vote on this country in an unconstitutional manner … as some members of the Liberal Party want to do … [They are] guilty of high treason and this law is intended for them.' In a speech in Durban in November 1962 the Liberal Party president, Alan Paton, described the Act, a creature of the Security and Justice Minister, John Vorster, as 'a totalitarian measure expressly designed to circumscribe the liberties of those with whom he did not agree'.

In protest, Ad – joined by Sammy van den Berg – planned to lay a wreath on the steps of the Supreme Court to signify the end of the rule of law in the country. They had agreed to it over the phone fully aware that the Special Branch would be listening, but then the *Pretoria News* asked if they could make it earlier so as to make their evening newspaper deadline and sent a photographer. Clearly the Special Branch had not caught up with this development because the wreath was laid, photo taken and Ad and Sammy had departed before officers rushed up, confused to discover it was already all over.

Government ministers and MPs took particular exception when senior Liberals started to organise in some of the Bantustans – so called 'homelands' for Africans designated according to their original chiefdoms, but which subsequent generations might never have visited. They were remote and desperately poor areas, covering just 10 per cent of the land for 80 per cent of the population. In the Transkei, where Nelson Mandela was born, they began working closely with his Thembu people. One National Party MP, viewing this activity as 'a cancer on the normal peaceful development of good relations between black and white in South Africa', urged measures 'to restrict the Liberal Party'. For organising alliances against the government's determination to segregate blacks into their 'homelands', Ad and Wal's good friends Randolph Vigne and Peter Hjul were both banned, and prominent Cape Town Liberal Patrick Duncan was exiled.

Despite Ad's by now decidedly frosty relationship with the Special Branch, she was caught by surprise at being semi-manhandled in public by Sergeant Jan Viktor, who had arrested her the previous year. With Wal standing by her she was trying to hand over a letter to a chunky, bespectacled United Nations envoy, Vittorio Carpio, in the foyer of a Pretoria hotel in May 1962, when the letter was grabbed from her and she was jostled back. Wrestling with Viktor she tried unsuccessfully to retrieve the letter as he stuffed it into his pocket. But suddenly she spotted Carpio striding hurriedly down a passage to get into a lift, and managed to force her way through to him. Confused that this determined young woman was saying to him 'Welcome, Mr Carpio, I was trying to hand you a letter offering to help inform you about the real situation in South Africa', the diplomat smiled but walked on. Wal quickly joined her and they made another unsuccessful attempt to speak to Carpio as the doors of the lift closed.

Later they were allowed to see him with Ernie Wentzel. But it was a big disappointment, not least because she found Carpio creepy, with 'octopus hands'.

By this time contacts with relatives had also become increasingly strained. Although the wider family was quite close, none of them apart from Jo was at all politically involved. Ad's eldest brother Hugh, also living in Pretoria, was by then the millionaire owner of a construction company and was worried that his business could be affected by association. Wal, *pro bono*, had designed a new holiday house for Hugh just down from Ad's parental home on the banks of the Kowie River, and also at Hugh's request an extension to the Christian Science church in Pretoria. When holidaying in Port Alfred, the children would be invited out on Hugh's speedboats. The children had also been regular visitors to Hugh's house in Pretoria to play with his own five children who were similarly aged, and to swim in their pool.

But these invitations suddenly stopped. Ad and Wal tried to explain the reason to their own children, shielding how upset they were, especially from Jo-anne and Sally, who were far too young to understand why they would no longer be seeing their close cousins and best friends, Annie and Liz. The family were not invited to the wedding of Hugh's oldest daughter, Barbara. But the day before that, Jo-anne and Sally were asked over to see the bridesmaid dresses fitted for Annie and Liz. Ad didn't want them to go since they weren't invited to the wedding, but the girls were keen so she relented.

Once, Ad was walking with her girls in a narrow Pretoria street with an Asian party member, Edward White, who was holding hands with them – highly provocative interracial behaviour at the time. She glanced up to see her brother Hugh coming in their direction on the pavement opposite. She was about to greet him, but then he turned his back to look fixedly in a shop window as they passed by. (Earlier, and after Ad made her emergency trip with the children to Port Alfred, Hugh called her to remonstrate, arguing she 'shouldn't have involved their parents' by journeying down to them.)

The schism had another effect. Ad, who had been brought up a Christian Scientist like her brothers and sisters – her mother though not her father devout – now felt estranged: what was Christianity about, if not to give support and understanding in times of difficulty? What was all that about the 'Good Samaritan'? Her brother Hugh and sister-in-law Margaret were staunch Christian Scientists, as were most of her wider family. How could the admirable principles of Christianity be reconciled with apartheid? How could the sometimes fundamentalist Christian churchgoers who ran the government possibly justify the human misery they deliberately inflicted? Some even grotesquely cited a section of the Bible – 'hewers of wood and the drawers of water' – to justify treating blacks as slave-like inferiors. What she came to feel was a stark contradiction between Christian Science's values and the tolerance of apartheid by active Christians like her brothers, which led her to become progressively disaffected from the church and then to lapse completely.

Their children used to go with their cousins to the local Christian Science Sunday school. Even though Wal was a convinced atheist, he was tolerant of his wife's faith and felt his children should make up their own minds. But during the period of Ad and Wal's imprisonment Peter realised that the person teaching them was a police officer – like the ones who had locked up his parents. He decided that neither he nor his brother and sisters would attend anymore; they never did again.

Wal's sister-in-law, brother Tom's wife Marie Hain, ran a travel agency in Pretoria and her boss told her to phone Ad to ask her to stop writing letters to the press under the name of Hain.

'No, Marie, I can't do that,' Ad replied.

When Marie persisted Ad laughingly retorted: 'No, Marie! I was a Hain before you were!'

Marie was then instructed by her boss to place an advert in the *Pretoria News* saying that her company had no relationship with 'the Mrs Hain of the Liberal Party'. Although Marie was embarrassed at the encounter, Ad and Wal treated it lightly – even as something of a vindication that their activities were having an impact.

Despite the absence of any personal hostility with relatives, a barrier grew as Ad and Wal moved in different worlds. When life later became extremely difficult and Wal was out of a job, their well-off relatives could have helped but chose not to. They remained in all other respects friendly and (within the white framework) decent, honest and caring family folk. It was simply that they were apprehensive of the impact of Ad and Wal's politics upon them, and feared it would be too risky to remain closely associated. This caused great personal anguish especially for Ad, who was close to her brother Mike and had always looked up to her big brother Hugh.

In December 1961 the ANC's paramilitary wing, *Umkhonto*, began a campaign of placing incendiary bombs in government offices, post offices and electrical substations, carrying out 200 attacks in the following eighteen months. Ad and Wal were amazed that the ANC were able to place some of these bombs in Pretoria offices where all government workers, down to the cleaners, were white – until their comrade Peter Magano said: 'Don't forget the "messenger boys" are still black!'

The term 'boy' was patronisingly applied by whites

to all black men, the spectacle of bumptious white kids casually talking down to greying black grandfathers tending their gardens epitomising the daily indignity of apartheid. On one occasion Peter's friend Dave Geffen knocked off the hat of an elderly man, Peter insisting he picked it up and gave it back. At school, one of Jo-anne's friends pointed to 'that boy over there'; she looked, but couldn't see any 'boy', telling her friend to call the elderly man by his name.

On 5 August 1962, having been seventeen months on the run, Nelson Mandela was finally captured near Howick Falls in Natal, after an informer tipped off the police. Mostly disguised as a chauffeur with uniform and peaked cap driving his white master, he had evaded the authorities and travelled throughout the country on secret missions organising the ANC underground, with the media dubbing him the 'Black Pimpernel'.[‡]

From October 1961 he had been based at Liliesleaf Farm, a smallholding in Rivonia, twelve miles north of Johannesburg, then set on its own amid untidy fields. Liliesleaf was the secret headquarters of his underground organisation, where Mandela masqueraded as a gardener and cook, wearing blue overalls and living – as was customary then for such black servants – in an outbuilding which also served as the office where he wrote his political and military strategies. His wife Winnie visited him there with their two little girls,

‡ See Peter Hain, *Mandela* (London: Spruce, 2010).

careful with her journey as she switched cars to and fro during the trips.

His trial opened at the Old Synagogue in Pretoria on 22 October 1962 and Ad covered it for the Liberal magazine *Contact*, enthralled as evidence emerged which had never made the papers of all his activities underground. Ad had tried to attend as a representative of the press but officials refused permission, and she was often the only one in the white section of the public gallery; once, a white couple spat at her as she was leaving. When Mandela entered court each day, after raising his fist in the traditional ANC *Amandla*! salute to the packed black section he would turn and do the same to her, an acknowledgement she returned and found very moving. Nearly thirty years later, when she met him in London as part of a group she said: 'I don't suppose you remember me,' to which he replied, giving her a great hug: 'How could I forget!'

As a crowd gathered outside the court Ad tried to take a photograph, but a policeman yelled: 'You can't do that,' clinging onto his hat as he ran towards her; she snatched a photo of him instead. Mandela's beautiful wife Winnie attended the hearings each day, often magnificent in African dress. Once, when Jo-anne and Sally accompanied Ad, Winnie bent down and put her arms around the two little blonde girls and kissed them, to the evident outrage of the onlooking white policemen bristling with machine guns and pistols. To them, the sight of a black woman – especially *that* woman, wife of the ogre Mandela – kissing white girls was plain *obscene*. Sally, then six years old, recalled: 'Winnie was stunning.'

Ad was to witness daily how Mandela's magnetic personality dominated the courtroom. He seemed to her almost regal, unflinching yet also courteous. Conducting his own defence as a practising lawyer, he knew all the court etiquette and exactly how to play the rules without transgressing any boundaries. She marvelled at his inner strength and the sheer power he exuded, enthralled at how the aggressive state prosecutor was repeatedly left floundering by Mandela's deft handling of his defence – clearly the superior lawyer. However, that did not prevent him being sentenced to five years' hard labour on Robben Island and he waved a defiant farewell to his supporters, Ad included, before being taken down and transported away.

Amid the increasing political turmoil surrounding the family, Peter became head prefect at Hatfield Primary School and Tom, very popular among the pupils, won the top School Good Fellowship prize. Ad and Wal instilled in their children a discipline to work hard, do homework on time and play sport virtually every afternoon. Certain teachers, aware of the Hains' growing notoriety, were quietly sympathetic. Others were not. Sally, newly at school, found her first teacher hostile and once was deliberately prevented from going to the toilet when she needed to, wetting her pants as a result.

However, none of the parents of friends of their children were difficult in any way and those of Peter's close friend Dave Geffen, 'Gef' and Gladys, were particularly kind. Dave commented in October 2012:

> I cannot remember my folks ever being critical of Ad and Wal's political views, even to the extent of expressing the opinion that 'everyone is entitled to their own opinion and view'. One thing was very clear though, my folks certainly respected them as parents, and the way they brought up their children. That also included the way they looked after me while in their care. Also, they did not try to force their politics onto others, only show them by example. In general, I think that most of our peers and their parents thought that they were a bit irresponsible, knowing that what they were doing was going to land them in some sort of trouble with the security police.

Meanwhile, Ad and Wal had become friendly with two sympathetic diplomats in the Netherlands and West German embassies, Coen Stork and Rudi Ernst. As they got to know the diplomats better, their families began mixing. Rudi and Wal swopped wartime experiences and found that even as enemies then they now had much in common, including their love for Italy. The

Italians, according to Rudi, had been very good to the German occupiers too, Wal noted wryly.

Both diplomats mentioned the difficulty of meeting black activists socially and suggested that the Liberal Party host gatherings to remedy this. Ad and Wal readily agreed and soon what became known as their 'diplomatic parties' were being held in their house. Special Branch officers parked outside noted all the diplomatic number plates and reported back that the Hains had embarked on a new scale of trouble.

The world was at last beginning to mobilise against apartheid and Ad and Wal were thrilled that on 6 November 1962 the General Assembly of the United Nations voted for sanctions against South Africa. Would this mark a turning point? Would the increasingly difficult position they were finding themselves in be reversed? It was not long before they were to find out.

❦

Of all the court cases in which Ad became involved, there was one that she would never for a moment have imagined, even under the often bizarre twists of apartheid: a trial for the ancient crime of heresy.

Albertus Geyser was a brilliant biblical scholar from a staunch Afrikaner family. Appointed aged twenty-seven as professor of theology at the University of Pretoria and a member of the synod of the Dutch Reformed Church, Geyser was asked to develop a biblical justification for the inferiority of blacks. But in an exhaustive study he came to the very opposite conclusion: that there was no such justification in the Bible.

Repeatedly pressed by both the Church and the Broederbond to change his mind, he refused because he felt it a matter of intellectual integrity. He and his family suffered enormous stress; his wife Celia had a nervous breakdown which led to her being admitted temporarily as a mental health patient. The Broederbond was outraged, and he was found guilty of heresy by a commission of the synod and expelled from it. He was also forced out of Pretoria University.

Early in the furore Ad was asked by Liberal Party leaders to contact Geyser and fixed to meet him at his home, arriving a little early and apologising. 'No, I'm glad you were early because my brother is just leaving and I might have hit him otherwise!' Geyser explained pithily, his wider family bitter over his stand. He was grateful for her message of solidarity from the Liberals, although he made it clear he was not a supporter of their universal franchise policy.

Geyser bravely appealed the synod's verdict to the Supreme Court in 1962, comforted by Ad's presence at the end of the case, though she was aghast at how his wife, a talented professional woman in her own right, had turned into a pale shadow of her former self. But he had a vindication of sorts: the case was resolved by an out-of-court settlement under which Pretoria University was required to reinstate him. Nevertheless, he remained in an impossible position and resigned of his own accord – still shunned in his own community. The more liberal Witwatersrand University in Johannesburg instead welcomed him as their professor of divinity.

By now Wal had taken over as chairman of the Pretoria Liberals and so he and his wife occupied what were effectively the two top positions in the city's only legal anti-apartheid force. As such they became even more prominent targets in this citadel of Afrikanerdom. They seemed to be permanently in the *Pretoria News* and, late in 1962, Wal began to write frequent leader-page articles for the *Rand Daily Mail*, the country's main liberal (though not *Liberal Party*) newspaper, which annoyed the Special Branch and government ministers even more.

Wal was also prolific in newspaper letter columns, with eloquent arguments based upon careful logic aimed at thinking whites, always signed 'W. V. Hain'. On 7 September 1961 he attacked

> the intellectually dishonest state of white South African sport today. Our white "sportsmen" have proved themselves completely two-faced – happy to play against non-whites on overseas tours, equally happy not to play against non-whites at home and so to support a system which denies non-white sportsmen access to representative sport.

On 15 October 1962 he attacked the National Party

notion that famine and malnutrition among black South Africans was their own fault:

> The chief cause given by all the experts is starvation wages and its inevitable corollary inefficient eating habits. The responsibility for starvation wages must rest in the first instance with the government, which is empowered to set a minimum wage above the breadline (as it has repeatedly been asked to do by commerce and industry, but which it has not done for purely political reasons). But commerce and industry must share in the blame, for when the government failed in its duty the onus was surely on them to take steps themselves to see that a country-wide living wage was instituted.

He also criticised the editorial stance of the *Star* newspaper on 3 December 1962, ridiculing its contention that there had been a lowering of racial temperatures on the same day that it commented on a riot in the town of Paarl in the Cape wine lands. Pointing out that attitudes had been hardening among Africans after the banning of the ANC and PAC, he was caustic:

> Your suggestion that there is a better chance of non-whites getting more when 'the country is prosperous and there is more of everything to go round' will surely evoke hollow laughter among them. The country is prosperous and has been for years, but the 'more of everything' predictably finds its way into white pockets.

In an erudite rebuttal of the racist prejudices of National Party supporters on 13 December 1962, he quoted Socrates, making an intellectual case for liberalism as being in tune with the advance of humankind. The Nats, he argued, were leading the country to

> eventual chaos and anarchy. In contrast the liberal aim is a positive one: by pointing out that the differences between peoples are insignificant compared with the similarities; that different races can and do live together in amity; that political integration is perfectly consistent with differing social and religious customs, to prepare the way for a peaceful and orderly change in our country. In this aim liberals have the moral support of mankind … These are the reasons why liberalism is such a powerful force in the world today, and the real reason why racialists have such a pathological fear of it.

In *The Star* on 13 February 1963 Wal took on specious claims by apartheid supporters that scientific evidence supported the doctrine of white supremacy.

> The great bulk of scientific observation and thought supports the view that psychological differences between racial groups (which of course exist between white racial groups, as well as between white and non-white) are primarily environmental and not genetic … Segregationists' attempt to give apartheid both a moral and a scientific basis should fool nobody,

> because it has neither. It remains today what it was in 1948 – a cynical attempt to maintain the privileges of the few, regardless of the sufferings of the many.

In these and other letters and articles Wal sought to persuade by rational argument, spending hours each time assembling his case, an honourable and worthy but in retrospect vain attempt to stem the onward rush of apartheid's deepening brutality.

Ad was meanwhile also prolific in print. To the Special Branch, 'Adelaine Hain' became an even more toxic name on letters and articles which bore the stamp of Wal's meticulous research. In a leader-page article in the *Rand Daily Mail* on 22 February 1963 she launched a broadside at dreadful health services and hospital facilities for black citizens. And to those who insisted the country could not afford to bring these up to the standards enjoyed by whites, she exposed the exorbitant waste of duplicating services in order to maintain segregation in health. 'There is no country in the world which can afford to duplicate such services,' Ad insisted. But then she went an important step further. Because they were so poor, Africans would not be able to afford hospital fees. Therefore, 'the only way to ensure that all who require health services obtain them when they need them … is by free hospitalisation, such as is provided by Britain's National Health Service, and is advocated by the Liberal Party here'. A few months later on 8 May 1963, Ad tore into the official opposition United Party (in which her father had once been active) for claiming that South Africa was a democratic country. 'Democracy in South Africa is merely a Nationalist myth told convincingly to the white electorate so that it will happily vote in Nazi-type laws to preserve the myth!'

Throughout the year 1963 the bylines 'Adelaine Hain' and 'W. V. Hain' provocatively poked at the underbelly of the ruling apartheid elite, especially its security apparatus. Among the many myths propagated to underpin an ideology of white supremacy was that Africans were 'primitive and uncivilised' and, on 7 March 1963, Wal confronted head-on 'a deep-rooted fear: that Africans are an essentially violent and brutal people'. Pointing out that, before they were banned, the history of the ANC and latterly the PAC was one of remarkable non-violence despite abject discrimination and oppression, he contrasted that with the recent violence of whites such as the IRA in Ireland, Jews in post-World War Palestine, Greek Cypriots and even the Nazi-supporting 'present Minister of Justice' [John Vorster], interned for sabotage during World War Two. For South Africa, he added: 'The lesson of history is that repression inevitably breeds violent reaction… And in making it virtually impossible for Africans to bring about change peaceably, the present government has ensured that political violence, which has hitherto been a stranger to the non-white South African scene, will in future become part of our lives.'

After Wal also made time to help his eldest boy Peter

with essays on current affairs at Pretoria Boys High School, a favourite teacher, Terence Ashton, remarked that Peter's writing 'seemed remarkably similar to that of W. V. Hain in the *Rand Daily Mail*'. Ashton taught English and, trying to explain the phrase *persona non grata* to Peter's class, said: 'Hain's parents are *persona non grata* with the government because they *think*.' The school had some liberally minded teachers, increasingly aware of Ad and Wal's growing role. While they never referred to it, some were quietly sympathetic. As a result, Ad and Wal had few concerns about their children being victimised. Equally, they had few illusions that for them the bell was tolling.

6

Banned

The Chief Magistrate of Pretoria, Mr D. J. M. Jordan, had his office in the building where Ad and Wal had got married fifteen years before, Ad recalled in amusement as she entered in January 1963. She had been served with an official summons to see him and, although this was something entirely new to her, she wasn't apprehensive, more intrigued as to what he would say.

Shown into Jordan's office, finding him formal, but courteous, it was immediately obvious to Ad he hadn't carried out this procedure before. Head down, reading stiffly from a prepared script he said: 'I have been instructed to warn you to desist from engaging in activities "calculated to further the aims of communism".'

'But what am I doing that I must stop doing?' Ad asked. She wasn't a communist – and she couldn't actually be accused of being a communist, because that was illegal and she would have had to be arrested and charged on the spot.

Jordan looked a trifle embarrassed, saying he was unable to specify which of her activities fell within this definition. 'I advise you to write to Mr John Vorster, Minister of Justice, for clarification,' he replied.

Then he stood to indicate that the strange encounter was over. Ad left none the wiser, later asking Ruth Hayman, her Liberal lawyer friend from Johannesburg, to draft a letter for her seeking clarification.

However, the reply from Vorster merely repeated the phrase and then stated: 'Should you so wish, you are of course at liberty to ignore the warning and, if as a result thereof, it is found necessary to take further action against you, you will only have yourself to blame.'

Her Orwellian predicament was brilliantly captured by a cartoon a few weeks later in the *Star* daily newspaper in February 1963, featuring Vorster and Colonel Spengler of the Special Branch.

Together with fellow party activists, Ad and Wal were tickled pink by this. 'Rather a badge of honour!' Ad remarked. Surprisingly perhaps, she wasn't at all worried – it just seemed to sum up her situation perfectly – and in any case, she was certainly not going to be intimidated: *that* would have meant giving in to the apartheid state and reneging on her comrades.

She never knew what was coming next, for instance when two women – the mother and daughter-in-law of a PAC detainee – came to see her one day while she was working in the Liberal Party's office. She was startled when they said: 'We have got bombs in our chimney.

What can we do? Can you help us?' Apparently PAC activists had picked them up from an army shooting range and hidden them there with the intention later of blowing them up in Pretoria. But winter was coming and 'the old man wants to light the house fire'. Ad had no idea what to do herself. She pondered, then asked, not looking at them: 'Do you know anyone who can remove them who you can trust absolutely completely?' The women chatted in their own language, then replied that indeed they did. To her relief she never heard from them again – nor of any bombs exploding mysteriously in a small, unknown township home.

Mamma Vorster: "Where's Adelaine Hain?"
Miss Spengler: "In the other room, I think, mamma."
Mamma Vorster: "Go directly, and see what she's doing, and tell her she mustn't."

Around this time Wal was driving their Volkswagen minibus through the Cape Reserve, having taken Asian and Coloured party members home, when the engine died. It just had to be *there*, he thought: in a section of the reserve where whites were not allowed to stop, even though they could drive through. White police soon pulled up remonstrating with him aggressively as he bent over the engine, having located a faulty electrical connection. 'Just fixing my engine,' he replied. They seemed doubtful, but fortunately the engine fired up and he drove off.

Meanwhile, Ad and Wal had been excited by John Kennedy winning the American Presidency and his sympathy for the civil rights movement with its charismatic black leader Martin Luther King. '*There's* the answer to white South African prejudice,' Wal used to say. 'How can anybody deny King is a highly intelligent man?'

Yet when confronted with this question, whites used to reply, 'Yes, but he is not like *our* blacks: ours are different, ours really *are* inferior.' Whites indulging in such sophistry and fantasy would even cite 'evidence' that white men's brains were apparently larger than black men's brains; to the counter that white women's brains were apparently physically smaller than black men's, there came no rejoinder. Such exchanges may have been droll and bizarre but they reflected a grim determination by whites to rationalise the mythology of racial superiority.

❦

With Liberal activists proving increasingly troublesome to the security police and ministers, the government set about the systematic destruction of the party. In Parliament the Minister of Justice, John Vorster, accused Liberals of being communists in disguise, tantamount to terrorists. Government ministers stated in Parliament: 'We will have to restrict the Liberal Party.' A cartoon in the *Pretoria News* of 11 March 1963, titled 'The Scapegoat', had a goat marked 'Liberal Party' being dragged by a knife-wielding Vorster up a hill towards a sacrificial pyre at the summit, with Prime Minister Verwoerd and other government luminaries forming an applauding procession behind him.

During 1963 many prominent Liberals throughout the country were banned and the fear of repression increased almost daily. Ad and Wal warned their children that life was going to get much more difficult as the government extended its police state by introducing the notorious law which increased to ninety days the twelve days for which people could be held without charge.

Although it seemed as if there was nothing they could do about this, it never occurred to either Ad or Wal that they should give up their ideals for a more comfortable life, still less turn their backs on comrades who had become closer to them than either their own former white circle of friends or indeed their relatives.

Then – a huge blow. The front pages of the main

newspapers luridly headlined a 'Rivonia plot', with pictures of Nelson Mandela's close leadership circle caught on 12 July 1963. The resistance high command was based secretly at Liliesleaf Farm and, worried their hide-away had been rumbled, they convened that fateful day to make emergency plans. It was to be their last meeting.

Before the police raid, a bird-watching enthusiast on a neighbouring residential caravan site half a mile away scanned continuously with her binoculars as she had done for ages. She had never been that interested in comings and goings at the farm but now noticed how workmen spent all day up telegraph polls adjoining it; isn't that odd? she asked herself.

On that fateful July day a dry-cleaning van trundled down the driveway to Mandela's hideout; an imposing farmhouse preserved almost unchanged as a museum,[‡] albeit now surrounded by suburban developments. As the vehicle came to a halt, armed policeman suddenly burst out. Although a tip-off had roused their suspicions, they could not believe their luck as they found all the wanted names they had been hunting for ages – including Walter Sisulu, Govan Mbeki and Ahmed Kathrada.

In a coal bunker a junior policeman poked about and to his astonishment discovered incriminating, hand-written documents by Mandela describing 'Operation Mayibuye', a master plan to overthrow the apartheid

‡ See http://www.liliesleaf.co.za

state. Mandela had passed out a message to his comrades when he was first captured the year before that his documents and a false passport, left behind when he was arrested, should be destroyed. But his wish was ignored – apparently they felt these might have some historical value – and that very nearly cost him his life.

Almost from the moment news of the raid broke, the word 'Rivonia' became synonymous around the world with further suppression of resistance to apartheid, as the leaders were charged and a mood of retribution swept through white communities. Absorbing the news, Ad and Wal said to each other: 'Just as you think "Well, it can't get any worse than this", it does.' They were by now in no doubt that their days too might be numbered.

They followed in dismay Nelson Mandela being brought back from Robben Island and what was to become known as the Rivonia Trial, commencing on their doorstep in Pretoria in 1964. Labelled 'Accused No 1', Mandela concluded his statement with the now famous words:

> During my lifetime I have dedicated myself to this struggle of the African people. I have fought against white domination, and I have fought against black domination. I have cherished the ideal of a democratic and free society in which all persons live together in harmony and with equal opportunities. It is an ideal which I hope to live for and to achieve. But if needs be it is an ideal for which I am prepared to die.

They read these powerful words as an inspiration for all involved in the struggle. But they also worried, because Mandela and his fellow accused were found guilty and faced the death penalty. In fact, after worldwide pleas for clemency, the defendants were all sentenced to life imprisonment, and in July 1964 Mandela returned to Robben Island, not to be seen or heard in public again for nearly twenty-six years.

The year before, in July 1963, the family had moved from Hatfield out to a smallholding at The Willows, to the east of Pretoria, partly because it fell within the catchment area for Pretoria Boys High School, which Wal had attended and where Peter and Tom also wanted to go.

The rented house consisted of two large thatched *rondavels* on a terrace well back from the road and at the foot of a *kopje* (small hill). With a small, leaky swimming pool and plenty of space to play, it was wonderful for children. Peter laid a makeshift cricket pitch which he used to water every evening, and Wal used to bowl to him and Tom. Nearby on rough grassy ground Peter and Tom used to play football against each other until it was too dark to see the ball.

Their move to The Willows took the security police by surprise. It was some weeks before they traced Ad and Wal, the first such feeling of freedom they had had in years. Their telephone had not yet been connected and the Special Branch were unable to discover them that way. Then one day their maid Eva answered the door to a man who asked her the name of her 'baas'. Eva did what she called her 'dumb kaffir' routine (with white strangers she always pretended to know nothing and understand less) and he was turning away when Ad went to see what was happening. He saw her, turned back and said that he was looking for a house that he'd heard was for sale. Eva was furious with Ad for showing herself. 'He is Special Branch,' she hissed, 'now they'll know where we live.' She was right. Thereafter the phone was speedily connected and tapping resumed.

But, with the usual Special Branch cars once more parked up outside the house, for Peter, Tom, Jo-anne and Sally there was also a sense of 'cops and robbers', which they found exciting. Wal would occasionally drive deliberately very close by the police cars as the boys hooted with delight and made faces.

On 13 September 1963 there was a knock at the door and Ad was confronted by the same two large security police officers who had arrested her and Wal in 1961 – Sergeants Viktor and van Zyl (the latter referred to as 'banana fingers' because of his huge hands). Their burly figures framing the door, they brusquely handed Ad an envelope containing a banning order which ran for five years and was expressly designed to end her role in the freedom struggle.

She didn't need to check all the clauses. She knew only too well what it meant to be a banned person. She was being prohibited from taking part in a political gathering and was forced to resign from the Liberal Party. She was now silenced as she couldn't be quoted in any publication. She was also barred from 'any social gathering, that is to say, any gathering at which the persons present also have social intercourse with one another'. In practice – her own family excluded – she had to assume she was now limited to being in the company of not more than one person at a time, although the courts were not at all certain of the law in all circumstances. A judge upheld an appeal of one banned person against a conviction for playing billiards with a friend, and a magistrate was unable to inform another banned individual whether or not it was legal to go to the local cinema. The standard clause prohibiting entry to educational premises meant banned university students were even refused permission to attend their universities, making it impossible for them to complete their degrees.

Ad's movements were restricted to the Pretoria magisterial district. She was prohibited from entering certain specified places such as factories, schools or university areas. She could not enter any 'native [African] location, native hostel or native village' or 'Coloured or Asiatic area'. Had she wished to, she couldn't even go to church – but bizarrely she was able to go with her sons to a sports match because apparently that did not involve her in a *social* gathering.

The order also included a section preventing going into any premises containing a political office – with

LEFT Wal, newly enlisted – eighteen years old, 1943

RIGHT Wal in the army with friend Loftus, 1944

Mentone, Port Alfred, 1947

Ad's parents, Edith, Gerald, 1947

LEFT Ad shows her leg to Wal, July 1947

RIGHT Ad and first baby, Peter, Nairobi, 1950

Ad with the Aprilia driving through Africa, 1951

Off to England, Cape Town, 1956

Peter, Tom, Jo-anne and Ad, London, 1956

Hilda Street House, Pretoria, 1958

Ad, Wal and four kids with Walter senior and Mary, 1960

Ad campaigning, Lady Selborne, 1962

Ad banned from attending Sally's birthday garden party, 1963

Ad and Wal at The Willows, Pretoria, 1964

Ad and Wal, John Harris's trial, Pretoria Supreme Court, 1964

Hain children representing banned parents at activists' farewell party, 1966

Family into exile: on board ship, Cape Town docks, March 1966

ABOVE LEFT John Harris's son David, Putney, 1968

ABOVE RIGHT Tom, Sally, Peter and Jo-anne, Putney, 1968

Greenham Common, protest against cruise missiles, Ad fourth from left next to Wal with grandson Jake on shoulders, April 1983

Free Nelson Mandela! Peter and Ad, Trafalgar Square outside South Africa House, 1987. For fifteen years protestors maintained a non-stop picket outside the South African embassy.

Wal visits Lanky's grave at the Commonwealth War Graves Cemetery for South African soldiers, Castiglione dei Pepoli, Apennines, 1996

Ad and Wal, Robben Island, 2000

Peter, Ad and Wal in Mandela's Robben Island cell, February 2000

Wal at Silverstone, 2001

Mandela with Peter, Elizabeth, Ad and Wal, 2003

Ad and Wal celebrating their 65th anniversary at their Neath Valley home, South Wales, 1 September 2013

inadvertent consequences. She regularly shopped in Hatfield Galleries where, during an election, the National Party once had a temporary campaign office. For the campaign period, she was barred from using their normal pharmacy or any other shop, so sent Peter there instead, sometimes on his way home from school. Alternatively she would phone the sympathetic Jewish pharmacist, and arrange for him to come out onto the pavement to hand over a prescription.

The ban ended her work as secretary of the Pretoria Liberal Party and stopped any overt political activity whatsoever. It was also unique: for the first time in any banning order she was prohibited entrance to 'any superior or inferior court in the land'. That was specifically directed at curbing her work seeking out and getting legal representation for defendants who had disappeared into the state's clutches. Ad's practice of haunting the courts to support political prisoners was probably the main reason for her ban. From then on all other banning orders included that clause.

She was now unable to attend the birthday parties of her own children held in her own home. She was not allowed to attend a funeral even of a close relative, or a family reunion or to visit a relative in hospital. It was hardly unexpected; she had discussed the possibility with her family and friends for months. But it left her feeling angry and frustrated. She effectively became a non-person and could not be quoted by the media. The restriction on meeting more than one person at a time was near-fatal politically and she was now prevented from continuing with all her work helping so many stricken people.

She was not even allowed to come into her children's schools and discuss their progress with teachers – that could only be done by standing outside on the pavement, which was just about feasible for the primary school, but not for Peter's high school because it was in the middle of large grounds. She could not attend a school prize-giving (upset for instance that she couldn't be present for Tom's Good Fellowship Award) or attend school sports meetings – a real blow because she had always taken a very close and active interest in their progress and was well known by teachers. Ad and Wal had become used to being targeted, but why should their *children* be affected? Why did *they* have to be picked on this way?

The banning order also required her to report to and sign in at Arcadia police station five miles away from home every Wednesday. So that she didn't forget, Ad established a routine of phoning her order for meat from her butcher and groceries from a nearby store before always reporting in. In the early days of this routine, the officers on duty in the small local police station didn't seem to have a clue what she was doing there and one week she was asked in a hushed tone: 'Mrs Hain, did you report to us last week?' Obviously they had made a mess of officially recording that she had done so. From then on she made sure she witnessed the signing in of her visits. It was an example of the way that the system operated: not every state official in every department or service was always up to speed with the latest development in apartheid's onward march – they were simply doing their jobs and getting on with life.

❦

Although shocked, Wal was not surprised at her ban and had little doubt that she would find ways to circumvent the restrictions imposed upon her – and, gradually, she did. Ad adjusted and worked out ways of acting as a contact for political prisoners whose relatives continued to approach her for assistance when they had problems. She seemed to be just as active. Although she could no longer participate openly in the life of the Liberal Party, she was kept in touch daily with events by David Rathswaffo, who took over from her as the Pretoria secretary. He would make a coded telephone call from a call box near the party office and she would then drive in to a pre-arranged rendezvous for an update.

Nevertheless, they decided to hold their 'diplomatic' parties again, with the security police loitering around the gate taking down the registration numbers. Party luminaries such as Alan Paton and Peter Brown attended in addition to Pretoria members. Ad's ban meant she had to sit in the kitchen and be visited by the guests one at a time; thirteen-year-old Peter enjoyed escorting them through for her. Tom (eleven years old) and Peter also had fun serving drinks under the guidance of a Coloured member and good friend, Alban Thumbran, who had been a professional waiter. Jo-anne and Sally, nine and seven years old, helped with the snacks. The Hain family had some fun, united and defiant against the enemy.

At one such party Peter heard a noise just outside the kitchen door. Peering through the window in the dark he was startled to catch a glimpse of someone lurking there, and called out 'Special Branch, Special Branch'. As Wal ran out there was a commotion and a figure began charging noisily up through the bushes and rocks of the dark *kopje*. Wal, running after his quarry, shouted 'Peter – bring the gun!' It was a ruse because there *was* no gun in the house. But the man ahead must have panicked. Before making off into the night, he picked up a big rock and threw it, glancing off a tree right in front of Wal's face. By now the partygoers had spilt out, all enjoying the excitement.

But the next morning Wal and his boys went up to have a look and found a large gash on the branch, forcibly bringing home that what had seemed like an exciting incident could have ended in a terrible family tragedy.

Soon afterwards they learnt of a real tragedy. When US President John Kennedy was assassinated on 22 November 1963, Alban Thumbran was distraught, immediately calling Ad with the news, stating: 'They've shot Kennedy.' She didn't know what to say to console him – because a symbol of hope had been extinguished in her too.

❦

Two friends, Fabian Ribeiro, a black doctor from Mamelodi, and his wife Florence, a sister-in-law of the PAC leader Robert Sobukwe, used to drop in regularly at The Willows. Sometimes their young children came and would play with the Hain children. Unusually for Africans, they were financially well off, but apartheid drastically restricted the way they could spend their money. They could not own a house in their township, send their children to the school of their choice, or take their family on holiday since there were no resorts for blacks. So they drove a Mercedes – way above Wal's pay level – and dressed very well, Florence at the height of fashion.

In those days non-whites were not permitted to try on clothes before purchasing, so absurd special arrangements had to be made for Florence to go in to Hamiltons, Pretoria's top clothes shop, which wanted her custom. The shop was kept open for her after hours so that she could try on her choices without upsetting white customers. (Two decades later the Ribeiros were both victims of state-sponsored assassinations: murdered by gunmen outside their home on 1 December 1986, as the Truth and Reconciliation Commission confirmed ten years later.)

Meanwhile, because of his political activities, Wal's work opportunities had been restricted to a limited number of private employers who would take him on.

He and Ad found increasing difficulty in making ends meet. Reluctantly, they decided they could no longer afford their maid, Eva Matjeka. So, to everyone's regret, Eva, who had become one of the family and a resolute political ally, had to leave.

However, her departure had one positive effect: the servant's room was vacant when Ad received a fraught telephone call from David Rathswaffo. Jimmy Makojaene, their PAC friend from Lady Selborne, had escaped from court. Jimmy had been involved in the 1963 campaign by the PAC underground group, *Poqo*, and had managed to flee until he was grabbed from a train on the Rhodesian border by the security police and returned for trial. But he managed to escape again during a lunch recess; astonishingly he had just walked straight out undetected. He later explained to Ad and Wal that he had actually been recognised by a black policeman who took it for granted he had been acquitted. Ad and Wal never queried this despite suspecting the policeman had simply turned a blind eye; their code was always 'don't ask questions'.

Now he had come to David for help and some money. Only too conscious of their tapped phone, Ad cut him short by saying she would come into town right away, asking Peter to watch over the other children. But when she got there, Jimmy had moved on so she picked up David to go looking for him, all the time conscious that she had to be incredibly careful because of her ban.

David guided her on a roundabout route towards

Mamelodi township. But suddenly they were through the gates of the township before she realised. 'David!' she shouted, 'I can't be in here! I am banned!'

'Fuck! he replied. 'I forgot.' He got out to search for Jimmy and she drove off at high speed.

David eventually found Jimmy and arranged for him to be dropped off late that night near their house and Wal carefully walked via a neighbour's garden through the surrounding bush, secretly collecting him away from the prying eyes of the Special Branch parked at the front gate. Before being installed in Eva's empty room Ad cooked Jimmy a meal in the kitchen-dining room. Afterwards she gave him magazines to read and blankets to sleep on in Eva's old room, attached to the back of their garage and shielded from prying eyes. The next day she took a meal in a cake tin, knocked on the door and left it outside for him.

Jimmy spent the whole day inside and, that night, having borrowed Maritz van den Bergh's car, with Jimmy lying down on the back seat and covered by a blanket, Wal drove him out to a nearby train station, attracting no interest from the security police, who were watching at the gate for the usual family vehicle. Jimmy got clean away, eventually ending up in Bechuanaland (Botswana).

But when the security police played back their phone tapes, they arrested David Rathswaffo, who said that Jimmy had told him he'd been acquitted, had 'borrowed ten bob' and disappeared. They held David for a few days, taking away his epilepsy pills to destabilise him. Fortunately, he told them nothing about Ad and Wal's involvement or they would have faced immediate arrest and prosecution for aiding and abetting an escaped political prisoner – Ad of course breaking her ban in the process.

She had been careful, as soon as Wal had driven Jimmy away, to wash all the bed clothes. She lit a fumigating tablet in the room and meticulously cleaned it. She wiped down all the furniture, including in the household kitchen where he had eaten, hoping to remove any trace of him ever having been there. Ad and Wal may have taken political risks but they were almost obsessively careful at times.

Throughout these years Wal and his boys remained keen on sport and learnt at first hand the extent to which apartheid infected it. Peter and Tom used to swim regularly at Pretoria's international-standard swimming pool at Hillcrest. In 1962 South Africa was involved in lucrative trade deals with Japan and visiting Japanese businessmen were granted 'honorary white' status, allowing them to stay in hotels and enjoy privileges usually confined to whites alone. A Japanese water polo team came over too and, after initially refusing it access to the pool, Pretoria City Council relented: business apparently triumphing over racism. But the decision caused such public uproar that the pool was drained and refilled after the team departed so that white customers could relax in 'untainted' water.

Attending a white state school (mixed schools being illegal) Peter and Tom had to play in whites-only school or club sports teams, and could not play against black teams. Sport was legally segregated from school and club right up to national representative level. Ad and Wal also used to join their boys watching the city's home football team, Arcadia Shepherds, at the Caledonian stadium. By some odd quirk they could even go to matches after they were banned – provided they did not meet anybody there.

Partitioned off on the other side of the stadium from whites were non-white spectators, some personal friends whom they might inadvertently bump into before the match, nervously looking around to see if anyone had noticed a potential breach of their banned status. As with other sports events, whites and blacks could not stand together or use the same entrances, toilets or facilities. Although Arcadia was an all-white team playing in an all-white league, black spectators were among the noisiest and most partisan fans. Then the government introduced proclamations banning non-whites from such major sports events, and their friends could no longer attend. The carnival atmosphere at Arcadia's home matches evaporated. But crowds of black fans still gathered outside the ground, listening to the match. Some of the keenest shinned up to watch from adjoining trees. But this so angered white neighbours that, as the Hains watched in horror and frustration, police dogs were used to drive them from these vantage points, some pulled down covered in blood.

Partly for these reasons, Ad and Wal along with fellow Liberals were enthusiastic advocates of a sports boycott in 1959 and in 1960, opposing a rugby tour by the visiting New Zealand side and a Brazil football tour, and working closely with Dennis Brutus, secretary of the South African Non-Racial Olympic Committee (SAN-ROC) – whose patron was Liberal president Alan Paton – for South Africa's expulsion from the Olympics. As state repression increased these were new phases of an escalating struggle against apartheid.

But SAN-ROC was later forced into exile, its leaders banned and harassed to such an extent that, like the ANC, it could no longer operate legally inside the country. For Ad and Wal the fact that sports officials too were victims of the police state gave another lie to the habitual cry that – at least under apartheid – sport could be divorced from politics.

7

The Hanging

Difficult though life had become for Ad and Wal, it was about to get a great deal more so.

Over five days in July 1964 many members of the African Resistance Movement (ARM), which had grown out of the National Committee for Liberation (NCL), were arrested. Some were friends in the Liberal Party who felt that non-violent means had reached the end of the road and that the sabotage of installations such as electricity pylons was the only way forward: sabotage against government installations but avoidance of injuring or killing people was their creed.

Ad and Wal's friend Hugh Lewin gave testimony in his trial when he was charged under the Sabotage Act, then aged twenty-four, on how he had been motivated to join up. Having first joined the Liberal Party at university, he became active. 'But my efforts seemed puny and hopeless,' Hugh told the court in a statement from the dock. He went on:

It seemed that nothing would awaken the whites. At about this time I was approached by a friend who asked me to become a member of the 'National Committee for Liberation', a secret sabotage group. My lord, I was terrified. Instinctively I was opposed to any form of violence and I knew that I was not suitable to the active role I was being asked to play. In spite of this, I decided to join.

Two factors in particular influenced me in making this decision. I was told that the NCL was a small group, consisting largely of young people, who wanted to make a demonstration of their protest, in the hope that by such demonstrations attention would be focused on the living conditions of the blacks. My previous attempt to do this had been completely ineffective. I thought that sabotage might shock the whites into an awareness of the conditions under which blacks were living and, in due time, change the system.

Secondly, I was told that the sabotage would be committed only against installations such as pylons, which were to be selected in a way which would ensure that the explosions would not endanger human life. The motive was to shock, not to injure. This, perhaps wrongly, I was able to reconcile with my conscience. So with some trepidation, I joined the organisation. I was a member of the NCL – later called the ARM, the African Resistance Movement – for about eighteen months. Our efforts were

> disorganised, our actions were sporadic. During that time I personally participated in three acts of sabotage ... but there were no changes and it seemed that what we were doing was futile. I was filled with doubts, and even thought of leaving my own South Africa. But always I came back to the sense of guilt and the feeling that I was part of a problem which I could not escape from by running away. So I stayed in the organisation and remained a member until my arrest.[‡]

The NCL's founders were ex-communists Monty and Myrtle Berman. Detained with others during the state of emergency imposed after the Sharpeville massacre, Monty and Myrtle had begun discussing the formation of the NCL with fellow prisoners. A key influence on Monty was his Second World War service with South African forces in Italy: occasional contact with Italian 'partisans' undertaking underground acts of sabotage against the occupying Nazis had made a big impression upon him.

Radical Liberals comprised the largest part of the NCL, which numbered no more than fifty over its life. One Liberal, John Lang, had first been active in the Torch Commando, a tiny all-white group formed in 1951 which tried to disrupt National Party meetings,

‡ Hugh Lewin, *Bandiet Out of Jail* (Johannesburg: Random House, 2002), a memorable account of his time in and reflections upon prison.

and then in a semi-paramilitary successor group in 1959 of ex-servicemen with access to dynamite. He too was detained after Sharpeville and joined in planning a programme of sabotage. (Lang went into exile in 1961 where he worked with ANC leader Oliver Tambo.) Members also included Trotskyists like Baruch Hirson. Most were young white idealists frustrated by the denial of legal and peaceful channels for change: with the ANC and PAC banned, for them the Sharpeville massacre symbolised the end of the non-violent era of resistance, with all lawful means exhausted.

However, black Liberal activists like Eddie Daniels were also members, so too were dissident members of the ANC Youth League – who felt, despite the formation of the ANC's underground group *Umkhonto we Sizwe* (MK) in November 1961, that their parent organisation was ineffectual: by this time the NCL had already destroyed two pylons and badly damaged a pass office. It had also received funding from the newly independent west African state of Ghana, leading NCL figures having met Ghana's President, the charismatic Kwame Nkrumah.

Small cells were established in Johannesburg, Cape Town, Port Elizabeth and Durban and, on 9 October 1961, NCL comrades brought down a pylon which blacked out a large area in Johannesburg East by sawing through it with hacksaws; a successful albeit amateurish effort which left them with badly blistered hands. At least in these early attempts, Eddie Daniels reported, 'we were complete amateurs as far as sabotage was concerned', describing shambolic attempts to blow up a pylon and a radio mast in the now plush Cape Town suburb of Constantia and various escapades learning how to handle explosives, at one point losing his revolver, which was fortunately found after a frantic search in the dark. However, Daniels's group was later successful in damaging railway signal cables, which brought Cape Town to a standstill. He was eventually arrested and sentenced to fifteen years (much longer than more prominent white ARM activists) on Robben Island. Decades later, he wrote: 'Many of us, through what some may consider foolhardy actions, had laid ourselves open to harsh criticism. But all we can say in our defence is, "We tried." Perhaps we failed and failed badly, but we did try.'

At the end of 1962, with the ANC and PAC paralysed and the NCL the main underground force, its leading figures drafted a political programme for a revolutionary group on which Magnus Gunther commented: 'The document was to the NCL what the eight-page plan for Operation Mayibuye was to MK: an egregious expression of hubris and desperate hope.'[‡] By May 1964 the NCL had mutated into the ARM, several of whose

‡ A good account of the NCL and ARM is Magnus Gunther, 'The National Committee of Liberation (NCL)/African Resistance Movement (ARM)' in South African Democracy Education Trust, *The Road to Democracy in South Africa Volume 1 (1960–1970)* (Pretoria: Unisa Press, second edition, 2010), pp. 193–233.

leading figures drew up a manifesto which insisted that only acts of violence would force the government to listen:

> ARM will avoid taking life for as long as possible. ARM would prefer to avoid bloodshed and terrorism. But let it be known that if we are forced to respond to personal violence – and we cannot forget decades of violence, torture, starvation and brutality against us – we shall do so ... For the present, ARM will inconvenience and confuse ... disrupt and destroy ... strike where it hurts most.

Gunther concludes: 'both high point and swan song of NCL/ARM' was the destruction of five pylons in the week of 18 June 1964, three in the area of Cape Town and two in Johannesburg – showing 'high capability and meticulous planning'. Up to that point the group had mounted twenty-five attacks since 1961: 'a considerable achievement given the sparse human and material resources at the organisation's disposal,' he argues, giving a favourable assessment of NCL/ARM as having had more impact than MK during its three years of existence between 1961 and 1964. 'For all their foibles, they would be remembered as ordinary people who endangered their own lives in order to keep the flag of freedom flying against immense odds.'

But for Ad and Wal the ARM's sabotage activities were pointless and, they thought, counter-productive. The government ensured news of blown-up pylons and attacks on other installations was suppressed, so they made little impact on the white community, who simply thought the occasional power blackout a technical failure.

Ad and Wal had heard of these activities and there was increasingly anxious, at times heated, discussion and argument within the Liberal Party. They knew that some Liberals must be involved, but their attitude was 'don't ask' – for if they didn't know, they couldn't be interrogated. Just as well, because their friend Maritz van den Berg had earlier been detained for questioning about sabotage activity and, curiously, Wal thought at the time, Maritz phoned to ask if he would come in to the police station to collect a cheque for his mother. Although wanting to assist a friend, Wal was suspicious, Ad even more so; she drove there with him and sat in a nearby cafe, waiting uneasily.

When Wal went in he was greeted by Maritz with the familiar Special Branch officer, Sergeant Viktor, present in the room. 'I've told them *everything*, Walter,' said Maritz disconcertingly.

'What do you know about the ARM, Mr Hain?' Viktor asked.

'Nothing,' Wal replied, 'I've only heard about it since the arrests.'

'Who do you know in the ARM?' the officer persisted.

'Nobody, don't know what you are talking about,' Wal replied.

As it happens that was true but his general dictum was: don't say anything. Once you started talking you never knew where it might end, he and Ad had long resolved when they had discussed the prospect of interrogation.

However, they had already been visited and confidentially sounded out to get involved in the NCL by their Liberal Party friends from Johannesburg, Hugh Lewin and Rosemary Wentzel. Certainly not, they said. 'But news of our sabotage will make headlines and create change,' Hugh and Rosemary argued. 'Virtually all legal means of resistance have been suppressed. We have no other option.'

It wasn't an acrimonious conversation but Ad and Wal were firm. Quite apart from the serious moral questions raised by violence, they considered such action naive and believed it would simply invite even greater police state repression without achieving anything tangible. Hugh Lewin later recalled: 'I really felt I had no alternative. But when I went to see Ad and Wal to try and recruit them, their position was very honourable. They said no and explained why but they were not judgemental or antagonistic. We remained good friends.'

To protect themselves, those undertaking the sabotage did not resign from the Liberal Party as its rules obliged them to do, and this occasioned considerable acrimony when their activities were eventually revealed. Ad and Wal had fraught discussions with close friends, including John Harris. Wal had witnessed the horror of the Second World War at first hand. The trouble with violence, he insisted vehemently, was that it tended to develop a life of its own. Whatever the intention, once started, it spread automatically. Also there was no way of containing it: even blowing up a remote pylon risked killing an innocent person who might be passing by, and Ad had been particularly impressed when a senior party figure, Jordan Ngubane, argued this point when staying overnight in their home.

Right across the country, however, ARM members were soon rounded up after the police discovered incriminating documents at the Cape Town flat of the national organiser, Adrian Leftwich, a prominent Liberal. Incredibly, he had kept a record of the entire cell structure of the ARM and its plans. Turning state witness, he was later paraded around the country giving evidence against his former comrades. Another Liberal friend of Ad and Wal (and an NCL/ARM activist), Randolph Vigne, got news that Leftwich was talking and immediately left on a Norwegian cargo ship from Cape Town on a borrowed passport. Among those arrested was Hugh Lewin – Leftwich had been best man at his wedding and now turned state witness to provide key evidence which was to convict Hugh. (Nearly five decades later Hugh wrote a soul-searching, beautifully crafted reflection on his experiences and how he eventually determined to meet up again with Leftwich in England.)[‡]

❦

Although the Hain family had always managed to live something akin to a normal life, they were now beginning to feel severely hemmed in. Then on 24 July 1964 a bomb exploded on the whites-only concourse of Johannesburg railway station, mortally injuring a 77-year-old lady, Ethel Rhys, and severely injuring her young granddaughter Glynnis; twenty-two others were injured, five suffering terrible burns.

Peter – having heard the news on a radio in the boys' bedroom – rushed to seek reassurance from his parents, not really thinking that they would be involved but needing to hear them say so and finding them both very upset. Wal sounded off against the 'idiots who did that sort of mindless thing'. Whoever was responsible had better not come to him for help, he said grimly.

A few days later, Ann Harris and her six-week-old son David turned up unexpectedly, driven by John's brother-in-law Drew Archibald, at the Hain home in The Willows. Her husband John had been arrested and was being held in Pretoria Local Prison, she explained. Ad and Wal had met John and Ann a few years earlier when

‡ Hugh Lewin, *Stones against the Mirror* (Cape Town: Umuzi, 2011).

they were new Johannesburg Liberal Party members, having joined in 1960. Both were teachers. John shared Wal's passion for sport, cars and motor racing (rather uncommon interests among the politically involved), so they got on especially well, as did Ann and Ad. There were exchange visits to each family's home in Pretoria and Johannesburg, and John went with the Hains to several motor races at Kyalami circuit.

For young Peter and Tom especially, John Harris was great fun. Once he drove the two of them fast around corners in his new Volkswagen Beetle as they exclaimed in delighted excitement. He became one of *their* friends too, and not simply one of their parents' adult circle. He was a real enthusiast for whatever happened to be the current one of his many interests. And he was very competitive, hating to be beaten when the boys or Wal played him at table tennis. He had a position on just about everything and loved an argument, disagreeing passionately with anybody who wanted to engage in an opposing point of view. Yet he bore no grudges, and when the argument was over, he would be joking and laughing again.

John had become active in the South African Non-Racial Olympic Committee (SAN-ROC) and succeeded Dennis Brutus as its chairman when Brutus was first banned then arrested and finally shot in the stomach while trying to escape from police custody. (An ambulance was called for Brutus, badly injured and spilling blood by the roadside, but when it arrived it turned away leaving him still bleeding because it was designated for whites alone.) As chairman of SAN-ROC, John in 1963 testified in Lausanne before the International Olympic Committee, seeking white South Africa's exclusion from the 1964 Tokyo Olympics. South Africa was indeed excluded. On his return his passport was seized and, in February 1964, he too was banned, later receiving death threats – and even gunshots aimed at his living-room window.

Wal recalled a fierce argument between them on a long drive back to Pretoria after a party meeting in the Cape. John was insistent that, although an act of violence might cause casualties in the short term, in the long term it could save lives if it hastened the end of the violence of apartheid. But, often in conversations like that, John was putting a position to test an argument, not necessarily espousing that position (he certainly never specifically justified violence against people).

Like Mandela's ANC by that time, he was deeply frustrated by the inability of young white radicals to accomplish anything against a police state that remorselessly crushed all peaceful opposition. John with other liberal friends was attracted to the sabotage movement, and deeply disappointed that Wal would have none of it.

When she arrived suddenly at the Hain home, Ann explained how she had been refused permission to see John in Pretoria Local Prison. But she had been told that she could bring food for him each day and collect his laundry. Could Ad and Wal put him on their list for food parcels? However, as she could not drive and was dependent upon others bringing her the forty miles from her home for prison visits, they suggested she stayed until his release. They assumed that John could not possibly have been involved because he had been under police surveillance after having been banned earlier that year – and he would probably be released in a week or so, they thought.

Jo-anne and Sally gave up their bedroom for the adjoining playroom and Ann and six-week-old baby David moved in, the girls excited at having a tiny child in their house. But instead of a short stay, Ann and David were to be there for nearly eighteen months and became part of the family, Ad and Wal observing with approval as their children helped look after and play with David as he grew from baby to toddler, including changing his nappies – an especially formative experience for Peter and Tom as teenage boys.

The Harris Volkswagen Beetle was collected and it effectively became Ad's car, Wal needing their VW minibus for work. Life revolved around a daily visit to the jail by Ad and Ann, taking food to John Harris, their friend Hugh Lewin, and others who were all held incommunicado under the ninety-day law. The extra housework occasioned by a tiny baby, coupled with the daily 25-mile round trip to the prison, and transporting children to and from school, meant Ad found it impossible to cope without help. So she contacted Eva, who was without a job and was delighted to take up residence again.

❦

Ann's arrival changed their lives forever. The station bomb had thrown the white community into a frenzy, and the security services were quick to exploit the resulting panic, giving Ad and Wal extra attention.

After a while, when all the other ARM detainees had been visited by relatives and Ann still had heard nothing, Ad and Wal began to realise that there was something seriously amiss. Then, in John's laundry, Ann was horrified at a blood stain on his shirt.

Immediately, she phoned the Special Branch: 'I have seen blood on my husband's shirt, what's wrong with him?'

'What's wrong with your husband, Mrs Harris, is that he is in ninety-day detention,' the officer sneeringly replied.

After John's lawyer Ruth Hayman had also queried this, two menacing members of the security police turned up with a letter for Ann. Ten-year-old Jo-anne was walking out of the house at the time to take Ad's newly baked cookies to the children next door when she was frightened to be confronted by the burly Special Branch officers.

Worried that her mom was going to be arrested again, she came running inside, tears streaming: 'The Special Branch are here – but I didn't cry in front of them.'

The letter was the first direct communication Ann or the lawyers had received from John. He wanted to reassure her that he had cut himself shaving – and he joked that he was unused to wet shaving as he'd had to hand in his electric shaver. In reality, he was still bleeding from horrendous beatings, including a broken jaw and damaged testicles. The letter somehow did not ring true for Ann, who suspected, rightly, that he had been forced to write it, and she was dreadfully stressed.

Ad meanwhile was ingeniously engaged in receiving and passing messages to her friends in detention, particularly Hugh Lewin. She regularly washed their clothes, recalling: 'They always smelt awful – completely different even from dirty socks after playing football, a real jail stink.'

Once after collecting Hugh's washing, Ann and Ad tipped it out to search it thoroughly. Ad noticed a filthy handkerchief with a large 'C' in ink on it. Odd, she thought. Wracking her brains, she recalled from her childhood that her older brothers used lemon juice for invisible ink. So she ironed it and was excited to find a message about Hugh's flatmate John Lloyd, and a love note to his girlfriend Jill Chisholm. But the handkerchief also contained information concerning other activists. Ad carefully cut out these bits and gave the remaining piece of cloth to Jill, saying to her: 'I've cut other names out because I am not sure what you know.'

Many years later Jill Chisholm (then political reporter for the *Rand Daily Mail*) recalled:

> Ad Hain taught me many things. Unusual things. Like how to peel away layers of an onion, slip a thin sliver of paper between lower layers and then 'reconstruct' the onion so that it appeared as complete as ever it was. Or how to unpick the stitches of a man's shirt collar … saving the original thread … again slide a sliver of thin paper into the collar … and then re-sew it leaving no evidence it had been undone. Strange skills for someone who could pass for a carefree, suburban mother-of-four. But then those were strange times in South Africa. Or, more accurately, brutal, oppressive and illegitimate years in South Africa. Ad was using these unusual skills to help get messages through – in food parcels – to young detainees held in isolation for months without any other contact with family, friends or lawyers.

Ad developed other methods: taking the pith out of an orange and gluing it back after inserting a message inside; or after cooking a whole onion sliding a note between the leaves to be covered as it cooled. She also put some pencil lead in a sausage to enable Hugh to write; in the same way she smuggled a needle inside. She learnt to look for cotton wound around the button of a shirt to signal there was a message in the collar which the prisoners had carefully unstitched. These messages were never discovered and formed an invaluable communications route. Once again, having been confronted with a problem, Ad found a way to solve it. But all the time there was an ominous momentum to her ever more daring activities.

❦

Hugh Lewin recalled what it was like for him on the inside of Pretoria Local Prison:

> John Harris was only one of a fairly large group of detainees who were incarcerated at Pretoria Local Prison – there were probably as many as twenty-four kept there in isolation and subject to only one consolation. This was that they could receive food parcels from outside. Strictly monitored, these parcels could be delivered to the jail each day, where they were carefully passed on to each of us, the detainees in their single cells.
>
> As I remember it, Ad was the delivery person. For some six months she arranged, every day without fail (except Sunday when parcels were not permitted), that each political detainee in the jail receive an individual packet of goodies: sweets, fruit, drinks, pies … the contents of these packages not only varied each day but each day the packages contained items which suited the specific delights of the detainees. Here an apple, here an orange, or *naartjies* [satsumas] or pears; a slab of milk chocolate rather than some dark speciality … Ad knew all the favourites. And day after day, she would arrive at the jail just before lock-up and deliver the brown paper parcels with the divine goodies for the prisoners.

Another ARM activist and political detainee, Fred Prager, wrote thanking Ad for strawberries, expressing astonishment at this rare delicacy in South Africa at the time. He was not to know they were provided by Lorna Bramley, a Liberal friend, whose parents had a strawberry farm.

Hugh explained:

> The food parcels became the focus of our existence in those barren days in the solo slammer. It was the key to maintaining morale to know that there, outside, was a group of supporters who were brought together each day to deliver the food parcels to Local.
>
> And not just the food parcels going in each day, but also (we discovered in time) the traffic somehow made its way out. Like the day I received a lemon in my food parcel … Why a lemon? Surely not to improve the occasional fish for Friday lunch? No, an evening whisperer told me, use the juice from the lemon to write a message on a handkerchief ostensibly being returned with the weekly washing.
>
> Or use the sewing needle mysteriously left alongside the communal toilet in the exercise yard, as if to repair a damaged button-hole, again sent with the weekly wash for 'treatment' by Ad.
>
> I once used the system to smuggle out some urgently required clandestine information. I didn't know Ad so well then, but I knew she made things happen, without any problems, which you could trust

> and know that it would work – and know that there was that other person at her shoulder, giving her total support: husband Wal. It was a remarkably powerful boost to one's morale.

Each day during his trial she used to stand and wait to wave to Hugh Lewin through the window of the police van as he was transported from jail to Pretoria's Supreme Court, something Hugh always found uplifting.

After Hugh was sentenced to seven years' imprisonment, Ad went with his girlfriend Jill Chisholm for her final permitted visit. She returned deeply upset because she wouldn't be able to see him again for such a long time, fighting back tears as she explained to Ad how Hugh had gallantly told her 'I don't expect you to wait for me' – but then kept wanting reassurance that she might in fact do so.

However, as John Harris's detention continued, Ad began to suspect that he must have had some connection with the station bomb. Even by the standards of the security constraints the family had got used to operating under (phone-tapping and not knowing whether or which rooms in the home were bugged), it was a particularly awkward period for Ad and Wal to communicate. They would walk outside in the garden to talk secretly.

Then, a month after the explosion, the old lady who

had been sitting near the bomb suitcase, Mrs Ethel Rhys, tragically died. Her twelve-year-old granddaughter, Glynnis Burleigh, had been left visibly maimed for life. Now John Harris was formally charged with murder. With Ernie Wentzel, Ruth Hayman, a Liberal Party friend and John's lawyer, was then able to visit for the first time, deeply upset to find him in a terrible state; he had only been charged after his jaw, which had been wired up, had mended enough for him to be presentable in court. The news was traumatic for Ann, Ad and Wal.

On Ann's first permitted visit Ad accompanied her, deliberately carrying little David as she followed Ann in. Before the warders realised she was there and aggressively demanded she leave immediately, Ad had seen John and shown him David – very important, she believed, that he witness his small son was being looked after and also that they were standing by Ann. (Because Ad and Wal were banned and John was banned, they had to apply to obtain special permission from Colonel Oukamp, in charge of the political prisoners, to visit him.)

She and Ad used to scour the papers daily to find out who else had been arrested. Then Ann noticed that an ARM colleague of John's, Ann Swersky's husband Barry, had been arrested. That triggered Ann's memory: a stubby key on John's key ring that she couldn't identify when asked by the Special Branch. *That's* what it was, she suddenly recalled: the key to the Swerskys' cellar where ARM explosive equipment was stored.

'Now I know John's going to be in prison for a long time,' Ann told Ad, deeply deflated and distressed.

John was indeed charged with the bombing on 14 September, and they told their children, finding Peter disbelieving: how could he have done this? It was shocking. They all felt numb – not so much betrayed as confused. Wal discussed it over and over again with Peter and Tom, as they all tried to come to terms with this savagely bitter twist.

Their feelings were torn. Although condemning without qualification what he had done, Ad and Wal remained convinced John never intended to harm anybody. He had meant it as a spectacular demonstration of resistance to tightening state oppression. Indeed he had telephoned a fifteen-minute warning to both the station police and two newspapers, urging that the station concourse be cleared.

It was later confirmed that on the afternoon of Friday 24 July 1964, John Harris called Johannesburg railway police with calm and precise instructions:

> This is the African Resistance Movement. We have planted a bomb in a large brown suitcase twenty feet from the cubicle above platforms five and six on the concourse of the new Johannesburg railway station. On the handle of the suitcase is tied a label bearing the words 'Back in Ten Minutes'. It is not our intention to harm anyone. This is a symbolic protest against the inhumanity and injustices of apartheid. The bomb

> is timed to explode at 4.33 p.m. Clear the concourse by using the public address system at once. Do not try to defuse the bomb as the suitcase is triggered to explode if it is opened.

However, as he later told Ann, his plans had almost come unstuck because the telephone in the first public kiosk he tried was not working and he had to race to find another one. That was not working either. He began to panic before he was finally able to make the call, also phoning the pro-government *Die Transvaler* and anti-government *Rand Daily Mail*, the latter immediately calling the security police. All three calls were noted down and admitted as evidence at his trial.

According to former South African spy and journalist Gordon Winter[‡] the head of security, H. J. van den Bergh, confirmed to him that the Railway Police had alerted him at 4.20 p.m. to an anonymous phone call two minutes earlier warning that the bomb had been planted. He had immediately used his hot line to talk to the Security Minister, John Vorster. But they resolved deliberately to ignore the warnings – better to exploit the subsequent and inevitable furore, they cynically calculated, than to use the station loudspeaker system to clear travellers from the concourse.

‡ Gordon Winter, *Inside BOSS* (London: Allen Lane, 1981), pp. 97–8.

Another twist by the prosecution to support their case of pre-meditated murder was to state that the suitcase was hidden underneath a wooden bench in a small cubicle on the station concourse, as if for deliberate concealment. Yet Gordon Winter persuaded Glynnis Burleigh to return to the scene ten years later and she recalled it being placed exactly as John Harris had described in his warning: with a label stating 'Back in Ten Minutes' in the middle of the concourse, which caused passers-by to step around it – more a deliberate advertisement than the furtive plot the state asserted.

At 4.33 p.m. the bomb exploded, causing devastation on the station and the pretext for the government to enforce an even more oppressive regime.

Despite their own horror, for Ad and Wal there was no question that their duty lay to their close friend John and his family. Equally they were in no doubt there would almost certainly be serious consequences for them and their young family. Perhaps if they had paused to give it too much thought, they might have been daunted, even terrified. But they were set on a course. They would not be cowed, and they could and would not abandon their friends or comrades. They ploughed on resolutely with quiet defiance. It was a solemn moment – but their values of loyalty and solidarity came before their own predicament. They carefully explained to their children that, despite deploring his action, they would be standing by Ann and giving what help they could to John in prison.

❧

Having long been targets for the local security forces, they were now principal targets for the whole state and its compliant media. Instead of being one of many enemies, it was almost as if Ad and Wal were now *the* enemy and the security service turned on them with a vengeance, their names now toxic in the white community. The harassment became vitriolic. Their house was now under continuous surveillance, with security police cars parked on the road outside twenty-four hours a day. As they drove out they would be tailed – on one occasion even when Peter and Tom rode down to the nearest shops on their bikes.

Raids on the family home also became more regular. Once, Peter cycled the five miles home from school to find security police turning over the house and searching through his school books and papers. Ad greeted him, upset and concerned that her eldest son might be intimidated. But to her relief he simply glared at the officers as they searched the family home.

Then their menacing presence took a comic turn. A young officer had discovered a list of names which constituted Peter's own chosen 'World XI' cricket team. It had stars like Gary Sobers, Wes Hall, Richie Benaud and even South Africa's Graeme Pollock, like Peter a left-handed batsman and his idol. But the names were listed at random and Peter had attached numbers indicating positions in the batting order. The officer thought he'd found a coded list and rushed excitedly to show it to his captain, who, after a quick glance, told him not to be a damned fool. Ad felt like laughing out loud, but sensed the officers' embarrassment and didn't want to provoke any of them in the brittle atmosphere. One up to the Hains, she and Peter both thought, exchanging glances: it was the kind of small victory which kept up their spirits then, and later on whenever they recounted the story.

Meanwhile, their Liberal activist friend Maritz van den Berg had been detained under the ninety-day law on 29 July and held in Pretoria Local Prison for a month before being unconditionally released. It was soon obvious that he had spoken freely because others were immediately pulled in for questioning. One of them, Alban Thumbran, was released again almost at once and telephoned to warn Ad: 'Maritz is singing like a bird.' This was to be the signal for messages to be relayed, by various covert means, to as many people as she and Wal thought might need to know. To confuse the telephone tappers, Ad and Wal had to develop their own code through which they could pass on sensitive telephone numbers.

Ad and Wal were never judgemental about comrades trapped and interrogated, often under threat of torture or physical assault. 'None of us really knows how we might react in detention and under that sort of intense pressure,' Wal would explain. With one important proviso, he insisted: those of their colleagues who did talk should never seek to deny it, as a few did.

Concerned that another party colleague, Derek Cohen, would be picked up, Ad quickly piled her children into the VW Beetle and sped off out of the front drive, security police vehicles in hot pursuit. She hoped all of the children in the car would provide cover for her as if on a routine family outing. However, in an exciting and pre-planned manoeuvre, she pulled up at traffic lights in the lane indicating left, then suddenly jumped the lights and tore rightward, leaving the tailing Special Branch vehicle blocked by oncoming traffic from following her. (As with her ingenuity over messages in and out of prison, Ad hadn't been trained in this sort of surreptitious behaviour: she simply used her common sense.) She drove undetected straight to Derek Cohen's house and into their garage, telling Jo-anne to jump out and quickly close the doors.

But his mother Anita explained that he had already left on the next plane for London. Shortly afterwards the security police called round looking in vain for him. Ad's resourcefulness had been unnecessary but at least she had welcome confirmation he was safe: another potential scalp for the Special Branch had been avoided. She drove back home passing police cars parked outside, unable to resist an impudent wave.

For the year since Ad's banning, Wal had taken over from her as the face of the Pretoria Liberals. He continued writing his leader-page articles for the *Rand Daily Mail* and regular letters to all the main newspapers. He also issued press statements.

But they both knew he was living on borrowed time. Then in September 1964, Wal was visited at his office and handed a banning order with a special clause inserted, quite different to normal banning orders. The same day a burly security police figure presented himself at the front door of their home and handed Ad an addendum to her ban, personally signed by the Minister of Justice, John Vorster.

It contained the same new clause giving them each special permission to communicate with each other – quite exceptional. A key provision of banning prevented any communication with another banned person. However, their situation was unprecedented and also potentially embarrassing to the state: they were the first married couple to be so banned. For Ad and Wal, Orwell's *1984* had arrived twenty years early with an exemption from the normal stipulation blocking banned persons from talking to each other.

His banning was clearly a reprisal for providing support to the hated John Harris and his family. It meant that Ad and Wal had no flexibility anymore for their political activism. She could not act behind the scenes for him as she had been doing for the previous year because he too was now barred from doing anything political or indeed meeting more than one other person at a time.

So they co-opted Peter as something of a surrogate. From then on, aged fourteen, he became increasingly active in a liaison role, taking and passing messages to individuals with whom they were prevented from communicating, such as journalists and other banned people, so helping them to continue much of their political work behind the scenes. But Peter's role was simultaneously a boon and a worry. What if this subterfuge were discovered? Might they be arrested for breaking their bans – or worse, might Peter be arrested too?

Wal had one panic moment. A requirement of being banned meant he had to report in weekly – in his case on a Friday to Pretoria Central police station. Once, under pressure of events, he forgot. Waking very early the next morning he realised his mistake. Eva was distraught, knowing how serious a breach it was.

Jumping straight into the car, he dashed off to the police station.

'Walter Hain. I should have reported in yesterday but I forgot. Can I do so today please?' he anxiously asked.

Fortunately, however, the duty policeman, used to processing defendants on bail, hadn't a clue who he was and seemed unusually cooperative and understanding. 'I will go and check. Maybe yesterday's report has not been ruled under yet.'

Mercifully, it hadn't. He came back with a copy and entered it right away, passing it to Wal for signing – the ever-vigilant Special Branch never discovering this oversight.

Another consequence was that Wal, who had often come to see Peter playing cricket or rugby on Pretoria Boys High School fields on his way home from work, was now barred from doing so, except when a game was near enough to the school fence and he could pull up on the road and look over, as he did occasionally. Peter was delighted to see him, a lonely figure staring from abnormality at normality. But Peter's uncomprehending teammates, familiar with Wal's fatherly support, couldn't understand why he didn't come over as before like all the other dads: none of the boys had even heard of a banning order.

But how were they perceived by colleagues? Jill Chisholm gave her insight of the Pretoria couple:

> Before I met Ad and Wal, I heard tales that there was a family in Pretoria who were Liberal – both capital and lower case Ls – and who were prepared to put themselves on the line for people courageous enough to resist the terror regime of the time. Not bloody likely, I thought. Pretoria! The entrance to this capital of the apartheid government was bracketed on one side by the massive Voortrekker monument to Afrikaner domination and on the other by the notorious Pretoria Central Prison, where black freedom fighters were among the hundreds executed by hanging. Not likely … not in Pretoria! I thought.

But it proved true, there was such a family. The determination of the Hains to resist the apartheid regime wherever possible had led to a spell in detention and to banning under the Suppression of Communism Act. For me, a young political journalist at the time, they became a source of accurate information and evaluation – they always seemed to have a finger on the pulse of resistance. They also became valued friends. Their dining table – an old door put into service – was a gathering place for people of all colours and political persuasions. There was a sense of freedom around it that was still decades away for most South Africans.

Because of their parents' involvement in the resistance, the Hain children developed a unique skill of their own, too. Their house stood a long way back from the public road. The children could tell the moment a car turned into their long drive whether it was a government-issue car – invariably driven by security police – or friends. Their banning orders meant Ad and Wal could never be in the company of more than one person a time. So the early-warning system of the children's enhanced hearing meant there was enough time for visitors to scatter into separate rooms or the garden if the security police were raiding.

Hugh Lewin gave a sense of Ad and Wal's role from his perspective, based forty miles away in Johannesburg:

As I remember it, I got to know the Hains best – that is, Ad and Wal, though not always in that order – during the year before the July 1964 arrests. Everything for them was always to do with the practicalities of running a political agitation group, small but effective. Posters for meetings, leaflets to announce the meetings, envelopes for leaflets, volunteers to address the envelopes, to organise the meetings' room, to organise the organisers, to organise.

And, if to organise, then to make tea. Tea for the members, tea for the organisers … tea, tea, but Ad and Wal were banned, so beware who makes the tea. Ad will make the tea while Wal, who can't make the tea simultaneously because he's banned, Wal will make the meeting.

The heck of it if the Branch are sitting in their cars outside the gate. Don't give them tea. Let them stew in their cars outside the gate. Stew and get furious because they've missed Wal. Slipping away on his way to town to collect the leaflets, and string for the posters. And slipping in again straight past the Branch in their cars, steaming. It used to be a joke; now it's plain aggro. Unnecessary pain. Tell the kids to take care – and no tea for the Branch.

They were both banned, which was a pain, but to the rest of us effectively it made no difference because they always worked together anyway. You couldn't separate them. That's how they always worked. Never apart. That's what gave them their strength and made them so effective.

At a time when it was increasingly dangerous to organise meetings, increasingly dangerous to visit friends from other parts of town, when any meetings were considered seditious, the Hains organised meetings, the Hains brought friends together. Once they were banned, they were living examples of the iniquity of banning orders. They didn't have to do anything to make a political statement. Their very existence made a political statement.

But anybody else would have cracked under the strain. Anybody else would have taken their children away, seeking to protect them from the looming presence of the Special Branch. Not the Hains. They were an inclusive family and what went for the parents went for the children too.

And for their friends too; and for their party friends and colleagues in their Liberal Party group. And when the family of John Harris came to seek temporary shelter that family became their family too, without hesitation.

Jill Wentzel, active in the Liberal Party with her husband Ernie in Johannesburg, recalled five decades later:

> After a life spent as a backroom political organizer in struggling, moneyless organisations, as a glorified telephonist, conning tired people to do all sorts of tedious

> work, I'd say, from my experience of very many salt-of-the-earth volunteers, that Ad was unique. With no ambition to be a great leader or struggle hero or any such thing, she just doggedly kept at it till the Pretoria branch was in my opinion the best thing in the Liberal Party. Her courage and Wal's was unsung because it was so simple and modest.

She added:

> I can't remember Ad and Wal being at all prominent in the many hefty arguments in the party. There were socialists and free marketeers sometimes at odds with each other, sometimes wanting the party's economic policy to veer towards one or other. There were those that wanted the party on a sort of ad hoc basis to back the PAC; others favoured cooperation with the ANC on specific campaigns, others altogether preferred the ANC, some seemed to want to muddle through treating each situation on its merits, some wanted the party to stick more specifically to its liberal principles (while arguing about what these actually entailed) – and amid it all few seemed to bother to stick to congress resolutions. The party was gloriously anarchic. Each group tried to prevent what the other was doing. They were a lawless bunch, but somehow it all careered along rather endearingly to a common purpose. Ad and Wal seemed somehow above or outside all of this. They just got on with it, and did their own thing fighting hard in Pretoria.

> The best of the party were its dogged, self-sacrificing volunteers of which the Hains were exemplars.

❦

Their bans meant that neither Ad nor Wal was able to attend John Harris's trial in Pretoria, which began on 21 September 1964, in Court C of Pretoria's Supreme Court. The court building, a British colonial period piece, faces onto Church Square, a grassed park in the city centre. The courtroom itself has dark wooden panelling and benches with crimson leather for lawyers, officials and defendants before a raised section for the judge and a place for a jury next to it. Spectators are seated on the same level, having entered from a columned atrium of which the building entrance is to one side and courtrooms the other. Ironically it has a somewhat egalitarian feel to it, the section for defendants not sticking up like a sore thumb, the judge not domineering from way on high as in old British courts.

To their shock Ad and Wal discovered that Harris's co-conspirator, John Lloyd, another friend of theirs and Liberal Party member, was to be the main prosecution witness. They immediately realised that they simply had to get news to Lloyd that, if he gave evidence, John Harris would be sentenced to death.

Ad, who had got to know Lloyd's girlfriend Jenny Corrigal, found a way of smuggling such a message in to him in an old Thermos flask with a shiny metal inside which she wrapped in tin foil containing a message. Jenny reported back that it had arrived safely.

Now the emotional stress became increasingly nightmarish, for Lloyd ignored this warning. At the trial he did not merely give evidence in corroboration of John's own confession (which would have carried a life sentence for manslaughter), but damningly went much, much further. Ad and Wal were aghast as Lloyd insisted that John had been willing to risk lives, in other words that John's act was pre-meditated murder. John consistently denied this and police testimony in court confirmed that he had indeed telephoned a warning to the railway police and urged them to clear the concourse, precisely in order to avoid injuring anyone.

Nevertheless, it became obvious that the judge accepted Lloyd's version – with fatal consequences. Ad and Wal were tense and upset as they described the savage turn of events to their children arriving back after school. Ann was stunned and Ad tried to console her while herself feeling much the same. They were all desperate. Nothing at all, it seemed, could be done as they were being sucked inexorably towards a horrendous end.

Then Ann indicated she wanted to speak privately to Ad and Wal; as usual for something confidential they moved out into the garden where they could be sure their conversation was not being bugged. The only time that Ann was ever allowed a contact visit with John was during court adjournments when he was taken down steps from the dock and then under the courtroom to a white-washed cell in the basement of the Supreme Court building. There they were able to put their arms around each other and whisper intimately, the warder standing in the corner of the cell (perhaps because he was a court official) taking no notice – special moments for them both.

On this particular day, Ann explained amid bushes in the garden, John had asked for a razor blade to be smuggled in. Distraught, she asked Ad and Wal: 'What should I do?'

They were horrified, their advice immediate and firm. 'No! You can't do that. It's far too dangerous. If John takes his own life or the razor blade is discovered, then you and not just John will be in the dock. Who will look after David then?'

However, John's lowest point proved transient, and the matter was never raised again. Looking back, Ad thought the moment must have come when he realised Lloyd's evidence would prove fatal and everything was so heavily stacked against him.

From the outset Lloyd was kept away from the other prisoners. When they were all transferred to Pretoria Local Prison at the end of July, he was housed on his own at a Pretoria police station, allowed frequent visits from his mother and given proper bedding with sheets. Evidence at the trial showed that Harris and Lloyd had been the only ones in their ARM cell still at liberty after the main arrests. The two had discussed a number of projects to 'make a big splash' to show that their ARM organisation had not been destroyed as the Justice Minister, John Vorster, had boasted on the radio. Among these were a bomb at Johannesburg station, a bomb in an underground car park and bombs in the private post boxes at Pretoria Post Office, all to be carried out on 24 July. John Harris was to carry out the first and Lloyd the other two.

However, Lloyd (the flatmate of fellow ARM member Hugh Lewin, who had been arrested on 9 July) was himself detained on 23 July, the day before John carried out his part of their project. It was not established whether the security services thereby had advance notice of the station bomb, but Lloyd's initial statement to the police mentioning John Harris and his proposal to plant a bomb at a station was made at 12.45 p.m. on 24 July, nearly four hours before the explosion. It may therefore have been that the security services had even greater forewarning than the fifteen minutes John himself gave. But, like the decision to ignore the latter, it suited their purposes to allow the bomb to explode as an excuse for the clampdown which then followed with a vengeance.

When it came to his judgment in the wooden-panelled courtroom – John sitting directly in front of him on a long, crimson-covered bench which had been occupied by Nelson Mandela and his Rivonia comrades some months before (and later Hugh Lewin) – the judge stated that Lloyd's evidence incontrovertibly proved that

John indeed had 'an intention to kill' and so was guilty of murder. There was no other evidence of the character necessary to sustain a capital offence and John's wife Ann, who had been present in court throughout, was now faced with the hideous inevitability of her husband facing the gallows. Although brave, she was inconsolable at home that night, as the family all waited for sentence to be passed. As the eldest, they had kept Peter fully appraised of the grim developments, but the younger Tom, Jo-anne and Sally had been shielded from just how desperate John's predicament was.

As the judge reconvened the hearing on 6 November 1964, Ad waited for Ann outside, parked on her own at the bottom of the wide court steps so that she did not break the terms of her banning order and find herself mixing with more than one other person; and also so that Ann could climb straight into the car and get away. Ad, careful that she did not break her ban by mixing with anybody, stood alone among scores of people gathering – party supporters, black and white, chatting as they anxiously awaited the outcome. Inside, the large marbled waiting area with a first-floor gallery on Roman pillars was packed. White office workers had poured in to witness the spectacle, staring morbidly at John's overwrought parents sitting on a wooden bench outside the courtroom. Also in the waiting crowd – quite extraordinarily, his young son with him – was the hangman, Chris Barnard, there to bear witness as he ghoulishly sized up his prospective victim. The executioner was not to be disappointed.

Ernie Wentzel came straight out to Ad with the shocking news that John had been sentenced to death by hanging – the first and only white in the struggle – an outcome cheered by the government-controlled media. As soon as Ann appeared walking down the court steps, Ad jumped out, opened the passenger door for her and they sped away.

Ad, deeply upset and shaking, came home as quickly as possible to speak to her children ahead of anyone else. Ann blankly stared ahead, and went straight to her bedroom. Peter seemed to have already accepted the inevitable but twelve-year-old Tom (also a great fan of John's) went completely white with shock. Jo-anne and Sally (nine and seven) could hardly take it in. The whole household was stunned.

During the next five months, as the shadow of the noose hovered over their family, Ad and Wal were involved in desperate efforts to save John's life. When his legal appeal on 1 March 1965 failed – because no additional evidence was forthcoming – they rushed about helping organise clemency appeals. Ann and John's father flew down to Cape Town to appeal to the Minister of Justice, John Vorster, but he was aggressive and dismissive. Petitions from a range of public figures were presented and the matter was even raised in the British Parliament.

A week after John's sentence four more ARM members stood trial in Pretoria including Hugh Lewin, who was jailed for seven years. Again – and although he had promised not to give evidence – John Lloyd was the main prosecution witness in Hugh's case.

Afterwards, Lloyd was released as part of an immunity deal by which he avoided being charged as an accomplice and very soon left with his mother for Britain, where a job awaited him. Soon after he was ensconced safely there, Jill Chisholm flew over to ask Lloyd to assist in John Harris's appeal by retracting his 'intention to kill' evidence. But he refused and instead threatened to tell the South African security police that she was 'trying to get him to perjure himself'. Then John's lawyer, Ruth Hayman, also well known to Lloyd as a fellow Liberal, flew over. Lloyd initially agreed to a draft affidavit retracting his evidence, promising to return in the morning to sign it. But he failed to do so.

There was a third similar encounter with Randolph Vigne, another ARM member who had escaped to Britain, who tried to persuade Lloyd to do an affidavit withdrawing key points of his evidence against John Harris. On a train from Bristol where Lloyd was based, Vigne got him to withdraw the evidence *in toto*. But when they reached London to meet solicitor Monty Cohen, a staunch South African Liberal, Lloyd refused to go with the wording he'd agreed and produced only a watered-down, anodyne statement. It was forwarded to the State President – but it was too little and too late. Lloyd even ignored Ann's final desperate cable – 'I plead for life in the knowledge that John and your friends would have done it for you.'

As the wife of a condemned man Ann was supposed to be allowed unlimited visits. However, the warders often claimed to be 'short of staff' and always tried to keep her waiting as long as they possibly could. Once they objected since she was wearing a dress without stockings and one Sunday they refused her entry because she was wearing trousers.

Ad and Wal paid regular visits themselves. John had meanwhile written a letter to a friend:

> The support and warm sympathy of friends has been and is among my basic reinforcements. I daily appreciate the accuracy of the observation that when one really has to endure one relies ultimately on Reason and Courage. I've been fortunate in that the first has stood up – my ideals and beliefs have never faltered. As for the second, well, I'm not ashamed – I know I've shown at least a modicum of the second.

Also while he was being held on death row he managed to convey a message to Ann. Despite the immense difficulty of talking to each other with everything being listened to, they knew each other so well they could talk in code. John had been approached by a warder who was a habitual smoker and who said he wanted to help him escape. This warder claimed to be 'a communist' – too clumsily contrived to be true, they immediately felt. John also told her that the warder insisted Wal must not be informed – further grounds for suspicion. He said that he would have to escape with John and that they both needed to go by motorbike and on to Russia. Ann asked a party friend for his passport so that John could use it.

Ad and Wal were torn. From the outset they were highly suspicious of a set-up designed to trap them, because they knew only too well the authorities were frustrated by being unable to bring charges against the couple. But if there was even the faintest chance to save John, of course Ann had to take it; otherwise none of them would ever forgive themselves. At great personal risk – they could have been found guilty of criminal conspiracy – they felt they had no alternative but to help her.

The warder arranged to meet Ann on a number of occasions. Ad – careful to protect herself as best she could – always dropped Ann off somewhere near the rendezvous or at the bus stop, but never at the spot in case it was being watched. One meeting point was a cinema while a film was showing, another in a Johannesburg restaurant.

Ad gave Ann the phone number of the telephone box she used regularly to speak to Pretoria Liberal organiser

David Rathswaffo and Ann passed it on to John in their usual code, for him to use if necessary when he got out. John had an almost photographic memory, with a brilliant mind, and had been known more widely as a star when he was a teenager on a radio programme called *The Quiz Kids*. Ann also gave John the number of a relative in England.

The warder explained to Ann that he would let John out of his cell and could then get them both through the prison ceiling and out onto the roof. A vehicle would be waiting to take them both. But he needed funds to get a suitable vehicle and make the getaway. After weeks of tense and contorted dealings with the warder, Ann posted him about 1,000 rand (a huge amount then) which she had raised partly from John's father; despite not knowing its exact purpose, he gave it to her without question.

Ad insisted that Ann had Elastoplast stuck discreetly over her fingertips so as to cover her prints and they both sat on the bed wiping the bank notes. The package of notes was marked 'cigarettes'. Ad also advised Ann to wear unusual clothing, including dark lipstick and a large turban-like scarf completely covering her hair, so that post office staff would not be able to identify her subsequently. But she emerged to tell Ad she was startled to be asked whether there were any matches in the package.

The warder notified Ann of the night the escape was planned and they spent a tense sleepless night waiting for news – or even her possible arrest, their emotions oscillating repeatedly between wild hope and cold instinct that it had all along seemed too good to be true. Morning came – and still no news. By now, fearing the worst, they resolved to stick to their routine daily prison visit. Ann went in as normal, and her spirit sank: as she had by now expected, there was no sign of anything different. He appeared for her as usual.

Ad went the same afternoon to see John herself. Entering the visiting room, there was a bench on the left against the wall with a green leather cover, and a thick perspex screen behind which John sat, with a warder further down on the same side. She smelt the tell-tale smoke identifying the presence of the warder concerned. 'Walter thinks you should try again,' she said deliberately, as the warder nearly jumped out of his skin, spilling his newspaper on the floor. John bent down to pick up his jacket and walked as if to go, then turned. 'No, it was a trap from the beginning,' he replied, looking more depressed than she had ever seen him. The security police had planned it all. There was nothing more that could be done to save him.

A date was set for the execution (1 April 1965) and a grim sense of foreboding enveloped the family.

On the occasions when Ann or Ad took little David in to see him, John was thrilled, remarking on how silky blond his hair was. Once they encouraged David to crawl along the bench so that John could see him do so for the first time. Prison regulations meant they were never allowed to touch – John was always shielded on the other side of the perspex screen.

Sympathetically patting David on the head, one of the warders said: 'Poor little chap.'

'He will be *proud* of his father,' Ad retorted sharply.

Ann and Ad would never let David out of their sight, anxious in case he might be snatched – such was the sense of siege under which they were living. Once, David was left sleeping outside in his pram in the garden, since they could always hear if any car was arriving. Then Ad heard an unusual noise. She rushed out, heart thumping, relieved to see the baby still safe and asleep. But to her astonishment a bouquet of flowers had been left on the pram.

Ad and Wal went together for their last visit, finding John remarkably stoic, almost his old cheerful self, wanting to know about arrangements for the funeral. Turning to a warder, he asked: 'What do they do with the corpse?'

Wal had previously shown him a photo Peter had taken of a new Ferrari Dino engine at Kyalami (Peter had wanted to take it in himself but prison chiefs prohibited him from doing so, Ad explained). 'We will help bring up David to be proud of you,' Ad promised John, tears rising in her.

On the day before the hanging Ann went for her final

visit, Ad taking her in, then leaving them to be alone. They were startled to see portable beds everywhere – along corridors, in offices, tucked around corners, everywhere. Perhaps, they wondered, a whole garrison was to be accommodated in case of some rescue assault and invasion of the jail?

The prison chaplain, a Catholic priest, Father McGuinness, sat with and comforted Ad outside, talking to her as she carried on with her knitting – she always did her knitting during the long waits for Ann. Despite John's continuing atheism the priest was due to be present at the hanging.

'If only we could have got the sentence commuted to life,' Ad told Father McGuinness. She was surprised by his reply: 'No, not in this place,' he shook his head grimly but sadly: it would have been hell for John.

In their last conversation, John asked Ann about the funeral. She explained it would contain the songs he loved including 'We Shall Overcome', and that 'The Battle Hymn of the Republic' was to be sung up to the verse that ended 'as he died to make men holy, let us die to make men free'. He was also pleased to learn that Wal would be reading the address. John wanted included Shakespeare's Sonnet 116 as a memorial to their deep mutual love which would not change, a constant despite their horrendous predicament and his own culpability. They went over the words together: 'Let me not to the marriage of true minds / Admit impediments. Love is not love / Which alters when it alteration finds...'

But he also insisted to Ann that she must leave the country or she would always be a target, and life would become impossible. (He was right: when Ann later applied for and was offered a teaching post at the prestigious Pretoria Girls High School, the Department for Education vetoed it. Shortly afterwards she received an official letter withdrawing her right to teach.)

To Ad and Wal's admiration, when she returned to the house, Ann seemed serene and almost relieved. 'I have just had such a lovely visit with John, we talked about everything,' she said.

The grisly, medieval ritual of being hanged by the neck until dead weighed heavily with Ad and Wal. Before he imagined ever personally knowing a condemned person, Wal had vivid discussions with friends and his son Peter about his total opposition to capital punishment: how an eye for an eye and a tooth for a tooth was the mark of an uncivilised society – how executing those convicted of murders did not affect the murder rate compared with equivalent societies without capital punishment – and how, once executed, someone innocent could not be reprieved by additional evidence gathered subsequently. The brutal violence of the act: trap door opening underneath, the sudden jerk of the body, jack-knifing as the neck bore all the weight and broke, blood spouting. This was all about to happen to their friend.

At John's request Father McGuinness helped him rehearse the words of the inspirational protest song, 'We Shall Overcome', so that he didn't get it wrong. The priest was often present before executions because condemned prisoners had known him to be supportive. But he found John, an atheist right to the end, markedly and admirably different. He later recounted that most prisoners 'went into a state of grace' at the point of their execution, whereas John remained calm and determined – as he had planned, singing 'We Shall Overcome' until the moment he died. These were his last words of defiance – they learnt later from Father McGuinness – as the noose was tightened around his neck, the trap door opened below his feet, and the last breath was torn from him. Years later, his hangman, Chris Barnard – who was responsible for 1,500 hangings as South Africa's longest-serving hangman between 1964 and 1986 – described John as 'very brave'.

He was hanged at 5 a.m., and across South Africa a lot of people rose unusually early, including Ad's mom Edith, way down on the southern coast of Africa. The Hain household was also up well before the moment arrived, with none of the clatter and chaos of mornings getting ready for school and work. Ann, Ad and Wal waited, still and silent as the darkness outside.

Then the phone rang, piercingly loud. The caller asked to speak to Ann. Ad refused, recognising the familiar voice of a security police officer who went on to say mockingly: 'Your John is dead.'

'Thanks for telling us,' she replied, deadpan.

Decades later she recalled: 'I felt like slaughtering him, but I was always determined never to give the Special Branch any sign that they might have stung us in the way they always intended with such nastiness.'

Both Ad and Wal were overwhelmed by a blank hopelessness combined with deep anger. They hadn't condoned what John had done; on the contrary they had bitterly condemned it both before and after they knew he was responsible. But, under any civilised system, he would have continued to devote his life to teaching children and would never have been involved in the sabotage which ended his life so grotesquely.

Wal and their barrister friend, Ernie Wentzel, had previously asked permission from the prison kommandant for the body to be released for cremation. This was not a normal procedure for the many black political prisoners who had been executed, but John was the first white. To everyone's surprise, the request was granted and a funeral was arranged at Pretoria Crematorium for 7.30 in the morning, just a few hours after his execution. (Ernie thought that the permission was given so that the security police could monitor who would attend.) As banned persons Ad and Wal required permission to go and this was duly given – again surprisingly.

But no sooner were their spirits raised than they were cruelly dashed. Wal returned from requesting permission to read the main address and told Ann he had been refused. It was the evening before the execution, Ann mortified because she had told John that Wal would be reading it. She didn't know what to do and Ad and Wal tried consoling her as she cried in the garden, the sun setting. Then Peter joined them, having ridden in from school, not quite sure what was going on. 'Anything I can do?' he asked. Ann turned, her face lighting up: 'That would be wonderful, Peter,' taking it for granted he would undertake the task.

Wal had painstakingly prepared a two-page funeral address to remember key people according to Ann's wishes and reflecting John's strong atheist convictions. Ad quickly retyped parts to make it easier for Peter to read. Dignified yet uplifting, it began with John's chosen Shakespearean sonnet and continued with John Donne:

> No Man is an Island, entire of itself. Every man is a piece of the continent, a part of the main … Any man's death diminishes me, because I am involved in mankind, and therefore send not to know for whom the bell tolls; it tolls for thee.

From the Bible was Matthew's 'Blessed are they which are persecuted for righteousness' sake' – specially for John's mother – and Ecclesiastes' 'To everything there is a season, and a time for every purpose under heaven', which was on an album sung beautifully by Judy Collins and often played in the Hain family home during those fraught months. The songs were 'The Battle Hymn of the Republic' (selected for Hugh Lewin), concluding with the Freedom Riders' song 'We Shall Overcome', immortalised at the time at American civil rights and peace demonstrations by Joan Baez.

The Rebecca Street Crematorium is set back in green spacious grounds, a serene, peaceful building, its chapel with a simple charm of its own.

Ad and Wal, not knowing what to expect as they arrived with Ann and their children, were gratifyingly astounded to find the chapel packed. The number and variety of people in attendance, apart from relatives of John and Ann, was deeply moving: the chapel was full, including non-whites unusually allowed to attend a white funeral. They were overwhelmed as they greeted many friends – Liberal Party members from both Pretoria and Johannesburg, people from the townships and even members of the diplomatic corps. All knew that, by attending, their names would be diligently recorded by the Special Branch officers grouped outside. Ann's parents, devout Catholics, had obtained special dispensation from the church, then required for them to attend a cremation. John's father and sister Jane were present but his mother, deeply traumatised, was sadly far too ill.

Twelve-year-old Tom, very small for his age, was angry and upset as he spotted prison warders carrying the coffin, and Ad gave him a hug. Gesturing to the procession, she said: 'Go and help if you want to.' The little boy in his khaki school shorts ran over and inserted himself among the bearers.

Ad and Wal led their girls to seats at the front of the plain wooden benches and ushered Peter, aged fifteen and dressed in his Pretoria Boys High School blazer, tie and grey trousers, up to the raised lectern before the assembled congregation. They worried that he seemed anxious, waiting as the coffin was carried through.

Although the ceremony had been carefully prepared and Peter had only to read out the address distributed to all who attended, Ad and Wal were very aware that he had never spoken from any platform before and had always avoided school plays or performances, being quite a private, undemonstrative and rather shy boy. The atmosphere had become tense, as if reaching a climax of emotion. Grown white men were crying and their black maid, Eva, was sobbing heart-wrenchingly out loud, resounding about the small chapel. They watched, tense but proud as Peter began, trembling a little, they noticed apprehensively, his voice seeming not to want to come out. Had he got stage fright? The proximity of the coffin behind Peter and to his left, containing John's body, life torn from him at the gallows only two hours earlier, made the ordeal especially distressing for them all.

But to their relief his voice picked up almost immediately, welcoming everyone as he began the reading. Then the congregation stood, their voices resounding through the small building, the Pretoria Liberal founder

Colin Lang playing the piano and accompanying the singing as best he could. Their spirits rising in defiance at the Special Branch outside and the evil system which had condemned a good man, they ended with 'We Shall Overcome' and Peter pressed the white button on a shelf immediately under the lectern marked 'push to move coffin'.

The last, totally irrevocable step had been taken by Ad and Wal's eldest son as the coffin moved eerily away out of sight, the body to be lifted on a trolley into an oven, taking half an hour to burn, with only the ashes of John's bones remaining.

That was it. Finished. All Ad and Wal's efforts – all that others had done to save John – a total, bleak and empty failure. A big piece of hope, of the optimism that drove people on in the struggle, died that morning too – and everyone there felt it very personally.

Peter stepped down awkwardly to a tearful Ann and hugs from proud parents. Tom, Jo-anne and Sally huddled tensely together, their minds swirling. To their embarrassment, people kept coming up and thanking the family. Smiles amid tears, Ad and Wal chatted to comrades they hadn't been able to see or talk to for what had seemed like ages; they had been given permission exclusively for the funeral to suspend the provisions of their banning orders which had made such conversations impossible. Then it seemed over almost before it had begun, and people drifted away to their lives and their work.

Ad and Wal dropped the children off at their schools – each with a note for lateness. Peter was photographed by the media as he got out of the car, before slipping into class, where his favourite teacher, Terry Ashton, gave him a knowing but unobtrusive welcome. Although they had warned the school that their son would be late that morning, none of his classmates knew the reason until a report with his photograph appeared in the papers the following day. Ad and Wal had worried about all four of their children, how they would cope after such a traumatic start to their school day. But they were pleased to discover later that Sally's teacher Mrs Parry played 'The Battle Hymn of the Republic' on the piano, not saying anything but giving the eight-year-old a comforting smile.

Wal went off to work and Ad took Ann home to be with nine-month-old David (who had been looked after by Wal's mother Mary), the tiny boy oblivious that he would never know the father he no longer had.

Eight hundred miles to the south near Cape Town, the political prisoners were already digging out limestone from the quarry on Robben Island, a gruelling daily process – especially in bright sunshine, which damaged their eyes. During their lunch break, John's ARM colleague Eddie Daniels called on all the prisoners to stand and observe a minute's silence 'to a great freedom fighter'. Nelson Mandela and all members of the ANC,

PAC, Communist Party and other political groups obeyed the call in honour of John.

Later, Father McGuinness came to see Ann and Ad at The Willows, as John had asked him to do. He had seen quite a lot of John in visits and found him widely read and interesting to talk to, always a great enthusiast as he asked what was going on in the world outside. The priest was also struck by how committed an atheist he remained – right to the end. Often, in his experience, condemned prisoners took comfort in Christianity even if they had never been religious. 'He went well,' he said, trying to comfort them both as Ann sat staring into space, her foot constantly swinging back and forward.

Nobody ever explained why, but after he was cremated the prison authorities kept John's ashes for years – apparently in the office of the commander of Pretoria Central Prison. Then they were handed over to the prison chaplain, who arranged for a burial in a simple grave in Rebecca Street public cemetery, a hundred yards from the crematorium, the prison authorities marking the spot with a stone bearing his name and dates – Ann not told about this. Only in 1998, apartheid having ended, and after a persistent search by her sister Meg, did his family finally discover the truth. Meg latter arranged for the words 'A True Patriot' to be added, as he had wanted, to John's gravestone. When his family travelled out in

2005 to mark the fortieth anniversary of John's death, Ad and Wal (invited but unable to attend) asked for a small stone to be placed next to the gravestone.

Then there was a 'Symbolic Cleansing and Wreath Laying Ceremony' at the Isivivane – a garden of remembrance – within the still unopened Freedom Park at Salvakop on a hill outside Pretoria, deliberately situated to the north of the Voortrekker Monument, a beautiful, tranquil shrine to all those who had fallen: from the colonial and Boer wars through the First and Second World Wars to the freedom struggle. Thousands of names were etched onto a light brown stone 'Freedom Wall'. Under a heading 'Executions' was 'John Harris 1937–1965'. 'This location', said Freedom Park's chairwoman, Gertrude Shope, officiating at a ceremony in 2010, 'is symbolical, in that we would like to give our backs to our past, while not forgetting it, and face the future as united nation.'

Later still, in December 2011, opening Pretoria's Gallows Museum at an event to which family members were invited, President Jacob Zuma spoke of those hanged for fighting apartheid, John the only white among them:

> The 134 men were terrorists or troublemakers to the authorities then. But to their people and families, they were freedom fighters who wanted to a see a free, democratic and non-sexist South Africa … Today, all 134 names are officially being enshrined for eternity so

> that future generations will know what this country went through, so that we never go through a similar horror ever again … All South Africans suffered for this freedom. Lives were lost and many families went through untold pain and suffering. We therefore open this museum as a place of healing … Let the blood of all the patriots who fell here inspire us to build a better South Africa that upholds human dignity and the right to life.

It was, Ann felt, sitting at the President's table, a fitting recognition at last; Ad and Wal hearing the news afterwards also felt a certain sense of closure – though for Ad especially, the deep, searing emotions surrounding the whole John Harris tragedy were never to go away.

8

Departure

Not only for Ad and Wal but also the whole nation, the station bomb was a pivotal event. But, although they sensed their lives had changed forever, they were not then aware it would propel them into exile. The Security Minister, John Vorster, made a bellicose attack on them both, fulminating (totally inaccurately) that John Harris had been recruited to the African Resistance Movement 'at the house of Hain'.

The bomb was exploited both to increase repression and systematically to discredit and destroy the Liberal Party. Its national chairman, the highly respected Peter Brown, was banned. Leading party figures up and down the country were also banned or detained or forced to flee to exile. In 1965 the period for which people could be held without charge was extended from ninety to 180 days; two years later it was to become indefinite. The Liberals' magazine, *Contact*, was closed after its fifth editor was banned. Alban Thumbran, the Coloured

Pretoria member to whom Ad and Wal were especially close, was banned. Ruth Hayman, John Harris's lawyer and their friend and legal mainstay, was banned and house-arrested. Their battered old Volkswagen minibus, for years effectively the Pretoria Liberals' main transportation, was stolen in circumstances which pointed to security police responsibility; it was eventually found months later in Hartbeespoort Dam west of Pretoria after the water level had fallen drastically in a drought.

Agencies of the state conducted other 'deniable operations' against leading Liberals. Randolph Vigne's house was petrol-bombed after he had escaped abroad. Peter Hjul's infant son narrowly missed being killed by a bullet fired through his front window. Alan Paton's car windows were smashed and iron filings inserted into the oil sump of its engine. The Liberals were subject to extreme harassment and intimidation by security forces, designed to terrify them into inaction. Their members were also fed disinformation leaflets and forged letters encouraging them to give up before they too were targeted.

But at the July 1965 Liberal Party Congress the party fought back defiantly, refusing to be cowed, and a motion was unanimously carried condemning 'savage, systematic and ... unconstitutional persecution' by the government. It also urged members: 'Now is the time to hold fast to our conviction and our faith.'

On the other hand the reputation of the party among the wider movement resisting apartheid had been damaged by Liberals such as John Lloyd and Adrian Leftwich turning state witness against former comrades – in stark contrast to the heroic stance of Nelson Mandela and his ANC comrades at the Rivonia Trial, taking place at the time. Ad and Wal felt bitterly betrayed.

Magnus Gunther argues bluntly:

> Sadly, not much pride, defiance or heroism was shown at the trials. It was not just police torture that broke ARM members. They seemed morally stricken … The fact that one of their members had killed someone and maimed several others seemed to drain all resistance from many, though … others [including Hugh Lewin and Eddie Daniels] refused to turn state witness … but it was the spectacle of Leftwich betraying his friends, himself and his ideals that personified the defeat of the organisation and led to others making statements. There were no stirring challenges to the regime from the dock, no expressions of pride about their considerable contributions to the struggle, as had been the case during the Rivonia Trial.

By now Wal's continued employment as an architect who specialised in hospital design was threatened. Soon after his ban the firm was told by the authorities that, if they continued to employ him, they would no longer receive any government work. He had to resign, and opened his own office – the firm continuing to slip him some work. It soon dried up, however, and although he had a few commissions of his own for projects outside the Pretoria magisterial district (to which his ban confined him), permission for him to leave Pretoria to inspect and survey the sites was refused by the Minister of Justice. An appeal by the head of the South African Architects' Association also fell on deaf ears.

The word went out in the profession in Pretoria that all private architectural firms seeking government work had better not employ him. Wal's reputation as an architect remained high: painstaking and inventive, he was in demand – if he had been a normal white professional. But of course he wasn't. He had some unfinished commissions, but the work they provided would not last much longer.

Ad and Wal were now trapped. Short of being imprisoned – which could still have been triggered at any time if they were caught in their surreptitious activities – their political work had been blocked. But while they still had an income, they could continue to play some kind of covert role. Now that had been blocked too. They were torn, desperate not to leave South Africa, but since they had no private means, Wal simply had to find a job in order to provide for their family.

With a heavy heart, he wrote to the architectural firm in London that had employed him in 1956 and was immediately offered a job. Now the question was: where would they live? Harold Smith presented the answer. A librarian, British Anti-Apartheid Movement member and former member of the British Communist Party who had subsequently joined the Labour Party, he had first visited South Africa with the British forces during the Second World War. He ended up working with a former Pretoria Liberal activist friend, Ansie Preller, who had gone into exile in London. She put him touch with Ad and Wal and he met them on a visit to South Africa in 1965.

'You can't do any more here,' Harold had tried to persuade Ad and Wal. They would be better off safe in exile than being dragged ever deeper into the clutches of the police state, he maintained, and offered to help. They had courteously rejected his overtures before, because they felt that, however difficult life had become for them, their duty lay to their comrades in South Africa. They always believed that whatever privations they had suffered as white activists were as nothing compared with the horror inflicted upon black activists, who were routinely tortured or simply disappeared.

In their new predicament, however, they turned to Harold Smith, who generously offered rented accommodation in an empty first-floor flat in his large home in Putney, south-west London. Nevertheless, their decision was a traumatic one. Wal, then aged forty-one, knew his already badly disrupted architectural career would be further undermined. They were both leaving the country of their birth which they loved and for which they had sacrificed many of the comforts and privileges of white life. They were also being forced to leave their parents – Wal's lived nearby in Pretoria, Ad's 600 miles away (she had not seen them since her ban in 1963 prevented her from doing so). They were only too conscious that by leaving they would almost certainly never see their respective parents again. Their children were aghast at the prospect, as children always are when required to leave their friends for a future unknown. They didn't want to move, and each resisted the idea until told it was inevitable.

However, for Peter and Tom, aged fifteen and thirteen, there was one small consolation: on inspecting a map of London, they discovered that Chelsea's football stadium, Stamford Bridge, was near what would be their new home; the team was doing well at the time and Ad and Wal were relieved that at least they had something to look forward to, the boys having resolved to become Chelsea fans. Then Peter was able to book special, cheap tickets for tourists for the 1966 World Cup football finals in England, so something else exciting awaited. They also talked of seeing cricket at Lord's and motor races at Silverstone and Brands Hatch – places of awe to a young 'colonial' boys like them which they could only imagine from magazine reports and photographs, or the crackly radio commentaries on the BBC's World Service. For Jo-anne and Sally, however, it was different: their lives might be more free in England, but they had little else to beckon them.

Friends raised the finance for their passages on a

Union Castle liner from Cape Town. Wal was eligible for a British passport because his father had been born in Glasgow and Ad was also eligible as she had married him three years before the rules had changed in 1951. Peter had all along retained his British citizenship, having been born in what was then the British colony of Kenya; but, unaccountably, his birth certificate was missing, probably, Ad and Wal suspected, taken by the Special Branch in one of their house raids. To compound the problem they now faced, Kenya did not recognise apartheid South Africa and so Ad and Wal had to obtain a copy of their son's birth certificate indirectly via Ansie Preller in London. Sally had been born in Britain. That left Tom and Jo-anne, and the British embassy helpfully registered them as British citizens.

The security police were unaware of all this. Whether they had explicitly calculated that by depriving Wal of a living they were thereby forcing exile upon them would never be known. But when Ad and Wal applied under the terms of their banning orders for permission to leave the Pretoria area, the Special Branch were initially obstructive. Then it was pointed out that the family had British passports and had already been issued with departure permits – clearly immigration officials had treated the matter routinely and had not thought to tip off the Special Branch.

The departure permits were then promptly withdrawn and replaced with one-way exit permits, which prohibited Ad and Wal from returning to South Africa and withdrew their South African citizenship. In the typically bloody-minded manner of the local bureaucracy, permission to leave Pretoria was then frustratingly delayed – at one point it looked as though they would have to postpone their departure, which would have triggered extra travel ticket costs and left the family without anywhere to live in Pretoria. However, at the last moment the authorities grudgingly granted them permission to travel to Cape Town. They had hoped to take the children up Table Mountain, but the permission to travel was strictly confined to going straight from the train which drew up at the dockside and onto the ship.

Although upset at their friends' impending departure, Liberals and other activists in Pretoria insisted on organising a farewell gathering in the party's office. The terms of their bans prevented Ad and Wal from being present, so they dropped off and later collected their four children to represent them. It was a sad yet joyous occasion and everyone there treated the Hain kids as surrogates for the absent parents they held in such high and affectionate regard.

Exile held no glory for them: they felt intensely guilty at leaving friends and colleagues behind, though simultaneously relieved that the all-consuming pressure under which their family had been living for the previous three years would now be eased. They wrote a press release which had to be issued in Peter's name and which he copied out by hand (because their bans still prevented them from saying anything publicly themselves). Dated March 1966, it said:

> My parents have reluctantly taken the decision to leave South Africa.
>
> Both are South African born and bred, and had hoped to live their lives working, as in the past, towards the attainment of a just society in South Africa; a society of which all South Africans could be proud, whatever the colour of their skins, whatever their religious beliefs, whatever their political convictions.
>
> But the Nationalists have made it virtually impossible for them to remain, for by direct pressure upon employers the government has made it extremely difficult for my father to obtain employment and by refusing him permission to inspect clients' buildings outside the Pretoria magisterial district it has ensured the failure of his architectural practice. The stage has now been reached where he is no longer able to make a living in his own country but must seek work elsewhere to support his family.
>
> This is the sole reason for my parents' decision to leave.
>
> They do not subscribe to the view that nothing more can be done within South Africa by radical opponents of apartheid and that there is

consequently no point in South African Liberals remaining here to continue the struggle for justice and equality. On the contrary they believe that the very scarcity of genuine opponents of racialism among white South Africans greatly magnifies the relative importance of white non-racialists here, and they point to the banning of nearly forty Liberals as evidence that the Nationalists share this belief.

The decision to leave has therefore been a painful one for them especially as it means leaving behind not only their parents, and friends – both white and non-white – but also the many Liberals who are also banned and so cannot communicate with them without risking prosecution.

We hope to return when South Africa is governed, not by narrow sectional government as at present, but by one that truly represents all South Africans; without the injustice of the pass laws, the Group Areas Act; when detention without trial laws are no more than a bad memory; when there is a decent, dignified life for all.

Edmund Burke once said: 'All that is necessary for the triumph of evil is that good men do nothing'; we believe that the evil of apartheid is temporarily triumphant in South Africa today because so few good men will become committed. And in Alan Paton's 'Cry the Beloved Country', the African priest, Msimangu, says 'I have one great fear in my heart, that one day when they are turned to loving, they will find we are turned

> to hating.' I and my parents share this great fear, and I urge my fellow whites to 'turn to loving' before it is too late.

Most of their household possessions had been previously placed into crates for despatch to England and it was early evening on 14 March 1966 when Ad and Wal finally packed up and were driven by his parents to Pretoria railway station. Gathered there were party stalwarts and friends. The tears flowed as they hugged and said their goodbyes on the first leg of their long journey. At the end of the platform standing quite alone as his banning order required, their former close comrade Alban Thumbran stood waving; his bereft sense of isolation and desolation gnawed at their emotions more than almost anything else. They were never to see him again.

Ad gave their maid and close friend Eva Matjeka a hug and kiss goodbye; Eva simply stood there as if turned to stone, knowing that if she let go of her emotions she would simply break down as she had done at the funeral, and her loud heaving cries would have erupted. Gladys Geffen, mother to Peter's school friend Dave, found her a job at a clinic in Pretoria and Ad and Wal offered her all their remaining household goods and furniture. As the steam train chugged out, Ad felt completely empty, drained of purpose and the bonds of comradeship: the waving figures becoming smaller and smaller then disappearing made it all so depressingly final. Wal simply buried his emotions.

Waiting on the platform at Johannesburg station as the train stopped were more party members to say their farewells and deliver parting gifts. John Harris's father, Frederick, was also there, a forlorn figure. Ann had already departed with David and they were his last connection to John.

Although profoundly upset, Ad and Wal were intent on making the best of it, as they had throughout the last eight years of activism. Their values and sense of duty had propelled them to this quandary, but they couldn't and didn't regret the stand they had taken. It had been the right thing to do, even if the consequences for them and their family were dire. Putting their own anguish to one side, they concentrated on comforting their children and encouraging them to find excitement in the novelty of the train journey and the waiting ship.

❧

As their train pulled into the station right alongside Cape Town docks, Special Branch officers waited and watched to ensure Ad and Wal complied strictly with the narrow terms of their permission to leave, by going straight onto the ship. They did, settling into their economy family cabin and then standing on the deck to wave a last goodbye to a small group of relatives and party friends on the quay.

But the ship remained berthed for what seemed like an age. By the time it pulled away, Ad was feeling terrible and ill. They steamed out and into the heaving Cape rollers, glimpsing Robben Island, grim behind the cold spray, where Nelson Mandela and his comrades were incarcerated in their harsh isolation.

Bereft as their beloved South Africa receded into the distance, they were depressed at what they felt was their legacy: part of a failed resistance. They had done all they could, but it was not enough. The principal liberation movement, the ANC, was outlawed and in disarray; its leaders were in prison; its military wing, *Umkhonto*, seemingly crushed. Other resistance groups including the PAC had similarly been banned or paralysed. The most militant white organisation, the Congress of Democrats, which had worked closely with the ANC, had suffered the same removal of its upper echelons and had been banned. The Liberal Party was badly damaged by the banning of over fifty of its activists, imprisonment of others and by the now imploded ARM.

Two years later on 9 May 1968, the Prohibition of Improper Interference Act came onto the statute book. Its purpose: making non-racial organisation and thereby specifically the Liberal Party illegal. It could not continue and met for the last time at the Guildhall in Durban, the party leadership issuing a final statement, 'a temporary farewell', appealing to all its supporters

> to keep open every channel of personal interracial contact you have, and to start others: to oppose racialism, black, white or brown, wherever you confront it;

> to keep alive the hope that right will one day triumph, apartheid will go, freedom and equal opportunity will come to every South African, and the non-racial society for which the Liberal Party stands and which is the only just solution to our problems will be born here in our country ... Liberty shall rise again!

Randolph Vigne comments in his history of the party:

> It ended with an appeal to Liberals to keep them ready for the day of the return of liberalism to South Africa. This seemed quixotic optimism then and for a quarter of a century to follow. In 1994, however, it was not exclusive Afrikaner nor African nationalism nor totalitarian Marxism-Leninism that triumphed. The liberal beliefs and ideals the party had championed against all comers were to arise phoenix-like and prevail at last in the first constitution of a new non-racial South Africa.

However, that new constitution was the brainchild of ANC leaders headed by Nelson Mandela and meticulously negotiated by the 1980s resistance leader Cyril Ramaphosa. The ANC and its partners were overwhelmingly the dominant force in the eventual overthrow of apartheid and the transition to the new South Africa. Yet the Liberal Party, during its short but eventful life between 1953 and 1968, was a catalyst for change, especially but by no means exclusively for whites. The banning of the ANC, PAC and Congress of Democrats in 1960 meant that the party was the only publicly active and, until it was forced to dissolve in 1968, legal anti-apartheid force. When Ad and Wal were most prominent – and under attack from the security forces and the state, in the period between 1960 and 1965 – there was no other visible and permitted political party committed to a truly non-racial society with equal rights for all.

Their departures had been marked by talk from friends that they would be back one day to savour the freedom of a new South Africa. But they felt these were only the ritual exchanges of close comradeship. Ad and Wal had no illusions. They were going for good. The apartheid state seemed immortal. Despite their very best efforts it had won.

But, as it transpired, their struggle was not over yet. They were to join other anti-apartheid activists in exile in what was to become a decisive era of international struggle against apartheid – there was another part for them to play in the eventual victory to come.

9

Exile

Southampton docks loomed, chilly and misty in the morning as the ship was piloted to its berth in April 1966, the weather a dank contrast to the heat which had accompanied them on the ship most of the way, and which they had left behind in their sunny homeland.

The two-week voyage had been an enjoyable relief as they put their troubles behind them and avoided worrying about the future. Living what amounted to a hotel life on board and eating out all the time was not something Ad and Wal had ever been able to afford for their large family, and so was a real treat. They struck up a friendship with a jovial Spanish waiter who regularly served them at their designated table in the ship's restaurant.

They discovered that by coincidence a fellow banned Liberal activist, Ann Tobias, was on board. But because she had been banned as well they couldn't speak to her until the ship had left South African waters and Peter was deputed to contact her and fix to eat at their dining table. (Ann had decided to leave after receiving a two-year suspended jail sentence for breaking her ban by joining two friends for a barbecue on Table Mountain, lamenting: 'Sooner or later I was going to jail for nonsense and it began to make sense to think of getting out.')

There was also an unexpected delight when they found their prosperous black doctor friend, Fabian Ribeiro, and his wife Florence also on board. Both Catholics, they were on a pilgrimage to Lourdes, the only way as Africans they could get a passport and permission to take a holiday. Their presence was much to the astonishment of white South African passengers, who had never encountered blacks doing that sort of thing before: holidays were what whites did. Ad and Wal asked two strangers on their table if they could switch places with the Ribeiros. But the two wouldn't move; instead they sat pointedly refusing to acknowledge the Hains throughout the two-week trip, Ad and Wal wondering if they were Special Branch eavesdroppers.

There was incredulity and some disapproval when, at a fancy-dress evening, Wal and Florence went jauntily dressed in their pyjamas labelled 'The Immorality Act' (the apartheid law banning both mixed-race marriages and mixed-race sex). Fabian and Ann Tobias – who, though 'white', had an oriental complexion – went as the first black President of Ghana, Kwame Nkrumah, and his Egyptian wife. Ad had Elastoplast sealing her mouth and a sash across her dress labelled 'The Perfect

Woman'. She and Wal always had an impish sense of fun and informality, even when their anti-apartheid activity had been so deadly serious.

Harold Smith and Ansie Preller kindly met the family at the dockside and drove them to his Putney home. For Ad and Wal it was a fillip to see Labour Party election posters still on display in Harold's front windows as they had arrived the day after Labour's huge general election victory in April 1966. A few days later they decided to join Harold and his friends on the Campaign for Nuclear Disarmament's annual Easter demonstration at Trafalgar Square, asking Peter and Tom if they wanted to come too. But their teenage boys preferred to go off on their own to see their favoured football club, Chelsea, for the first time. The boys were squeezed into the car on its way to the demo and were dropped off into what seemed to Ad a massive crowd (the ground had a 60,000 spectator capacity): 'Will I ever see them again?' she briefly wondered.

But the CND march and rally was an eye-opener, with a real sense of freedom compared with what they had become used to. The police were very different: no guns, no snarling dogs and no nastiness. There seemed almost a carnival atmosphere.

Meanwhile, they were relieved that their children were excited by watching Harold's television for the first time (there was then no TV in South Africa).

However, there was an early worry. On what they felt in retrospect was a peculiar recommendation from

Harold Smith, their English landlord and ex-communist, Wal had taken his two sons to enrol at what turned out to be the local state grammar school, Emanuel, in Battersea (years later it became a private school). When they later understood the system of secondary schools in Britain they were horrified: their strong preference was for comprehensive schooling – without any academic selection, like they were used to in South Africa.

The boys arrived for an interview with the head teacher, Charles Kuper, lugubrious and ruddy faced with whiskers and, Wal thought, an aroma of alcohol. A written recommendation from their old head teacher impressed the new one. But Wal took exception when he was asked to explain the reasons for their exile. 'I am not surprised you were treated that way,' came Mr Kuper's reply. Nevertheless, the boys were accepted.

He returned home with Peter and Tom, who had taken an immediate dislike to Emanuel, its class-ridden culture – uniforms had to be purchased at Harrods – a world away from Pretoria Boys High. Despite Ad being furious with Wal for enrolling them, in the circumstances there seemed no alternative but to proceed.

Placed into 'Lower 5 General' – the bottom-performing class of the year – Peter was told by the head to spend an additional year there catching up with the curriculum for the 'O' level exams the other boys his age were sitting in six weeks' time. He baulked at losing a year like that and, against strong official school advice, resolved to enter the exams anyway. Ad and Wal were happy to back him, paying a special fee for late entrance. Peter quickly threw himself into preparing for the exams and was given extra help by his teachers. Using excellent revision and exam techniques learnt at Pretoria Boys High, spotting likely questions and boning up intensively on areas of his strength in each subject, he was able to assemble sufficiently high marks across his areas of expertise in each exam to offset questions where he was either weak, or in some cases knew nothing whatsoever. To parental relief his pass grades awarded in all ten 'O' levels entered – which included Afrikaans, coached by Ansie Preller – were creditable, even if not as consistently high as at Boys High. Tom, also coached by Ansie, later got a higher Afrikaans grade.

However, Ad and Wal's concern about the school was growing, especially as Tom was evidently and deeply unhappy there, despite becoming a cox in one of the school's rowing teams – Emanuel had an excellent record at rowing and Ad took the boys to see the 1st VIII compete in the Henley regatta. Eventually they moved Tom to Wandsworth Boys Comprehensive School, wishing they had been directed there in the first place, as Tom was much happier.

The stress of the build-up, first to John Harris's execution and then to the funeral, had meant Ad and Ann especially lived for nine months on adrenalin and nerves, battling against an all-intrusive police state and a hostile white public.

But the aftermath was extremely traumatic too. Suddenly there was a void. They had failed to save John. Readjusting to a more orderly life proved very hard. Ad had watched constantly over Ann. With her all the time, Ad had been privy to all her emotions, from her steadfast courage in public to her anguished desperation in private.

Now they were both in a bad state, reaction setting in, but in different ways. Where they had been unswerving together in the fight, they naturally began to get on with their own lives, and perhaps inevitably there was some friction between them.

John had pressed Ann to get involved with another man who could offer her the companionship he felt she needed and to marry again – and Ann soon fell into another relationship. But Ad didn't approve, believing the mutual friend wasn't right for Ann, that it was too rushed and that she needed time to find herself after such a horrendous, life-changing ordeal.

When Ann accepted a kind offer by an anonymous well-wisher to pay for her travel for two weeks' holiday in London and stay in Harold Smith's house where Ansie Preller had a room, Ad had been delighted to look after David for her. However, Ann said that her new partner thought Ad was trying to get 'control' of David, which naturally hurt her deeply, and their relationship suddenly changed. Later on, having arranged to travel with Ad and Wal and their family into exile, Ann decided not to and instead went ahead with what proved to be the temporary man in her life. With David, nearly two years old, she moved into a tiny flat above the one the Hains had been offered in Putney. So Ad was surprised and rather disconcerted when Ann was there to greet them on their arrival in Britain as if nothing had happened between them.

For his part, Wal was upset too and supported Ad as he always had through thick and thin. It was a wrenching episode, churning away inside Ad, making her feel guilty about her behaviour, yearning that Ann might in future come to understand. With hindsight Ad felt she should have let Ann go her own way and given her more of her own space.

One of Ad's personality traits was to take a strong line on what she thought was right or wrong. This expressed itself positively in an indomitable spirit when fighting against injustice or carrying out her strong sense of duty when she became almost fearless, and in intense loyalty to friends and family. But, if she disapproved of the behaviour of someone close to her, she could also be negatively judgemental.

It was only later, after Ann – by now on her own again – had returned with David from a spell teaching in Uganda that their friendship was fully restored. Ad was thrilled when Ann remarried, to Martin Wolfe, who gave David (then aged six) a happy upbringing, and later Ann another son, Toby. And when

Toby was born Ad travelled to stay with them in Cambridge, to look after David, from where Wal fetched them both for a holiday at their friends' home in the Dorset village Burton Bradstock, joined by their own children.

Ad and Wal concentrated upon building a fresh life on the assumption that they were never going back. As they discovered, many South African exiles in Britain then lived a kind of limbo existence – waiting to return. That was their choice and their dream. But Ad and Wal were determined to put down roots, to get involved in the community and to make a new future. Britain was now their home, they made clear to their children.

Nevertheless, being exiles was tough – very tough. Willingly choosing to move to another country, as many people do, is one thing. It involves disruption and adjustment for any family. Children rarely like big change, and worry about a new and foreign school and finding new friends. But at least families taking that course usually do so out of choice and for positive reasons. And they know they can return – either on a visit or even permanently if their new lives don't work out as hoped. But political exile is completely different – not positive, overwhelmingly negative. Emotions are not balanced, they are simply torn asunder. In a revealing comment on Thabo Mbeki – in 1962 pitched into exile in London against his will but on his father's instructions so that he could be groomed as a future ANC leader – a friend described that Mbeki's exiled comrades had a 'sense of exile, of being in constant pain … exile became an internal condition that shaped and affected the way they saw things.'‡

For Ad and Wal their new freedom from surveillance and restriction was hardly compensation, for they had got used to coping at home – it was part of their lives, they had learnt to handle the stress. Instead – their children and their close relationship apart – they had lost everything that really mattered to them. But they refused to pine after their old life, their comrades or their parents. Instead they chose to cope by closing down their emotions and the pulls of home, simply getting on with their new existence. Outwardly at least, they seemed cheerful compared with other exiles with whom they mixed and who were often depressed.

But, where Wal was able to bury himself in work and return home at night to be with her and with his children, Ad was stuck in the house – very different indeed from the role in Pretoria to which she had become accustomed and in which she was so proficient. Within a couple of years she had to be hospitalised with severe meningitis, looking ghostly white as she was carried by stretcher into an ambulance. She had been prescribed

‡ Mark Gevisser, *A Legacy of Liberation* (New York: Palgrave Macmillan, 2009), p. 107.

Valium tablets back home during John Harris's trial and was now prescribed more Valium than she would have liked – mild anti-depressants they may have been, but she worried that they still created their own dependency. Nevertheless, she told herself, she was fortunate in comparison with other exiles. Exile may have been more benign – or Ad and Wal may simply have been more resolute in keeping with their values and disciplined upbringing – but it certainly took its toll.

As it did on their friends, for example the family of Donald Woods and his activist wife Wendy. Late in 1977, they and their five young children were suddenly uprooted from their large family home in the Eastern Cape, for a dramatic escape from their beloved South Africa into exile in London.

His transformation from respected, conventionally anti-apartheid editor of the *Daily Dispatch* into 'subversive' friend of black consciousness leader Steve Biko turned the family's life upside down. Security police wired each light fitting of the Woods' house with surveillance microphones and recorded all telephone calls. Twice they fired bullets into the house, one landing right next to a bedroom entrance when Donald was out of town.

Steve Biko was then brutally murdered by the security police while Woods, who had exposed the murder, was banned. Their five-year-old daughter Mary received a T-shirt through the post, packaged as a present but which the security police had laced with acid powder, burning her face and arms. Now there was no alternative but painful exile.‡

As Jane, the eldest of the children, recalled:

> We arrived in London on 6 January 1978 with one suitcase and £150, five days before my fifteenth birthday, which passed without cards or gifts. Understandably my parents were busy with things like finding somewhere to live and buying us clothes, but it made me even more miserable and homesick.
>
> On our way to London from the airport I was somewhat surprised to notice rows of very shoddy homes. Oh shame, I thought, the housing situation here is not much better than our townships back home. It was later explained to me that these were called allotments, places purely for British people to grow vegetables and plants.
>
> Two weeks later my father gave me an *A–Z* and a tube map and told me to go to the Alien Registration office in Lamb's Conduit Street urgently. 'What?' I wailed; the only venturing I had done on my own up to then had been to the 'bioscope' [Afrikaans for cinema] and down the local beach in sleepy East London. My apprehension it turns out was justified, 'Why has it taken you three weeks to register?' barked the intimidating official as I tried not to cry.

‡ Donald Woods, *Asking for Trouble* (London: Victor Gollancz, 1980), and Richard Attenborough's acclaimed film, *Cry Freedom* (1987), a dramatisation of the story.

Our exile was compounded by the fact that we were not just adapting to life abroad. Being from a small provincial town, we were adapting to life in a big city as well. We were also without the domestic help we were used to and laughed at ourselves as we sat in a rented flat not much bigger than the pool room in our former home and made weekly trips to the grotty Laundromat at the end of our road.

Not long after I had settled in school, a friend asked for someone to cover her after-school job for a few days, babysitting three children until their mother returned from work. I jumped at the chance to earn extra money and turned up to find an extremely wealthy Nigerian family living in a huge house with a pool and quite naughty children. As I tidied, cleaned and picked up after them, I giggled to myself, wishing Evelyn, our African nanny back home, could see me now.

On my first day at my new school, mid-week, mid-term, I was greeted with 'nobody told me I was getting a new girl' from the stern, somewhat unwelcoming teacher. I attempted to settle in, swapping Afrikaans, netball and 'takkies' for French, lacrosse and 'plimsolls'. Girls asked me 'When did I get back?' which puzzled me until I realised I was being lumped in with girls who had lived in South Africa for a few years because of their fathers' job. They hadn't met a white African before. 'It's hardly the same,' I wanted to shout.

Adelaide Tambo, wife of ANC Leader Oliver Tambo and the mother figure of the exiled community, welcomed my parents quite literally with open arms. I recall her giving my mother a huge bear hug on their first meeting. Her children spoke with the plummy English tones we'd heard in films, in sharp contrast to our thick Eastern Cape accents. The exile community were close and my parents found it a great support, because it was very difficult coping.

It was hardest for my mother though. Having survived the escape and the extremely stressful period prior to it, she found herself dealing with five children and no money, while my father dealt with the press and the publishers of his book on Steve Biko.[‡] She was an extremely stoic person, however, and slowly built up a life for all of us. The long periods of absence from my father, who was trying to earn some money for the family by doing lecture tours in America and also in tireless anti-apartheid campaigning both internationally and across Britain, proved difficult, however.

We also mixed socially with draft dodgers, those in self-imposed exile who objected politically to the apartheid government's call-up to national service. They seemed to find it especially tough and were constantly homesick. Very few stayed on in the UK permanently.

‡ Donald Woods, *Biko* (London: Paddington Press, 1978).

All five of us kids survived and adapted to life in London, but it wasn't easy. On the plus side, after years of threats and attacks, both verbal and physical in South Africa, it was a strange and liberating feeling to walk around anonymously in the big vibrant city. I also discovered with glee that, unlike home, teachers were not allowed to administer corporal punishment, so no more canes, whips and 'hold out your hand Miss Woods' anymore. That's something I definitely didn't miss.

Her brother Duncan added:

We didn't have our own house and we had left our home. I am still impressed that my parents got us all through all this. They had no money, no jobs and no possessions. They were winging it, and as difficult as it was, they made it work.

My brother Gavin and I arrived mid-term at a boarding prep school. There was no space in any of the dormitories so we slept in the infirmary. For the first few nights, we got into one single bed and cried ourselves to sleep. We missed our parents and felt very alone.

Living in exile is profoundly discombobulating. You miss your country of birth and are constantly aware that you are a guest and not a native of your host country. I have always failed Lord Tebbit's 'cricket test' and at the same time felt a loyalty to a country that

> has welcomed me and allowed me to thrive. I have never forgotten the extraordinary hospitality that we were shown when we arrived in the UK. People that we had never met offered up their houses to us. I have also never forgotten that this country granted us political asylum.

Three years after the family arrived in Britain, Wendy Woods told her husband's old paper, the *Daily Dispatch*: 'I've met lots of exiles who feel they're living in two places at once and can't live properly here.'

Ad and Wal were shattered when tragedy struck the family of their close friends Ruth Hayman – John Harris's lawyer – and her husband Merv Lazar, who had similarly been forced into exile in Britain. In a shockingly salutary indictment of the psychological pressures South African exiles were going through, their son Alan, the same age as Peter, abruptly committed suicide a year after moving to London, also in 1966. An extremely bright school student and a very talented young cricketer, nobody who knew him could find an explanation except that he hated his new (private) school ('It smells of cabbage,' he complained) despite it having been recommended by his favourite teacher in Johannesburg. Alan's suicide was a dreadful, albeit delayed, reaction to the family turmoil created by his parents' involvement in the struggle and their enforced departure from their homeland. (Several years later Ad and Wal were also left devastated by another suicide in exile, this time their close friend Ansie Preller, by then living in America.)

Ruth Carneson, teenage daughter of ANC and South African Communist Party activists Fred and Sarah, also found exile harsh. She was admitted to hospital in London in 1967 after taking an overdose and slashing her wrists. The following year, Ruth began running away from home and then hospital where a psychiatrist was disbelieving about what had happened to her family in South Africa. Her dad was in prison 6,000 miles away, her mother in a constant state of shock, desperately trying to cope with her daughter's predicament, the dislocation of exile and a job that left the family very short of money. Ruth later told her sister Lynn: 'When I came to England I had a total identity crisis. I lost all sense of self. There was no reference point. I was unfamiliar with the British social rules, I was still only fourteen … There was nothing familiar to measure myself against. There was a great big void of nothing that I could relate to. I felt nothing. It was much worse than being depressed: I couldn't see a way out. All I wanted to do was to die.'[‡]

Another prominent white ANC and communist activist, Hilda Bernstein, escaped with her husband Rusty, a defendant in the Rivonia Trial. But she 'felt

---

‡ Lynn Carneson, *Red in the Rainbow* (Cape Town: Zebra Press, 2010), pp. 196, 203–4.

deeply depressed after coming to London', her children 'uprooted and disturbed', and later wrote:

> There was a considerable group of political exiles from South Africa living in London, and while our children began putting down their roots and gradually adjusting – with some difficulties – to their entirely different and physically restricted environment, we formed a rather incestuous entity, with our political and social life focused on the fact of our exile. I am not sure now whether I am British or South African. I feel that I belong to both – yet to neither. Travelling in the past I had a sense of a loss of identity, not sure of who I was, in what I believed – what I would call 'exile politics'.[‡]

Hilda also wrote a mammoth survey of different experiences which revealed 'the pain, the loneliness and alienation of a life of exile'. Children 'often express deep anger and resentment towards their activist parents, while at the same time revealing their love and admiration for them'. Tellingly, she added:

> Many political activists, dispersed across continents, were to suffer an even sharper sense of loss. In South Africa they had enjoyed a status, a purpose, and a

‡ Hilda Bernstein, *The World that was Ours* (London: Persephone, 2004), pp. 383–4.

> strongly-knit comradeship, bound together by mutual danger that demanded mutual trust. In exile they often found themselves parted not only from their families, but also from their comrades ... The bonds that had held them together had been essential for their survival. In exile the purpose that had fired their lives was fractured. They ceased to belong to the coherent community they left behind, and could not find – or did not wish to seek – a way to belong to the new world in which they found themselves.[‡]

She found that, at its most extreme, alcoholism, breakdown and mental collapse were all products of the trauma and disorientation of exile. The exiled South African writer and poet Breyten Breytenbach tried to explain: 'You are engaged with an elsewhere that cannot be reached. Isn't that the defining characteristic of an exile?' The exiled Palestinian professor Edward Said grappled with the torn complexities: 'Most people are principally aware of one culture, one setting, one home; exiles are aware of at least two, and this plurality of vision gives rise to an awareness of simultaneous dimensions, an awareness that – to borrow a phrase from music – is contrapuntal. For an exile, habits of life, expression or activity in the new environment inevitably occur against the memory of these things in another environment.

‡ Hilda Bernstein, *The Rift: the Exile Experience of South Africans* (London: Jonathan Cape, 1994).

Thus both the new and the old environments are vivid, occurring together contrapuntally.'‡

Ad and Wal's family tried their best to settle down quickly into their new life, albeit missing friends and the sunny, outdoor existence, feeling rather subdued amid the indifferent and mostly grey London weather.

But there were things to do for the boys at least. That summer of 1966 Peter and Tom went to see the visiting West Indies cricket team play England in three test matches. Lord's, the venerable home of English cricket, and the Oval, were stadia of awe they had only ever read about. Ad also drove them up for a day to Nottingham's Trent Bridge ground, where they watched English batsmen like Colin Cowdrey and Tom Graveney, figures of distant wonderment back in South Africa. But they were all especially excited by West Indies legends like Gary Sobers, Wes Hall and Lance Gibbs – seeing them in the flesh was a tonic because Ad and Wal had always supported them back in South Africa. Black cricketers playing as well as, and usually better than, whites proved what they had always believed when combating prejudice at home.

Then for Ad and Wal there was the extraordinary – and uplifting – sight of Basil D'Oliveira, a Coloured cricketer

‡ Edward W. Said, *Reflections on Exile: And Other Literary and Cultural Essays* (London: Granta, 2001).

who was selected that year as an English test player, having been barred from playing for his own South Africa because he wasn't white. They clapped joyously as D'Oliveira scored freely and took wickets, establishing himself as a key member of the England side.

Ad, Wal and their boys were also able to go to Wembley with bargain World Cup football tickets purchased back in Pretoria for overseas visitors, and Peter was lucky enough to win a ticket in the draw for the final between Germany and England, cheering on his new country to an exciting and historic victory, and coming home flushed with excitement to tell them all about it.

They found it a revelation to view leading politicians being questioned on television, and top quality current affairs investigative programmes like *World in Action* and *Panorama* – a stark contrast to the state-controlled propaganda of South African radio and its deference to the select group of favoured white apartheid politicians allowed on it. Ad and Wal also enjoyed the luxury of reading the liberal *Guardian* and *Observer* – such a contrast to most of the newspapers back home.

But all these happy benefits were clouded by looming problems as Ad and Wal tried to cope with the 'sex, drugs, rock and roll' culture of London in the late 1960s, so at odds with their free-spirited but traditional, rather puritanical upbringing. If the way they treated their children had not been an issue in Pretoria with its traditional family mores, it certainly was in swinging London. Where Tom, Jo-anne and Sally had thought they had the best parents in the world back in South Africa, now they found them at times insensitive and uncomprehending of London teenage adolescence. The three still loved their mom and dad but also felt increasingly alienated and rebellious: over boys in the case of the girls, over experimenting with cannabis in Tom's case – the latter a total anathema to Wal especially.

At the same time Ad and Wal constantly worried that they had made a mistake about Tom's schooling at Emanuel and Ad often gave him hugs when he came home upset. She was distressed, feeling that she had let him down. But it wasn't as if they neglected any of their children. On the contrary, they were as attentive and supportive as any parents could have been while trying to cope with adjusting to exile and a more permissive lifestyle.

Tom got caught up in the bohemian youth culture of the late 1960s, and later explained how he felt:

> Mom and Dad were such terrific parents in South Africa. If I had misbehaved they would always explain why it was wrong and why I shouldn't do that again. For instance I still have a shocking memory of the day I was playing with matches in the bush around the spot at our home in the Willows where we used to burn rubbish. Suddenly, before I knew it, a fire started and just seemed to race away in the wind

through the bone-dry bush around our house. I was aged eleven and it was terrifying. There seemed nothing we could do to stop the fire burning down our thatched *rondavels*. The flames were raging towards the house, really high, until dozens of black farm workers appeared from somewhere and managed to beat the fire out.

Mom and Dad could have beaten me to a pulp. They were obviously very angry with me. But instead they told me firmly never to do anything stupid and dangerous like that again. So I remember being full of respect. They were also such fun. We had a great time as kids. When I look back at what they were going through with all the intimidation and attacks from the Special Branch and other apartheid forces, I am amazed at how they somehow managed to shield me from it. But they did and I never really felt worried or frightened.

So I couldn't understand how they seemed to change completely when we got to Britain. I found our move really upsetting and adjusting to school and life in Britain really, really difficult. I had to change schools because I was unhappy at the first school we went to, Emanuel, a sort of would-be upper-class school which was the pits. At my new school Wandsworth I did better and was the star actor in *The Ragged Trousered Philanthropists*, a socialist play. It was great having Mom and Dad coming to see me perform.

But otherwise I didn't seem to get any recognition

from them. Everything I did was wrong. In retrospect I suppose I was behaving as an awkward adolescent made worse by having left South Africa. They wouldn't let me do anything – go to a film with my mates, or things like that. It was just 'NO', and never an explanation like always used to be the case at home in South Africa. I started to think, sod it, I will do what I want to do anyway. I wasn't doing well at my school studies and in the end left home and ran away, hitching down to South Dorset where we had spent summer holidays at a friend's house in Burton Bradstock, by the sea. All I wanted was for them to understand me and to respect me like they always used to.

Dad was at work during the day and would come home to give me a telling off. Mom was having to cope with all of us. And she was having a tough time. I remember Peter gathering Jo-anne, Sally and I together and explaining that Mom was really stressed and we should all try to be more supportive.

In the years that followed I went my own way, dropping out I suppose, not following a conventional career path Mom and Dad wanted. I don't think they ever listened to me, what I had to say, what my views were on life. Sad really because I loved them at the time and I still do. I know they have always loved me in their own way even if they couldn't always show it during those early days in London.

The three younger children found adjusting to their new life in England much more difficult than Peter did. That, Ad and Wal later freely admitted, perplexed them. They had been more worried about Peter than their other children, because he had been more exposed and was at a critical moment in the final years of his high school career. In retrospect, as they would later readily and self-critically volunteer, they should have been more focused on the younger ones, because Peter was soon to find his niche in all-absorbing political campaigning. And in a way they were to rediscover their own thwarted anti-apartheid activism through him. But they never really came to terms with what they saw as the self-indulgent, materialistic, amoral culture of the late 1960s. They were certainly not prudish or intolerant, more contemptuous and bemused by those caught up in this permissiveness – and worried about its impact on their own children, now teenagers.

Jo-anne, then aged eleven, remembered being 'very excited' about coming to England:

> Despite leaving everything we knew behind, I had only positive feelings about it. I thought England was a land of freedom and equality, where they made films and pop stars – important to me, because I wanted to be an actress or singer.
>
> In London, I went to a local primary school for a term. When they heard I was from South Africa, the children asked why I wasn't black and wearing

a grass skirt and did I used to live in a mud hut with a grass roof? They found my accent fascinating and kept asking me to repeat words. We all spoke English, but the culture was so different it was like another language. Then a teacher who'd been to South Africa decided to test my Afrikaans, our second language. 'What's "Horlinks"?' he said. It sounded like a bedtime drink to me. When I didn't know, he ridiculed me. 'Keep left!' he sneered, having pronounced the Afrikaans so badly that I didn't recognise it.

At Mayfield, the 2,000-strong, all-girls comprehensive school I went to, there were girls from all strata of society. Back in South Africa it was easy: you were either white or you weren't. Here there were lots of black girls, but it wasn't about colour, something much more complicated, maybe class. I couldn't get my head round it and never knew where I belonged.

Inside I always felt different and because as a family we never talked about any of these negative feelings, I just tucked them away and soldiered on. I tended to bounce from one situation to another. Never sure of myself or where I fitted in, I'd attach myself to people or situations, instead of ploughing my own path. I often felt depressed that there was something wrong with me and worried that I would eventually become one of the one in four – the number that succumbed to mental illness.

> It wasn't until I was aged forty-four that I embarked on a counselling course which involved two years of personal therapy. Revisiting my past and experiencing my true feelings was painful and frightening, but I began to understand better why I am myself.
>
> I am very proud of my Mom and Dad. To have the strength and bravery to fight for what you believe and to make such a big difference is fantastic. They lost everything – both sets of parents, brothers, sisters, nieces, nephews, comrades in the struggle, and a way of life that could never be replicated in the country to which they had to flee. Often I looked at my parents and wondered how they'd borne it.
>
> They instilled in me my love of humanity and a belief that change is always possible. They helped me to become the caring, compassionate person I'm proud to be. But I will always carry a great loss inside. Looking at it and understanding it doesn't make it go away.

Aged nine years at the time of the move, Sally had similar mixed feelings.

> Sad as I was to leave my country I believed that coming to London would be our saviour, because life had become pretty scary. I believed that once we got here everything would be wonderful and that we would all live happily ever after. But arriving at Southampton

> docks was a bit of a shock. I can still remember the greyness of everything which continued throughout the drive into Putney.
>
> In South Africa often it was us four kids with Mom and Dad against the world. But in London we were just individuals who happened to be part of the same family: adults and children struggling in their own way to survive, fit in and find their place. It was just so different and I suppose a huge anti-climax and disappointment.

One media commentator in 1972 referred to the 'tight little Hain clan in Putney', but four decades later Sally observed:

> If I had to sum it up in a few words, exile left us rootless. I don't blame anyone for this – except the leaders of apartheid. And, through everything, we stuck together – the four of us joined later by our children and grandchildren, with Mom and Dad always at the very centre of their ever-extending and loving family.

Many people looked up to Ad and Wal for their courageous anti-apartheid record, their dedicated, principled lifestyle and attitudes. Peter's contemporaries, for example, at least twenty-five years younger than Ad and Wal, would often remark at how easy they were to get on with, ruefully comparing them with their own staid parents. Their generosity and neighbourliness was renowned among friends – no kindness, large or small, seemed too much for them.

In the 1980s and 1990s Wal organised a cricket team in Putney made up of his workmates and friends of his children. He would gladly be led astray when malt whisky was on offer and his *pièce de résistance* was donning a kilt and sporran to celebrate Burns Night, or to first-foot after New Year, in honour of his Scottish parentage. For her part Ad was always at the centre of community activity – campaigning on local issues and later involved in her grandchildren's nearby primary school. They both engaged busily in local politics, first with the Liberals, later with Labour, leafleting and helping at jumble sales. Both were active in the Putney branch of the United Nations Association. As their years in exile continued, they were also increasingly at the fulcrum of their burgeoning family in Britain: grandchildren and great-grandchildren idolised them, periodically enthralled by stories from a strange world far away, of outwitting the Special Branch, of prisons, bannings and struggle.

However, at least in early exile, relations with some of their relatives remained awkward. Wal's brother Tom and wife Marie – she still ran a Pretoria travel agency – called by the family home in Putney, with a bottle of brandy which they shared with Wal. But the convivial occasion soon deteriorated when Tom made clear he thought the South African authorities were correct to have treated Ad and Wal the way they had. Wal, normally meticulously polite, but with inner steel when provoked, calmly took the glass of brandy from his brother's hand, put the stopper in the bottle, and handed it back over. 'Get into my car, you are going back to your hotel right now,' he instructed. They left immediately as Wal drove them into central London never exchanging a word.

❦

Ad and Wal joined the local Liberals in Putney and the Anti-Apartheid Movement (AAM) almost immediately on arriving in Britain. The AAM had been formed in 1959, in response to a call from then ANC president Albert Luthuli for an international boycott movement, which later gathered momentum after the 1960 massacre at Sharpeville. Among its prominent members were other exiles including old friends, but it took a while before Ad and Wal were thrust into hyper-activism again.

Although they had never exhorted their offspring to follow them into political work, they were pleased when, about a year after arriving and aged seventeen, Peter expressed an interest in joining the AAM, going to meetings with them.

They were also supportive when he was going on eighteen and at school in his final year doing A levels, Peter gradually became more politically involved, following current debates, avidly discussing topical issues like the Vietnam War with Wal, who was hostile to American intervention. But both Ad and Wal were concerned when Peter and Tom decided to go on the big anti-Vietnam War demonstration in Grosvenor Square in October 1968. The media were predicting violent clashes between police and protesters determined to storm the US embassy. It was one thing for them to have taken risks under apartheid, another for their young sons to get innocently caught up in conflict in Britain. At the same time they were rather proud. The centre of London was eerily boarded up as the marchers set off from Victoria Embankment up to Mayfair. Watching on television, Ad and Wal saw pictures of repeated confrontations between demonstrators and police – some on horseback.

Then Peter came home looking for Tom, thinking he must have got home first and aghast to find he hadn't. They had got separated in all the melee and violence in Grosvenor Square despite having been on the periphery of the trouble. Ad was frantic with worry. She didn't know what to do. There had been lots of arrests but there was nobody they could check with.

But what seemed like hours later Tom suddenly turned up, chanting, 'Ho, Ho, Ho Chi Minh! Hey, hey, LBJ [US President Lyndon Baines Johnson]! How many kids have you killed today?' Cheerfully brandishing a red banner given to him by a Marxist group, Tom was still exhilarated by the experience. For years afterwards he used the banner as a bedspread.

Meanwhile, Peter had decided he wanted to join the Young Liberals, having read in his dad's *Guardian* of their vibrant, irreverent activities and ideas. Ad and Wal were once more encouraging, and helped him when he was involved in setting up a 'Medical Aid for Southern Africa' appeal in 1968 to assist the ANC and other liberation movements. Many people sympathetic to, or actually involved in, anti-apartheid movements would not associate themselves with guerrilla activity, but would back medical aid. With Ad's help, he typed up and printed on a second-hand Gestetner duplicating machine (similar to her old one in Pretoria) copies of a pamphlet supporting the medical aid appeal. Wal did the artwork for the cover, including the white and black clasped hands emblem of the South African Liberal Party.

However, that was to prove only an appetiser. Within a year the Hain family once again found itself at the eye of a storm – this time in their adoptive country.

Ad and Wal had been pleased, though also apprehensive, as Peter started to get caught up in the radical politics of Britain's late 1960s. The Young Liberal activism quickly took over his life and he seemed to be out a lot at evening meetings and especially weekends. They fretted about his coming A level exams. 'Your exams must come first. They are a ticket to a university degree and then a decent job,' Wal repeatedly told Peter, explaining his firm view that without such a platform to build a life, it would be very difficult to be politically active. But it was very apparent that their son was enthralled by an exciting ferment of the era's new and left-wing ideas shaped by passionate debate in teach-ins, conferences, demonstrations and sit-ins. And he was inspired to adapt tactics of non-violent direct action – such as student sit-ins like that at Hornsey College of Art in 1968, worker occupations, and squats in empty houses – to confront sports apartheid. It was not enough simply to bear witness, their son explained: protest needed to be militant to be effective.[‡]

The spur to his militancy was anger – very much shared by Ad and Wal – at the way the English cricket authorities brazenly announced in January 1969 that they would proceed with the scheduled 1970 cricket tour to Britain by a white South African team. Incredibly, this announcement was just four months after universal outrage at the apartheid government's cancellation of the planned tour by England to South Africa because the English team included Basil D'Oliveira.

Peter was the first to advocate direct action against white South African touring teams: physically disrupting the matches in a manner which could not be ignored by the sports elites, who had been impervious to moral

‡ For the background see Peter Hain, *Outside In* (London: Biteback, 2012).

appeals and symbolic protests previously organised by the AAM.

He discovered that a private tour by an all-white South African club side sponsored by a wealthy businessman, Wilf Isaacs, was due in July and August 1969, and organised the first ever direct action against cricket anywhere, by leading a group of Young Liberals onto the pitch at a game in Basildon, Essex, having borrowed Ad and Wal's car to drive there; in his absence they worried both about him and their family car, a Volkswagen Beetle, on the back seat of which their four (now teenage) children would often be squeezed. Once more borrowing their car, he did the same at a Davis Cup tennis match in Bristol between South Africa and Britain, Ad watching live coverage on television, both thrilled and apprehensive to see her oldest boy sitting down on the court. Later she was worried when Peter, permitted to make one phone call, said he was speaking from Redlands police station where he had been detained (only to be released without charge and given a ticking off).

A few weeks later the Wilf Isaacs team played in Roehampton, near the Hain family home, and Ad drove her children to the cricket ground. Tom, Jo-anne, Sally and Peter ran onto the pitch to stop the match and were photographed by the media. Ad and Wal were simultaneously elated but also anxious that their children might get into trouble. Yet, what could they say? They had taken much bigger risks themselves back in Pretoria.

Because sport was being targeted by such direct action, the protests were highly newsworthy, encouraging other anti-apartheid activists to adopt similar protests. With what began as a small group Peter decided to launch the Stop the Seventy Tour Committee (STST) at a press conference in September 1969. Aged nineteen – and little more than three years into the family's exile – he was pressed by South African Non-Racial Olympic Committee exiles, Dennis Brutus and Chris de Broglio, into a leadership role. Ad and Wal, enthusiastic albeit as bemused as he was by his sudden elevation, found him leading the new campaign to stop the 1970 cricket tour. However, its immediate target was the Springbok rugby tour due to arrive in under two months.[‡]

The night before the Springboks arrived at London's Heathrow airport in October 1969, Peter and Tom again borrowed the family car and – their parents approvingly but fretfully aware of what they were doing – slipped out to paint a large 'No to Boks' sign prominently on a wall adjoining the carriageway the team bus would travel along in from the airport; it remained there for years. A day later, with Peter stuck at his university lectures, Ad took Tom, Jo-anne and Sally to try and disrupt the Springboks training session at Richmond in south-west London.

'We are South Africans and we'd like to come in

‡ For an account of the campaign see Peter Hain, *Don't Play with Apartheid* (London: Allen & Unwin, 1971).

and see the players,' Ad told officials, who were pleased to welcome a young South African mother and her children. Then she spotted an opportunity and they all scampered on. There were photographs and television shots of her running with other protestors amid the players, her skirt lifting above her knee. Amid the frenzy she spotted a bunch of astonished officials heading determinedly towards them and shouted to her children: 'Run!' She didn't want them grabbed, and turned herself towards the officials. As she did so she was struck on her temple with an umbrella by the irate official who had let them in; stunned, she put her hand up to feel the spot, now starting to ache, as they were all hustled away.

On the back of growing excitement and publicity, the campaign simply took off, but without any administrative infrastructure – except for Ad and Wal's modest first-floor family flat in Gwendolen Avenue, Putney, which became the headquarters address and 'office'. Volunteers turned up to help and Ad – well versed from her Pretoria days in running an organisation – found herself willingly performing the crucial role of unofficial campaign secretary, fielding phone calls, keeping in touch with local branches, coordinating information and helping with correspondence and posting batches of leaflets.

The whole family was involved, directly or indirectly. On her way to and from school Sally would telephone South Africa House and deliberately leave the phone off the hook, jamming one of their lines as the technology of the time permitted. When Tom got home from school he would take piles of mail and packages down to the Putney post office in Ad's shopping trolley.

Ad also got used to encountering hostility: for example, when she tried to pay in cheques carrying donations, a local bank official initially refused to accept them out of antagonism to the campaign, which had aroused fierce opposition. However, she would not be deflected from what had become virtually a fulltime, albeit unpaid, job. A member of the Young Communists volunteered to put the card index of over a thousand contacts into regional geographical order as Ad had little idea of where the towns and cities were.

Wal came home from work to write leaflets and background briefs – experienced at writing from his days penning articles in South African newspapers. He would also stand in the bedroom doorway next to the phone as Peter was quizzed by the media, prompting and guiding Peter to give suitable answers. 'It was uncanny how the two of them worked this together without the journalist on the other end of the phone ever being aware,' Ad recalled.

In a reversal of roles from their life in South Africa, Peter had now become the front person in what was to prove perhaps the biggest and ultimately most successful single anti-apartheid campaign in Britain; but he could not have accomplished it without their constant support in the background.

All this activity and energy coincided with the start

of Peter's mechanical engineering course at Imperial College, University of London, to which he cycled daily. Decades before the era of mobile phones, he used to spend lunch breaks with his mother's homemade sandwiches in a phone box talking to journalists and local organisers through messages relayed from Ad at home where the phone rang incessantly. As she kept Peter in touch, journalists used to call one of two telephone box numbers where Peter was ensconced for an hour or so each day. Often she had to reassure them that he was there when the line was busy with other callers she had referred. So constant was the stream of incoming calls at home that at times she could not even find a moment to go to the toilet. The campaign had taken over Ad's life and – with Wal supportive in the background – their family was back at the centre of the struggle in a way they never for a moment envisaged when they left their homeland.

Wal was initially troubled at the element of law-breaking involved in Peter's direct action disruptions of the rugby matches, and challenged his son closely about it. The direct action he had backed was in South Africa's undemocratic society; whereas Britain's was democratic, he argued. However, he was persuaded that the strategy was necessary and that over the generations non-violent direct action had been a catalyst for change and probably always would have a role to play. Ad felt differently: she automatically supported the militancy, seeing it in the tradition of Gandhi and Martin Luther King.

They were both thrilled as each one of the twenty-five matches in the Springbok tour saw protests, some heavily disruptive. Ad liaised with her sister Jo, also living in London, and a family friend, Phoebe Brown, wife of Peter, the banned former chairman of the South African Liberals, to acquire tickets for the games at Twickenham. On one occasion, their thick South African accents and respectable middle class appearances acting as perfect foils, they were able to purchase over 100 tickets on the pretext of needing them for a South African schools visit; by then, well into the tour, tickets were very difficult for the protest organisers to obtain.

Their son Peter's sudden elevation to notoriety attracted some of the intimidation and pressure which they thought had been left behind in their homeland. The family telephone was tapped – this time by the *British* Special Branch, disconcerting because they had always looked up to Britain and always considered it a model democracy to which South Africa should aspire. The British Security Service, MI5, opened a file on Peter. Ad was highly suspicious that at least one of the volunteers who helped out at their home was an informer. (Four decades later Special Branch documents in official archives confirmed that was indeed the case.) Threatening, anonymous letters poured in – some of the crazed 'green ink' genre, some viciously racist and some asserting that Peter was her child by a black father. Others contained ugly, perverted themes of sexual fantasy and racism.

Ad and Wal worried that all these threats meant Peter might be physically endangered, especially since he was often travelling the country on his own or returning from meetings at night. In fact, although he was frequently targeted, they were relieved that he managed to remain unscathed. Meanwhile, Tom, Jo-anne and Sally remained supportively in the background, showing no resentment at the manner in which their lives had once more been overtaken by anti-apartheid activism, even enjoying the excitement and helping out whenever they were asked – which was often; Sally also accompanied Peter to most of the Twickenham demonstrations.

Having initially felt they didn't really belong in Britain, their all-absorbing involvement in the campaign gave them again an invigorating sense of purpose and even a recognised new role in their adoptive society.

Eventually, after the Springbok rugby team, battered by demonstrations, had limped home, the focus turned to the original remit of the campaign – to stop the cricket tour that summer of 1970.

Ad was also covertly involved in supporting the work of an 'inner group' of some of Peter's most trusted and experienced activists – several years older than him, like Mike Craft, Ernest Rodker and Jonathan Rosenhead, who had years before participated in nuclear disarmament direct action demonstrations. Called the Special Action Group, it was established to work on undercover projects, its existence known only to a very trusted few.

Both Ad and Wal were confidentially forewarned about one such project. Late in the night on 19 January 1970, anti-apartheid activists simultaneously raided fourteen of the seventeen county cricket club grounds. All were daubed with paint slogans. In addition a small patch in the outfield of Glamorgan's Cardiff ground was dug up and weed killer was sprayed on Warwickshire's Birmingham ground. Pre-planned reports from each small, tight group were telephoned in throughout the night both to the Press Association news agency and to Ad and Wal's home; sometimes they answered and took down details, sometimes Peter did. In the morning the coordinated protest dominated the radio bulletins and there were screaming headlines with pictures in the evening papers, television programmes and the following day's national newspapers.

The protest was a devastating shock to the cricket authorities because the widespread strength of the STST campaign had been starkly revealed in an operation seemingly carried out with almost military precision. More than this, the fear at the back of the cricket authorities' minds had suddenly crystallised: if protesters could daub paint slogans seemingly as easily as they had, it raised the spectre of the tour collapsing amid damaged pitches and weed killer.

Even by the standards of the previous few months, media telephone calls answered by Ad were relentless. Journalists were desperate to find out who was responsible, the impact heightened because that was not clear. The STST national committee had not authorised or approved the action, thereby distancing Peter and the campaign from it. But in truth it was indeed a covert operation by key STST activists executed from the centre with deadly efficiency and effect. Within weeks, 300 reels of barbed wire arrived at Lord's and most county grounds introduced guard dogs and security. The pressure on the cricket authorities was mounting relentlessly.

They responded by cutting the number of matches in order to defend the grounds more effectively. Then the pressure increased weekly in the build-up to the first match due on 6 June 1970 – dubbed 'D Day' or demo day. African, Asian and Caribbean countries threatened withdrawal from the planned Commonwealth Games due in Edinburgh, also that summer, which would have left the event a sad rump with only white nations competing.

Plans for huge demonstrations and ingenious disruptions went ahead, as Ad and Wal found themselves at the eye of a national storm. She used to watch every television news bulletin to keep track of what was happening as the phone calls continued to pour in. Eventually, at the direct request of the Labour Home Secretary, James Callaghan, the tour was cancelled. 'Hain stopped play,' was the cricketing headline in a sympathetic feature in the *Guardian* newspaper, causing much celebratory mirth in their household.

Uncomfortably for Ad and Wal – who when in South Africa had always seen Britain's rule of law as a model for their aspirations – the right-wing press trumpeted darkly about 'anarchy', 'lawlessness' and the threat to England's 'green and pleasant' civilisation. But they were proud and elated that the campaign had grown from an original few to one with mass support. Furthermore, STST was one of the very few British protest groups to have completely achieved its objectives. For the first time in ten long bitter years since the Sharpeville massacre, black South Africans and whites involved in the resistance had something to cheer about.

Ad and Wal were especially moved to receive a telegram from the Cape Reserve in their home town of Pretoria. It contained a simple but moving message signed by their activist friends Poen Ah Dong, Alban Thumbran and Aubrey Apples, who had waved them goodbye in 1966: 'And so say all of us.' (To have said anything more explicit would have invited police attention.) Other messages of congratulation poured in to their family flat. In Britain there was ecstasy from disbelieving supporters absorbing the full extent of their momentous achievement.

On Robben Island, Nelson Mandela and his comrades heard from their apoplectic white prison warders – sports fanatics to a man – about the demonstrations and the stopping of the cricket tour. The warders vented their fury on the prisoners, blaming them for the mayhem and horror inflicted upon white sport, seemingly oblivious that they were communicating something very precious through the news blackout then in force on the island and to political prisoners elsewhere. Serving his sentence in Pretoria Local Prison, Hugh Lewin also learnt from his furious warders of the demonstrators – *betogers* – and of 'bastard traitor' Peter Hain, whom he tried to equate with the quiet young teenager he had last seen six years previously.

Wal's brother Tom shared a negative attitude to his nephew Peter, for whom he had been a favourite uncle. Both the boys used to idolise Uncle Tom, an excellent craftsman who built a small steel racing car for them. They always jumped at the opportunity to spend time with him. But, when he and his wife Marie visited London, Uncle Tom refused to acknowledge Peter when the family went to see them at their hotel. He was also surprised and disapproving when the hotel concierge, recognising Peter from television, delightedly met and congratulated him and his family on the Stop the Tour success.

Peter was labelled 'Public Enemy Number One' in the South African media, vilified by whites for having 'betrayed' his people. As the victory they had helped secure gradually sank in, Ad and Wal permitted themselves a quiet celebration. How paradoxical that, in forcing them to leave the country, the apartheid state had unwittingly given birth to a Hain-led campaign which had just struck a decisive blow against white supremacy.

But retribution was swift. They were alarmed when Peter was almost immediately prosecuted for criminal conspiracy over the sports demonstrations. Two years later a tense four-week trial followed, at the end of which he narrowly escaped being convicted by successfully appealing to the jury that he was the victim of a political prosecution. Wal came when his work permitted, but Ad attended the court every day. Sitting outside in a corridor, she apprehensively waited to give evidence, wondering what was happening to her eldest son inside and chatting to his legal team, journalists and supporters.

Then the defence team decided both her evidence and that of others closely involved, far from supporting her son, might actually implicate him because the conspiracy charge was so enveloping it seemed that he was culpable for almost anything connected to the campaign. Huddled together with Peter and his solicitor, she learnt that they planned a surprise, abrupt closure of the defence case. The prosecutors, well aware of both her crucial involvement and that of others, were furious and frustrated.[‡] Ad was elated: it almost seemed like old times, outwitting the enemy.

Before that, at the end of the prosecution case, both Ad and Wal were (most unusually) invited to attend an important legal conference in the chambers of Peter's QC, Michael Sherrard. Although she had been practised in scurrying around Pretoria's courts, the cloistered old alleys and buildings of the Temple where the top legal firms were based seemed quaint, quintessentially English – and somewhat intimidating. With Peter they crowded into Sherrard's room with the full defence team. The occasion had the familiarity of a meeting rather than the normal august conference between client and QC. The problem, Sherrard explained, was the catch-all nature of conspiracy as a charge: if the judge asked his lawyers what his defence in law was, they would be forced to concede that Peter didn't actually have one. In which case the defence case would quickly collapse and the only role of his QC would be to make a plea in mitigation over the sentence.

The solution, they collectively decided in the cramped tense room, was for Peter to 'sack' his lawyers and appeal directly to the jury by conducting his own defence and thereby avoid giving evidence through which he would probably convict himself. It was a sombre conclusion

‡ Derek Humphry (ed.), *The Cricket Conspiracy* (London: National Council for Civil Liberties, 1973).

and, although fully persuaded, Ad and Wal were now extremely worried. Judge Bernard Gillis was noticeably hostile and they feared – as did his defence team – that their son would be imprisoned. They had come to Britain partly to avoid such a calamity for themselves, but now it was threatened for Peter.

After four weeks of legal proceedings, the jury was finally sent out to reach a verdict mid-morning. Ad had almost lived at the court the entire time, participating in regular decision-making meetings with Peter's solicitor, Larry Grant, who became a close friend, normal family life suspended. She was on tenterhooks as Peter was escorted away to a cell downstairs – previously he had been permitted to go home at the end of the day and join them all at lunchtimes. She stared at members of the jury as they filed out to decide her son's fate, wondering about their attitudes.

The seven and a half long hours dragged by for the jury's verdict, Wal joining her after work. What could be happening in the jury room, they wondered? Was it hopeful or fateful that they hadn't reached a quick decision? Waiting, they were desperately anxious. Then the tension was broken – but only temporarily. After six hours the jury, looking stressed and glum, were called in by the judge and asked to return to reach a majority verdict because it was evident that they could not agree unanimously. Ad and Wal's hopes and emotions rocked. Maybe Peter would be acquitted? But then maybe a majority verdict would make a conviction easier? They had no way of knowing how divided the jury was and which way the majority were leaning.

An hour and a half later the jury trooped back in, even more fraught – except, Ad noticed with her uncanny sixth sense for people, the one black juryman and the one Asian one seemingly almost serene. Her spirits rose but her stomach was tightly knotted. Wal stared fixedly ahead.

Finally – relief. The jury remained implacably divided on the three major, more serious and imprisonable charges. The judge – who they noticed could hardly contain his fury – directed that their son should be acquitted. The only charge on which a majority verdict could be reached was to convict for the minor offence of peacefully interrupting the Davis Cup tennis match by sitting down on the court. To Ad and Wal's inner elation all the prosecution had been able to secure – after weeks in the top criminal court in the land – was a £200 fine, money easily paid by the defence fund which supporters had set up on his behalf. As their son stepped down from the dock, a free man again, Ad rushed to hug him, Wal beaming.

By now they had been fortunate to move half a mile away in Putney to 90 Fawe Park Road, which was under compulsory purchase order for an urban motorway and was therefore at a lower price and with a 100 per cent

Greater London Council mortgage which they could afford; Putney prices were otherwise way above their means (though in fact the motorway was never built).

However, at their new family home they encountered a more horrifying attempt on their lives than had ever occurred in their Pretoria days. One Saturday in June 1972, a package addressed to Peter, postmarked from France, arrived in a large pile of post on the family's dining table. It was opened by their youngest daughter Sally, excitedly helped by John Harris's then eight-year-old son, David. Ad was upstairs working at the time and came downstairs to discover confusing consternation in the house. She froze in horror. There was a letter bomb sitting on the table.

But, mercifully, there was a technical fault in the bomb's trigger mechanism – otherwise their home and all the family would have been blown to smithereens, Scotland Yard's bomb squad ominously reported, having made the device safe and taken it away. The South African security services had specialised in sending letter bombs which assassinated anti-apartheid leaders across the world, from Paris to Maputo (where their friend from London anti-apartheid circles Ruth First was a victim).

The appalling threat was suddenly over just as quickly as it had happened, Ad and Wal simultaneously terrified and relieved. It took some time to sink in. But they were unsurprised that the British security services seemed to have little interest in following up the Hain letter bomb.

Insultingly, one of the bomb squad investigators even speculated to Ad that some Young Liberals opposed to Peter's leadership of the movement (he had been elected national chairman the year before) might have sent it – 'Don't be ridiculous,' Ad snapped back. At the time British officers worked closely with their intelligence counterparts in South Africa. It was the height of the Cold War, when white South Africa was seen as an anti-communist ally and the anti-apartheid resistance as an enemy.

That also helped explain another, even worse family trauma, when Peter was surreally arrested and charged in October 1975 with snatching £490 in five-pound notes from a Putney branch of Barclays Bank several hundred yards from their home. The theft was committed by someone looking rather like him and – despite the audaciously improbable and contradictory nature of the case against him – Peter only narrowly escaped conviction for something he knew nothing about.

Ad came home both astonished and shocked to discover from a neighbour that her son had been arrested when police had swarmed all over the flat a few doors away to which he had moved, having recently got married. Instantly recalling how she had helped arrestees back in Pretoria she immediately phoned Wal and also Larry Grant, Peter's solicitor in the conspiracy case three years earlier. She asked Larry to discover what was happening as she had no idea why he had been arrested. Nobody seemed to know what had happened. Whatever it was Ad was absolutely certain her son would not have committed a bank theft, because he had called by to see her when it had apparently happened. When he came home Wal went down to Wandsworth police station to try and find out what was going on, but to no avail. 'What's he done *now*?' Wal wondered to himself.

Although hours dragged by with still no news of Peter's detention, Ad and Wal just took it for granted he would be released. But then in the early hours of the following morning, their son finally returned escorted by his solicitor, John Dundon. They were flabbergasted that he had been charged with the theft. It was unbelievable. Next morning the news sank in, and soon the police leaked it to the media. They were horrified at the front-page headlines. It was so totally bizarre and yet it had happened.

Ad was furious, more than at any time since she had been in England – and also frustrated that she couldn't do anything about it. Wal was very upset too, unusually for him revealing his emotion in a television interview when his eyes moistened. Being framed was the norm in South Africa – but surely not Britain too?

During a two-week Old Bailey trial, Ad gave alibi evidence from the witness stand. But the aggressively hostile judge, Alan King-Hamilton (a member of the Marylebone Cricket Club for whom her son was a *bête noire* during the Stop the Tour campaign), implied she had been lying. Ad was infuriated, struggling to stay composed as she knew she must. The case against Peter was preposterous, how could this be happening? There was another gruelling wait, this time for six long, edgy hours, and another divided jury, until finally on a majority they returned a not guilty verdict. Ad felt she had aged during the whole saga but now there was joy as pandemonium broke out and the public gallery erupted with cheers and clapping. Bewildered court ushers rushed about shouting 'Order, order'. The floor of the court was alive as Ad and Wal were hugged by a smiling jumble of people, Wal struggling to curb his normally buried emotions.

The whole episode was an ordeal for Ad and Wal too as they worried about the consequences of this latest attack on their family and found themselves spending hours being visited by a series of questionable figures alleging Peter was a victim of a South African-inspired plot. It emerged long after Peter's eventual acquittal that the bank theft had indeed been committed by his 'double', a South African agent flown over and assisted by elements in British intelligence.‡

If Ad and Wal had envisaged a more normal life when they went into exile, it hardly materialised. And yet in

‡ See Peter Hain, 'Under Attack', in *Outside In*, and *A Putney Plot?* (Nottingham: Spokesman, 1987). Also Winter, *Inside BOSS*.

a curious way they thrived on it just as they had back in their beloved South Africa.

Wal was active in Architects against Apartheid, which pressed for South Africa's suspension from the Royal Institute of British Architects until apartheid was overthrown. In a double-page interview with *Building Design* on 19 January 1973, he argued: 'As I understand it the RIBA abhors racialism. All I want my Institute to do is practise what it preaches and to stand by that. I don't see this as a political issue at all. I see it as an issue of common humanity, nothing else. I hope that the RIBA will sever links with the Institute of South African Architects in the interest and cause of humanity and architecture.'

Meanwhile, Ad and Wal found themselves in a new and fulfilling phase of their lives. Tom was the first to bring them a grandchild, Lila, in 1973 – though he was then living in Scotland and they didn't get to see her until she was a few weeks old. But soon more grandchildren followed. When Tom's second child, Jethro, arrived he had begun squatting across the road from their house in a prefabricated home erected after bombing in the Second World War and now awaiting demolition for a new build. Ad was thrilled to be present at Jethro's birth. Then Jo-anne's first child, Hannah, was born in 1975, to be followed the next year by Sam, Peter's first. Within a few years they had six grandchildren, most living nearby, as they became the fulcrum of their extended family.

Over the years they were to spend a great deal of time

with their new grandchildren, but that joy had been tempered by the successive deaths of their own parents. The biggest bolt from the blue was the death of Ad's mother Edith in Port Alfred on 13 January 1970, aged seventy-seven. Perhaps because of the family's Christian Science convictions, nobody even told Ad that she had been ill. Her father Gerald died aged eighty-five on 30 November 1973 under anaesthetic while having a bladder operation in Pretoria after an intermittent illness – also tormenting because she felt so powerless, but at least it was not so shockingly sudden. Both their deaths left her with a numb emptiness. Wal bore the passing of his parents with his customary fortitude, mainly because his father Walter had long been ill with throat cancer and his mother Mary had first had a colostomy before her bowel cancer became fatal. Enforced exile had not only torn Ad and Wal away from their country but from their parents.

❧

When the change finally – miraculously – came, they witnessed it from London. On 2 February 1990, they gripped their chairs, disbelieving, at the live television broadcast of President F. W. de Klerk opening the first session of the new Parliament in Cape Town. De Klerk made good his promise of a 'new South Africa' and surprised everyone by boldly announcing the unbanning of the ANC and other outlawed organisations. He also gave notice of the impending release of Nelson

Mandela and hundreds of other political prisoners. And he declared his readiness to negotiate a new constitution in which everyone would enjoy equal rights.

Ad openly sobbed with joy, Wal's eyes welled up. Relatives, friends and colleagues phoned each other or chatted excitedly. They could hardly comprehend it. The new South Africa for which they had struggled now beckoned at last.

But that was only the first act. Nine days later on 11 February 1990, they were transfixed as the world's most famous political prisoner, kept out of sight for over a quarter of a century, walked to freedom through the gates in the fence around Victor Verster Prison in the magnificent winelands outside Cape Town. Viewing it from their Fawe Park Road home in Putney, Ad, Wal and their family hugged each other, tears flowing, just as millions of viewers across the world also wept openly.

They watched, as with his wife Winnie by his side, Nelson Mandela walked towards the massed ranks of TV cameras and spectators. Except for his obvious humility and humanity, he looked almost regal, a giant among his people. The government had carefully pre-released the first photograph of him for decades, meeting President de Klerk. It had revealed not the burly, big, bearded freedom fighter in the prime of his life whom Ad and Wal remembered and who for years had appeared the world over, but a slim, dignified old African statesman with a smile of destiny that hovered somewhere between the benign and the all-knowing. Mandela then climbed into a car in an ANC cavalcade for the 35-mile drive to Cape Town along a road lined with smiling, waving crowds of all races.

Later, on the balcony of the City Hall, with the eager upturned faces of the crowd filling the Grand Parade below, raising his fist in the ANC salute he cried out, '*Amandla! Amandla! Mayibuye iAfrica*!' ('Power! Power! Let Africa return'). With Cyril Ramaphosa, a leader of the 1980s internal resistance headed by the United Democratic Front (UDF) and Congress of Trade Unions (COSATU), holding the microphone he said: 'Friends, comrades and fellow South Africans, I greet you all in the name of peace, democracy and freedom for all. I stand here before you not as a prophet but as a humble servant of you, the people.'

Ad and Wal also watched as Mandela gave a commanding performance at a press conference the next day, staged before 200 of the world's media seated in the sun-drenched garden of the Archbishop of Cape Town, the irrepressible Desmond Tutu. Mandela had never appeared on live television; when he had gone into prison there was no television in South Africa. Yet he looked a natural. He was masterful, charming the hard-bitten journalists, who gave him a spontaneous ovation at the end. For days afterwards almost continuous live broadcasts covered his exhilarating appearances, enchanting not just black South Africa but a watching world.

An Afrikaner president was at last prepared to negotiate with the 75 per cent of South Africans who had never enjoyed democratic rights in their own country. But although the new South Africa beckoned, its birth pangs were still fraught with anguish as over the next four years more people – overwhelmingly Mandela's ANC supporters – were killed than at any time in the country's history. If only, if only, Ad and Wal both thought, those in power had listened to the demands for change when they had been active thirty years earlier. So much bitterness, bloodshed and terror could have been avoided.

Eventually, however, the country's first ever general election did take place on 27 April 1994 and Mandela and his ANC were overwhelmingly elected. Ad and Wal queued up joyfully outside South Africa House on a clear day with hundreds of other exiles, carrying the old South African identity cards they still possessed which made them eligible to vote. They were babysitting their granddaughter, Sally's child Connie, and took her with them. Ad explained afterwards: 'I put my cross on the ballot paper next to the smiling face of Mandela.'

They couldn't quite believe they were participating in a process for which they had fought so long and hard: it seemed the consummation of a mission accomplished.

By the time of that triumph Ad had assumed another political role. Experienced and proficient from her days in Pretoria, aged sixty-four, she had been asked by Peter to work for him and to take her first paid job for over forty years as part-time secretary in the House of Commons. Peter had been elected Labour Member of Parliament for Neath in April 1991. Working partly from home, she came in regularly to the Palace of Westminster on her senior citizen London underground pass, helping to set up his new office and taking piles of work back home where she had learnt to use a desktop computer through trial and error, mainly helped by Peter's son Sam, then aged fourteen, who set it up for her.

Busily in and out of the House of Commons, she often chatted to other MPs who admired her anti-apartheid record. She loved the job, conscientious to the point of over-diligence for the next eighteen years until she finally retired in 2009, by then aged eighty-two, still very capable. However, there was a sour note to her retirement. Several months before, some MPs had become embroiled in the scandal over parliamentary expenses, and in a newspaper report one journalist outrageously questioned whether her role was a family sinecure rather than a real job. Ad was furious. If anything she had been grossly under-paid for her devotion to the job. When informed that her salary at the time was a paltry £5,000 per annum, some journalists then reversed their spin on the story to assert she was being exploited. Although hurt, nothing in this surprised Ad, as she had a long memory of media unfairness and inaccuracy. 'Never let the facts get in the way of a story,' was one of Wal's sayings.

Earlier, during the epic, year-long miners' strike of 1984–5, she had volunteered to deal with correspondence and the logging and banking of donations to the Miners' Christmas Appeal Fund, which raised hundreds of thousands of pounds, having been launched by Peter with Glenys Kinnock, wife of the then Labour Party leader, and other prominent people. Hundreds of letters containing large and small donations poured into the family home. Ad read the letters – moving tributes to the miners and their desperate struggle, reflecting her own values of justice and fairness.

Meanwhile, in 1991, the same year as Ad had begun working for Peter, Wal was still at a large architectural practice in Epsom, half an hour's drive south of London from their Putney home, and had his sixty-seventh birthday. However, his employers didn't realise his age and the next year told him suddenly that they didn't employ anybody over sixty-five and promptly retired him on a pension. He was shocked and disorientated, having loved the job, specialising in hospital design, notably at Addenbrooke's in Cambridge and Great Ormond Street in London. But they still wanted him to carry on working for them from home in his speciality – laboratory design, a subject on which several years later he wrote a popular textbook.[‡] When that work ceased he did designs for free for friends and family on their house and office alterations.

‡ Walter Hain, *Laboratories: A Briefing and Design Guide* (London: E & FN Spon, 1995).

Being retired left plenty of time for Wal to give to his grandchildren, particularly Peter's sons Sam and Jake, who lived just around the corner. They were always popping in for food and treats, and Wal used to take them to play football and cricket when their parents were too busy. Sally and her partner Arthur McGuinness lived in a flat underneath Ad and Wal after they had divided their home and her small daughter Connie was constantly up the stairs or seen being carried around the neighbourhood on Wal's shoulders.

When Connie began school, Wal used to take her and was a daily volunteer reader to her class. One vulnerable little boy loved Wal – and his mother, a victim of wife-battering and living in a refuge, later thanked him profusely. 'I don't know whether my son would have come through our trauma without your support,' she said. Wal also used to give talks to older pupils on his wartime experiences and sometimes he would be joined by Ad to talk about apartheid as well.

By this time they had long left the Liberal Party and were active members of Putney Labour Party, attending its meetings, with Wal regularly leafleting. They became local stalwarts and were given special service awards in 2009.

In May 1997, when Peter was promoted into the new Labour government by the Prime Minister, Tony Blair, Ad and Wal were proudly delighted, albeit nervous since they had never warmed to Blair's 'New Labour' project. Like many fellow party members they became increasingly estranged the longer Labour was in power and the letter pages of *The Guardian* or *Tribune* contained an occasional sharp rejoinder from 'W. V. Hain' to what he saw as the latest policy departure from the Labour values of social justice and democracy to which he and Ad had devoted their lives.

Their strongest and most anguished disagreement was over the Iraq War, which began in March 2003, Peter by then a member of the Cabinet. For the first time, their close family was split. Sally accepted Peter's view that what he honestly believed was evidence of weapons of mass destruction held by the Iraqi tyrant Saddam Hussein justified the invasion, but Tom and Jo-anne were firmly with their parents.

On 13 March 2003, a week before the invasion of Iraq, in 'Iraq – A Statement', sent to their family, friends and Labour Party members, Wal set out their strong views based on careful research, which showed uncanny foresight:

> Saddam Hussein is clearly an amoral, cruel despot who cannot be trusted, who has already attacked two neighbours (Iran 1980–88) and Kuwait (1990), who has used gas against one section of his own people, the Kurds in the north (about 25 per cent of population) and attacked Shia in the south. Nothing has been shown to have changed in Iraq since the 1999 report by the UN Inspectors after they were withdrawn in 1998. They confirmed that Iraq had not had

> nuclear weapons, that most of its pre-1990 stockpile of biological and chemical weapons were destroyed either in the war with Iran or under supervision after the Gulf War, and that any remaining would no longer be viable (most of them go off after about 3 or 4 years). Nor has any evidence been produced to show that Iraq has repaired the facilities for producing Weapons of Mass Destruction (WMD) which were destroyed after the Gulf War. So Bush's claim that Iraq is a threat to the USA is risible to anyone but a fundamentalist American and it appears obvious that it will take years before it can again become a threat even to its own region.

They continued:

> We consider any war to be a last resort, embarked upon only after all other avenues have been exhausted, which as regards Iraq is demonstrably not the case. However well intentioned, the attack proposed by Bush and Blair would inevitably cause civilian casualties in Iraq – Hussein can be depended upon to ensure this. In the medium term it will further damage Iraq's fragile infrastructure, depressing existing dismal living standards and could even lead to civil war in a country of such ethnic and religious diversity. It could also destabilise the region if not the whole Middle East, and an attack on Iraq could trigger an attack upon Israel, spreading the conflict to a Muslim/West confrontation. Another reason for not subjecting Iraq

to the turmoil of war at this stage is that, whatever the US's optimistic promises made for post-war rehabilitation and unification in Iraq, experience in Afghanistan would suggest that these are more likely than not to be empty ones.

Although Ad and Wal didn't question their son Peter's sincerity, they vehemently insisted that the war would have disastrous consequences, and supported the massive, million-strong march in protest through the streets of London. Friends like David Evans, who had been a political prisoner under apartheid and in exile resigned from the Labour Party over Iraq, recalled their stance:

> Intensely political, Ad and Wal also maintain deep and affectionate family relationships. I particularly admire them for their continued support for son Peter while disagreeing strongly with his enthusiastic backing for the military action in Iraq. That is love. And, though they can both be sharp and critical where they see a need, love and tolerance are key attributes of their exemplary lives.

Epilogue

They had never expected apartheid to be abolished in time for them to return. Indeed, because they told themselves they never would, that acted as a spur to the relative success they made of assimilating into Britain and their local community. For nearly thirty years they had suppressed their inner longing for 'the old country' and just got on with it.

But, having been exhilarated on *his* return when acting as a British parliamentary observer for the first democratic South African elections that Mandela's ANC won in April 1994, Peter pressed Ad and Wal to go back on a family holiday. They *must*, he insisted, if only to experience the new rainbow democracy they had helped to create.

Ad and Wal were initially reluctant, then finally persuaded – but remained extremely apprehensive. Although it was now a new South Africa, they feared the old one might be lurking somewhere to settle scores, memories still too raw, even after all that time. And, they were hesitant to admit, they were also emotionally conflicted. Going back would require them to see, to breathe, to listen, to smell – all that was familiar but long banished to their inner recesses, to again meet people once left in anguish, to experience the beautiful homeland, the special, evocative sounds and light of Africa, which they had been able to survive without only by telling themselves it was gone forever.

Finally, they were persuaded on a three-week visit over Christmas and New Year in 1994–5, which proved a roller-coaster of fun, joy, reunions – and also a welling up of emotions from deep, very deep, inside their souls.

Eagerly they peered out of the jumbo jet as it swept around Table Mountain, glorious in the early morning sun, a white cloth of cloud draped over it, Cape Town stretching out magnificently below. Accompanied by Peter and his wife Pat, their sons Sam and Jake, Sally and her partner Arthur and baby daughter Connie, Ad and Wal's arrival could not have been more different from their departure. Instead of security police surveillance to hustle them out, there was a surprise welcome back with VIP limousines waiting on the airport tarmac.

The daughters of her eldest brother Hugh, Liz Smith and Annie Bodenstein, with whom Ad and Wal maintained regular contact, kindly made the arrangements with their brother Brian – a director of the airport. Officials warmly greeted them and courteously attended to all the arrival formalities, including collecting the family's many cases and dealing with immigration formalities, as they were shown into a smart lounge normally deputed for kings, queens and presidents, and served tea and coffee.

Their nieces and their husbands, Kent and Pete, eagerly whisked them away to settle into their homes in Noordhoek, down the breathtaking Cape Peninsula. (Liz and Annie later explained how as little girls they had never understood why they had suddenly not been allowed to see their close cousins Jo-anne and Sally anymore.)

On the way they drove specially past Pollsmoor Prison, where Nelson Mandela and his close comrades had been imprisoned in later years after being moved from Robben Island. The day was packed with old memories and delightful vignettes of just how dramatically the country had changed.

For lunch the family drove up to the Cape Town waterfront, where they could still see the old dockside railway tracks where Ad and Wal had arrived after their Berlin-corridor-type journey from Pretoria to board the liner for Britain. It was hard to imagine those grim dark days as they lunched with glasses of Wal's favourite Castle lager at the old docks, now a marina, seals lazily bobbing up and down at the quayside. And what a joy it was to sit among black families and couples being served drinks and snacks by white and black waiters.

Later, it was up the majestic Table Mountain by cable car to look out and savour 'the fairest Cape in all the circumference of the world' according to sea warrior Sir Francis Drake. And, yes, there beyond the Atlantic breakers, shimmering in the haze, Robben Island, where Nelson Mandela, Walter Sisulu, Eddie Daniels and so many others had spent the prime of their lives. It had somehow lost its grim menace, with day trips and visits to Mandela's old cell a top tourist attraction: they saw the Robben Island ferry taking visitors out to the island.

Mandela sat astride his nation almost godlike. Even whites, fearful before the elections, now worshipped him. 'Isn't our President wonderful,' they would tell Ad and Wal. He symbolised the transformation from evil to hope. That evening, invited to a *braaivleis* (barbecue) at the home of Peter's friend Andre Odendaal, they encountered a poignant tribute to Mandela's extraordinary influence. Andre, a white Afrikaner involved in the anti-apartheid struggle, told how his mother had for several years refused to recognise his marriage to Zohra, an Asian and former activist herself.

Indeed his mother had refused to meet Zohra or their mixed-race first child. Then her fears ebbed as Mandela mutated from Satan to saviour. Blacks weren't going to burn her out of her farm after all (although a neighbour had been killed in a PAC attack). She reluctantly agreed that Andre bring his wife and daughter to the farm – but only after dark. A mixed marriage would still shame her in the eyes of her neighbours. They booked into a hotel in the nearby town, and the meeting took place outside her house. She took her granddaughter, paused, then cradled the baby gently in her arms. Suddenly she seemed to emerge from a trance, inviting his wife, who had remained discreetly in their car, into her home. And they ended up sleeping there rather than the hotel after all, Zohra warm in an insistent mother-in-law's dressing gown.

As Ad and Wal and their group enjoyed their first South African *braai* in three decades, Grandma was upstairs babysitting – Andre's first Christmas with his mother since the marriage. But she was still apprehensive at meeting the 'notorious' Hains until Andre insisted on introductions while she hugged the baby.

It was as if a great millstone had been lifted. Whites could for the first time ever be themselves, at ease with the world. Ad and Wal were reminded of their friendliness and old-fashioned courtesy – something they missed in bustling, impersonal London where care and community often seemed to be lost. There always had been a *personal* sense of decency in most whites but it did not extend to *public* decency, buried by complicity in the institutionalised racism and brutality of apartheid.

The old South Africa they had left had been descending relentlessly into a pit of human depravity. The new one was buoyed by an infectious optimism from whites and blacks alike – though they too were caught by the same sense of wondering whether it was actually true. For Ad and Wal it also appeared difficult to find anybody who admitted to ever having supported apartheid – rather like Germany after the Nazis, he remarked ironically. And of course most whites had just gone along with it, turning a blind eye to the misery and the oppression, choosing not to know, while enjoying the immense privileges.

But there seemed to be a desire to exorcise guilt. During the three-week visit, some of the same relatives who had kept a studied distance when Ad and Wal most needed support in the dark early sixties now gave them generous hospitality. It was a small example of the healing process which they found to be such a moving feature of the new country.

The dramatic change was everywhere. A Coloured car park attendant at Table Mountain enthused: 'Visitors used to say "South Africa is wonderful". Now they say to me "*Your* country is wonderful".'

After a wonderful stay in Noordhoek, the family left in a minibus to drive around South Africa, visiting relatives and former Liberal Party colleagues. They travelled nearly six hundred miles eastward along the coast from Cape Town, past long sandy beaches on the turquoise Indian Ocean. It was delightful but strange to experience mixed-race swimming on previously segregated beaches. Near George, where they stopped overnight, they found themselves amid a school of dolphins surfing in the waves.

Stopping for petrol, Wal found himself standing at a urinal when he heard someone walking to the one next to him. 'I glanced up and saw an African standing next to me. Then I *knew* things *really* had changed!' he recounted back in the minibus.

Then it was on to Ad's home town, Port Alfred, now expanded with a population of around 20,000. She and Wal enjoyed idyllic summer holidays there until her 1963 ban. 'Never go back' is often a wise axiom. And Port Alfred, like the country, had changed an awful lot in thirty years. They disliked the yuppie marina. But her old family home, Mentone, had been preserved unchanged and the wide, flowing Kowie River was as they had remembered it, especially upstream where it was protected by a nature reserve. The expansive cream beaches remained a delight. 'It's not right. We should never have been forced to leave all this,' said Ad, tears streaming at the emotion of her return as she stood on Mentone's front lawn, looking out at the Kowie: her parents had died there during her absence and of course she had been barred from attending their funerals, a non-person, a non-daughter.

Her brothers Hugh and Mike had also died but Hugh's eldest daughter Barbara welcomed them to Masuri – the family riverside home Wal had designed and where the group stayed. She arranged with her brother Brian a lunch party and *braaivleis*, joined by some of Ad's nieces, nephews and relatives who were also staying in their holiday homes for Christmas.

Ad drove to Kowie's Queen Alexandra Secondary School, up a hill which didn't look anything like as steep as when she remembered climbing up it starting at age six. Signs depicting the old separate boys' and girls' entrances remained, but the school was now multi-racial. Sports fields stretched out behind, the outdoor life of her childhood a fond but very distant memory now.

As arranged in advance, she made time to go to a bank in the seaside town containing an account with a small amount of inheritance money which had been previously frozen by the authorities; now she was able to draw it all out and close the account. 'It was quite exciting being able to do this after such a long time,' she remarked. (Most of the money had been used to pay off Wal's university loan before the account was frozen.)

There was another nostalgic return to nearby Grahamstown and Victoria Girls High School, much the same as before the war, when Ad went there. The English colonial feel of the town had been engagingly preserved, with covered decorative walkways still adjoining its old shops. But Ad and Wal were struck seeing blacks and whites in the same queues in shops and banks.

On Christmas Eve they were welcomed by their old Liberal Party comrade Peter Brown, wife Phoebe and family at their farm, Lion's Bush, in the midlands of Kwazulu-Natal, north of Pietermaritzburg where they stopped briefly to view the small town where they had once lived in the early 1950s. Peter Brown was celebrating his seventieth birthday as they arrived – a reminder of another talent wasted. He should have been in government instead of being imprisoned, then banned. A few days later Wal celebrated *his* seventieth birthday at the Browns' holiday cottage in the misty Drakensberg mountains, his baby granddaughter Connie given her first swim in a nearby stream.

The peaceful atmosphere was striking: just ten miles away at Mooi River there had for years been scenes of awful carnage between the government-backed Zulu Inkatha movement and ANC supporters. Yet political violence appeared to have vanished just eight months after the election.

And Christmas Day itself was wistful too: instead of the now familiar British snow, cold or rain, it was sunburn weather by 7.30 in the morning, pre-lunch drinks on the lawn and roast turkey on the veranda – an action-replay from the old days.

But they were struck at how the British colonial connection had survived. It felt almost like home to a British visitor. On the drive up from Natal to Johannesburg, they stopped at Ladysmith, scene of a famous 118-day siege during the 1899–1902 Anglo-Boer War, where Tom was born, and found the home where they had lived for a couple of years and staged their first Liberal Party meeting. Nearby was the site of another battle, Spioenkop (from which Liverpool football supporters named their haven at Anfield, The Kop), and to the east Rorke's Drift and Isandlwana, of 'Zulu War' fame. In need of a swim and lunch, their party stopped by chance at the Inkwelo Motel below the towering aMajuba Hill – where a British defeat in 1881 ended the first Boer War – and were shown unmarked British graves. The local area is called *Ingogo* – Zulu for 'half a crown', which is what local women asked for in return for sexual favours to the British soldiers: a small mixed-race community the result.

By late afternoon, Johannesburg was in sight, the yellow glint of its gold mine tips visible through the baking heat haze. Another group of old Liberal Party comrades embraced them in a welcome-back party. One remarked how the Stop the Tour sports protests in 1969–70 had been 'decisive' in rocking whites into accepting change. 'The government must have bitterly regretted kicking out the Hains,' she chuckled. The goodwill among black South Africans remained remarkable.

The only upsetting thing was the ubiquitous wave of crime and muggings. However, another old white friend brushed this aside (rather too airily for Ad and Wal's taste). 'It's just redistribution of wealth. What else do you expect with black male unemployment at over 60 per cent?' But in the Jo'burg suburb where Ad and Wal lodged with their old Liberal friend Jill Wentzel, every home seemed to be guarded by security gates and burglar alarms. Whites travelled only by car – and even then were vulnerable to hijacking at gunpoint. It was almost as if crime had become a means of exacting compensation from whites for the grim decades of oppression.

Although South Africa had been liberated from

constitutional apartheid, crime, poverty and destitution were much, much worse than when Ad and Wal had lived there. Over seven million black South Africans – a quarter of the total black population – subsisted in squatter settlements ringing the white cities. On the Cape flats, they were guided to the latest grim squatting areas, not by accident named 'Beirut' and 'Vietnam' by their inhabitants.

Soweto Cricket Club's new Elkah Stadium was the only decent cricket ground in the township, serving twenty-five school and four club teams amid a population of three million. They were welcomed there by Khaya Majola, now deputy director of the new non-racial United South African Cricket Board, and his players and officials; under apartheid Khaya had refused overtures from white cricket officials to play a 'token black' role and decorate their racist game, instead sacrificing his career as a first-class cricketer to support the non-racial game. The club's chairman, Edward Cebekulu, had been one of those involved in the Soweto 1976 uprising when white police opened fire on peacefully protesting school students. He pointed out schools that had taken part and the memorial to Hector Petersen, the schoolboy photographed dying in his brother's arms, a symbol of the atrocity which shocked the world.

After this it was on to the Kruger National Park game reserve for a delightful few days with Jill Wentzel. On the way they stopped at the farm which she had owned with her husband Ernie, yet another comrade from their activist days who did not live to see the new South Africa. Ernie's gravestone up on the kopje was a tribute to his record as both legal advocate and political activist: 'Ernie – the best labourer dead – and all the sheaves to bind 1933–1986'.

In the wildlife park itself, Ad and Wal were again reminded of what they had given up. Nwanetsi camp's isolated location on the Mozambique border gave a real feel of the primitive African *bushveld*: hyena and baboons patrolling the perimeter to a cacophony of birds and Christmas beetles. They held hands outside at dawn soaking up the smell, the Highveld sounds and the distinctive African light they loved. The experience made Ad weep and Wal almost, as they confessed to their family something repressed for so long: how sorely they missed their old homeland.

And then the *pièce de résistance*. Some of the black activists who had struggled alongside them in Pretoria, suffering much worse harassment than the Hain family ever did, celebrated Ad and Wal's return home. The last time they had all met was at Pretoria railway station when they waved goodbye into exile. Poen Ah Dong and Aubrey Apples turned out with dozens of their relatives. Back in the 1960s, they lived in shacks in the Cape Reserve. Now they partied in the garden of the sumptuous family home in Pretoria's exclusive Waterkloof Glen owned by Poen's daughter, Mee Ling. She would never have been allowed to live in such a 'white' area in the old days, and it would have been illegal to hold such a multi-racial party where liquor was served. Again unthinkable in the past – two white Afrikaners *braaied* a lamb for the predominantly black guests. And Ad met her godson, Edward Rathswaffo, whose late father David had been her close friend and successor as Pretoria party secretary. Moved to meet him, especially as his father had meanwhile sadly died, Ad gave him a huge emotional hug. She hadn't seen him since she cradled him at his christening as a baby all that time ago, but over the years she had sent small amounts of money and presents for birthdays and Christmas.

They had previously been welcomed to stay by Wal's brother Tom at his home outside Pretoria, his antagonism now gone with apartheid. Their children's old schools were much the same. At Pretoria Boys High, Wal pointed out where, as a banned person, he had watched Peter play cricket from outside the school fence. Hatfield Primary School, where all four children had been educated, had an honours board in the quadrangle in front of which assemblies were held in the open. It still bore the name 'P. Hain Head Prefect 1962': the gold lettering had survived even Peter's denunciation in the media and by government ministers in the early 1970s (though apparently a member of the administrative staff had unsuccessfully tried to get it scraped off). Also still there proudly was Tom's award: 'T. Hain Good Fellowship Prize 1964'.

The seat of government was at the Union Buildings, a sandstone building designed by Sir Herbert Baker and started in 1910, its colonial architecture lording it over the city from high on a hill. There, Ad recalled the spot where she'd been spat upon by civil servants during a Black Sash protest. Now all was at peace in the morning sunshine, the new South African flag fluttering proudly overhead. Once the seat of white oppression, it now housed Nelson Mandela's presidential office.

The Old Synagogue, which had acted as a court when Ad had attended Mandela's trial in 1962 and where she and her two girls had been kissed by his wife Winnie to the disgust of white security officers, was now boarded up. But she couldn't help breaking down outside the Supreme Court where John Harris had been sentenced to death and Hugh Lewin given seven years in jail. The two separate prisons where Ad and Wal had been jailed, another where Hugh Lewin had been imprisoned, John Harris had been executed and where in the old days black prisoners were hanged at the rate of over a hundred each year, were hidden behind a new, less threatening, facade.

Where were all those agents of the police state who had intimidated, tortured and killed in the name of apartheid? What were they doing with themselves these days? Were they passing by unknowingly as Ad and Wal walked like tourists past the city centre statue of Paul Kruger, the Afrikaner leader and South Africa's first Prime Minister?

❦

After an almost breathless three weeks revisiting old familiar spots and reunions, Ad and Wal returned home safely to London. They had fought to defeat the old South Africa, but were now unapologetic evangelists for the new one.

Much of what they had rediscovered was no surprise: people hospitable, weather warm, food and wine a delight. Nowhere else in the world, they reminded themselves, could be found such a rich variety of animals, birds and flowers, and such breathtaking variations in landscape, with an infrastructure that made visiting so effortless, whether in the Mediterranean-type southern Cape, the hot humid littoral of Natal, or the dry heat of the Transvaal Highveld. They were thrilled that their old country, for so long a pariah, was now at last able to reveal itself, in Alan Paton's immortal words, as 'lovely beyond any singing of it'.

Nevertheless, their return to Britain did leave them both deeply unsettled, and for months their close family noted that they were not quite their normal phlegmatic, lively selves. They had experienced what they thought they never would: going home. But where *was* 'home' now? They didn't really feel British, because they weren't. But they were not South Africans anymore either. What *were* they?

As Hilda Bernstein noted of the 40,000 South African exiles who returned to settle, going back was invariably very far from straightforward. When the dream became a reality, returnees found themselves conflicted. They had been changed by exile and their country had meanwhile changed without them, bringing a fresh emotional turmoil. Some couldn't cope – some even returned back to 'exile', whatever that now meant.

Other reunions and visits followed, always a mixture of joy, jarring nostalgia and jangling emotion. In February 2000 they were chief guests at the British high commission's official reception in Pretoria to mark Peter's visit as Britain's Africa Minister, wryly observing how Wal's sister-in-law Marie, whose travel agency back in 1962 had publicly disavowed Ad as an altogether different Hain, now basked in the admiration from guests for being Peter's aunt.

During that visit they also stayed overnight on Robben Island, guests of Peter's friend, anti-apartheid activist Andre Odendaal. It was both eerie and thrilling, a place which had once been synonymous with horror and oppression now a gentle environmental sanctuary and an historic memorial to hope and the triumph of human spirit.

In December 2004, Wal delighted in a surprise eightieth birthday party organised by Sally at Liz and Kent's home in Noordhoek. Present were some friends and activists from the past, including Eddie Daniels and Randolph Vigne, both Liberals and African Resistance Movement cadres. They reminisced over past struggles and campaigns, bannings and detentions, breathing the air of democracy and freedom on a warm, sunny Cape day.

Invigorating though these visits back to their homeland were, they nevertheless still found them psychologically charged. 'I like visiting but I don't like leaving,' Ad would explain. Perhaps that is why – apart from the length and cost of the flight – they preferred to holiday on the southern coast of Spain. The dry heat, the soaring Andalusian mountains, the outdoor life and the freedom in his late eighties for Wal especially to swim out into the warm sea – occasionally glimpsing the African coast across the Mediterranean – were all reminders of what they treasured from 'the old country'. So too in its way was the home to which they moved in 2009 to be near their daughter Sally, who acted as unofficial carer. The house, where they celebrated their 65th anniversary in 2013, stands high on the side of the Neath Valley in Peter's parliamentary constituency, in an old mining community. 'Especially on sunny days it reminds me of Africa,' said Ad, 'its panoramic views, the sense of space, are lovely.'

In any case Ad and Wal's close family were almost entirely British and their strong family attachments meant they never really had any inclination to return to live in South Africa. Although Tom had moved to Australia and Jo-anne had a spell living in southern Spain – both in search of a life similar to the sunshine one they still missed – almost all their children, grand-children and great-grandchildren lived in Britain.

Family came first – almost ahead of themselves – and, through email and texts, which she was taught to use by her grandson Sam, Ad kept in close touch with all her family members, acting as their *de facto* centre. She also maintained regular links with old comrades and new friends in South Africa. Wal, however, would have nothing to do with this 'new-fangled technology'. When he drafted his own articles and letters, or drafted sections on apartheid for Peter's books, he always did so in his handsome handwriting; Ad would then type and email them for him. Inseparable in struggle, they remained inseparable.

❦

In their late eighties, while this book was being written, Ad and Wal remained unequivocal that they had acted out of conscience and for a necessary and just cause: the triumph of freedom and human spirit over tyranny and evil. They were modest about their role in helping to defeat apartheid, and of the subsequent transformation of the country, notably under Nelson Mandela.

But they worried about the failings of Mandela's successors: Thabo Mbeki over his denial of HIV/Aids and pusillanimous stance towards Zimbabwe's tyrant Robert Mugabe; and Jacob Zuma over his personal lifestyle and the rampant corruption at all levels of government. Yet, they always insisted, the legacy of apartheid was a haunting one for the new democracy: widespread poverty, black unemployment rates of 50 per cent and more in some areas, dire educational performance and chronically low skills in a world increasingly dominated by the ravenous economies of China and India. By 2012 no country was spending as much of its GDP on education as South Africa and the ANC had doubled school attendance since the dark apartheid days. Yet out of 137 countries in the 2011 Global Competitiveness Index, South Africa ranked 130 for the quality of its overall education – public service delivery overall a serious problem.

In August 2012 Ad and Wal were horrified by the lethal conflagration at Lonmin's Marikana platinum mine near Rustenburg, where thirty-four striking workers were killed and seventy-eight injured by black and white police armed with automatic rifles, pistols and shotguns. After the initial confrontation, twenty-two of those killed were hunted down as they cowered in a cluster of boulders and shot in cold blood. Witnesses were later detained and some tortured. Inevitably, the ugly clash invited immediate comparisons with massacres by the apartheid regime, including the sixty-nine innocent people shot at Sharpeville fifty-two years earlier. (Ronnie Kasrils, former ANC underground intelligence chief and subsequently an ANC government minister, insisted it was actually *worse* than Sharpeville, because some evidence suggested the attack had been pre-planned as the ANC state turned its firepower on its own people.)

They were haunted by the growing recognition that Marikana had broader roots in the mostly simmering but sometimes explosive resentment at the chasm between expectations and delivery. Despite millions having received running water, electricity and better housing from the ANC, in other respects living conditions of poor blacks, including miners, had hardly improved in the years since apartheid ended. As in most other countries, the gap between rich and poor had widened – with South Africa one of the most unequal societies in the world – and a new black middle class including ANC politicians and ANC-linked trade union leaders was enjoying enrichment, with corruption also breeding grass-roots bitterness.

At the same time they remained proud that the dark, imprisoned country they had left in 1966 remained such a marvellous, uplifting one to visit. The once omnipotent fortress had been breached, the awful oppression and gross indignity banished. They enveloped themselves in the joyous, bubbling spirit of a new beginning, reassured that the new constitution was a beacon to human rights the world over, and that independent voices inside and outside the ANC spoke out in protest at transgressions or betrayals of the freedom struggle.

How then might their contribution be assessed?

It made a huge impression on the youthful Nelson Mandela when in 1943 he first met white activists allied to the ANC: 'I discovered for the first time people of my own age firmly aligned with the liberation struggle, who were prepared, despite their relative privilege, to sacrifice themselves for the cause of the oppressed.'[‡] And he never tired of thanking those whites who did, against their own private interests, join the struggle, for the contributions they had made, big or small.

Eddie Daniels also paid tribute to the white South Africans who spurned skin colour privilege, fought apartheid and paid a heavy price in the process.

> Blacks like myself ... were shackled by the racial laws of the land. While White South Africans, under apartheid, were the most privileged of any citizens of any country anywhere in the world. And yet, there were those tremendously courageous men and women, such as members of the Congress of Democrats and the Liberal Party of South Africa, heroes and heroines one and all, who made outstanding contributions to the Freedom Struggle. And who, in spite of their white skins and the tremendous privileges that their skin colour bestowed on them, spurned those privileges, risked all, and joined the Liberation Struggle to help rid our beautiful South Africa of the curse of apartheid and in the process suffered bannings, detention, torture, exile, imprisonment and death, while many Blacks, such as the Bantustan leaders, among others, cooperated with the regime to line their deep pockets with their ill-gotten gains.[§]

‡ Nelson Mandela, *Long Walk to Freedom* (London: Little, Brown, 1994), p. 85.

§ Daniels, *There and Back*, 3rd edn, p. 261.

Jill Chisholm said: 'Of all the things Ad and Wal taught me the most important was that an indomitable spirit coupled with integrity will always survive an oppressive power. Even if it sometimes takes a long, long time. There are many examples of this in South Africa's history, and Ad and Wal have their place in that history.' In July 1996, Walter Sisulu wrote of how Ad and Wal 'joined many thousands of other South Africans, black and white, in the internal resistance – and we salute their courage. If others had done the same, much suffering, much pain and much killing could have been avoided.'

Eddie Daniels observed:

> Of all the stories extolling their courage the ones that touched me deeply were those which spoke of the tremendous courage and loyalty they showed to Ann and John Harris, and their son David, before, during and after their terrible and harrowing ordeal that they endured during John's arrest, detention, guilty verdict, death sentence, appeal, dismissal of his appeal, his execution and after. Their courage and staying power during that terrible journey was tremendous.

In England, Ann remembered:

> Ad and Wal had a simple but happy family life with which they seemed very content. Despite their having known me only a little before, when I arrived on their doorstep with six-week-old David and explained that

> John had been arrested, they immediately pressed us to stay with them to be closer to the prison – our home was an hour away. Over the next year, they made us part of their family, however unpopular that would have been with their wider families, the public and the authorities. I learnt hugely from their personal values, about how to enjoy a simple life, about how to cope with trials and tribulations (the Special Branch particularly!) and about how to support your friends.

Her son David added:

> Ad and Wal took us in and cared for us when others would have turned away. They did the 'right thing' despite the risk to themselves and their family. That has been a lifelong inspiration to me. I am eternally grateful to them and to Sally, Jo-anne, Tom and Peter.

Myrtle Berman with her husband Monty was a founder member of the National Committee of Liberation and then the African Resistance Movement, and formerly in the South African Communist Party. No fan of the Liberals, most of whom activists like her saw as insufficiently committed to the resistance, she nevertheless said of Ad and Wal: 'They were always spoken about positively, with high regard: people with integrity who had lived their beliefs. Somehow set apart by their actions, consistently so.'

Liberal Party and ARM activist David Evans, who

in 1964 was sentenced to five years as a political prisoner and then house-arrested on his release, saw them this way:

> Adelaine and Walter Hain made the ordinary extraordinary. On first acquaintance they struck you as nice, middle class, professional, orthodox, decent, family-oriented people. What that reasonable description missed was their energy, dedication to creating a better society, loyalty to their friends and family and a certain toughness. These qualities made them formidable opponents of apartheid in the country of their birth.

But when asked why they chose to be one of those whites who rebelled, Ad and Wal would invariably reply: 'Anybody would have done what we did.' And they would quickly add: 'Others did much more and suffered far, far more than us.' But only a tiny minority of whites *did* rebel against apartheid and join Nelson Mandela's freedom struggle; only a relative handful showed the same courage and self-sacrifice that they did.

There were indicators in the way their lives developed as to why they may have been so different from their relatives (Ad's sister Jo excepted), their friends and their peers. But these do not by any means tell the whole story. Discovering why only certain people get involved in politics, anywhere, at any time, in any country, even when injustice stares all in the face or affects them directly, is always tantalising. Certainly Ad and Wal could never provide a comprehensive account as to *why* in their case.

They may have seen themselves as 'ordinary' people – and in a way they were: not schooled in the ideology of liberation, for instance, and living in other respects a fairly conventional family life. But, motivated by their values and their sense of duty, they did extraordinary things. Which, living in exile for the rest of their lives, would always remain their proud legacy.

Appendix

I CANNOT ACT ON WARNING –MRS. HAIN

Pretoria Reporter

MRS. ADELAINE HAIN, secretary of the Pretoria branch of the Liberal Party, has told the Minister of Justice she cannot act on the Supresssion of Communism Act "warning" given her on his instructions last week.

In a letter to Mr. Vorster, Mrs. Hain has asked him to explain in detail which of her activities he believes are furthering the cause of Communism. The letter was airmailed to Cape Town yesterday morning.

Mrs. Hain was called before the Chief Magistrate of Pretoria last week, and was told to stop activities which were said to be in the interests of Communism. When she asked which activities she should stop, she was told to approach the Minister direct.

Common courtesy

Last night Mrs. Hain said: "Obviously, for reasons of common courtesy, I cannot disclose the text of my letter at least until it has been received by the Minister.

"I deny emphatically that any of my activities are furthering the aims of Communism in any way, and I have made it very clear to the Minister that I cannot act on his so-called warning. I am at a complete loss to understand to which of my activities his warning refers. Like all true liberals adhering to a great philosophy and political creed, I am vehemently anti-Communistic.

"I cannot see what the Minister is getting at. But over and above all this, and even though I am not a Communist, I still question most strongly the Minister's right to try to muzzle anybody or condemn anybody out of hand without access to a trial before a court of law."

News by J. B. Richards, Van der Stel Buildings, Pretoria Street, Pretoria.

Mother banned from sports

A MOTHER stands, alone, outside a Pretoria primary school ground, watching her three children compete in the annual sports. SHE IS FORBIDDEN TO ENTER.

MRS. ADELAINE HAIN, banned former secretary of the Pretoria branch of the Liberal Party, was refused permission this week to attend the sports because they constituted a gathering of an educational institution.

For Mrs. Hain, banned under the Suppression of Communism Act, this was the second disappointment within the last fortnight.

A week ago she was refused permission to go to the school to discuss her children's progress with their teachers — and was told that under the terms of the banning order she might not even enter the school premises.

Liberals only party which can condemn new Act

Sir,—The new proposals embodied in the Population Registration Amendment Bill for determining the racial identities of South Africans can only lead to increased friction and to further deterioration in race relations.

They have been bitterly criticized in Parliament by the Opposition but it is open to question whether these critics are really in a position to attack the Act itself.

For all three parties—the United Party, National Union and Progressives—propagate policies which differentiate between racial groups and which therefore require some mechanism for determining racial identity if they are to merit serious consideration. Such a mechanism must inevitably result in the same injustices as does the Population Registration Act.

The Liberal Party stands alone among South African political parties in considering race to be an accident of birth which has no relevance where individual rights are concerned.

The Liberal Party is therefore the only party which has no need to determine the racial identity of South Africans and which can with honesty condemn the Population Registration Act for the revolting and degrading piece of legislation it is.

W. V. HAIN.

Pretoria.

SUNDAY EXPRESS, Jan. 27, 1963 9

Mr. Vorster has failed to scare us —Liberals

MOTHER, WHO WAS WARNED

MRS. ADELAINE HAIN with her four children. They are Tom, 10, (left) and Peter, 13, and Sally, 6 (left) and Jo-Anne, 8.

SUNDAY EXPRESS REPORTER

MEMBERS of the Liberal Party in Pretoria — probably the most active branch of the party in the country — have refused to be intimidated by the "warning" given to one of their members on the instructions of the Minister of Justice.

They have taken the warning to their secretary, 35-year-old Mrs. Adelaine Hain, a mother of four, as proof that the Minister is now extending his activities to include even the legitimate and legal Left-wing bodies.

Mrs. Hain was warned on Thursday by the Chief Magistrate of Pretoria, Mr. F. J. Mostert.

He told her that he had been instructed by the Minister of Justice to warn her under the amended Suppression of Communism Act—but could not tell her what she had been doing wrong.

Yesterday Mr. Walter Hain, Mrs. Hain's husband and chairman of the branch, told me: "Since the warning does not stipulate which of Mrs. Hain's many activities are upsetting the Minister, and cannot therefore be acted upon, its real purpose is clearly to frighten her into withdrawing from the struggle against racialism."

As such, it was the latest of many similar attempts against members of the Liberal Party, beginning with the imprisonment without trial of Liberals during the state of emergency in 1960, he said.

Other attempts included the imprisonment for two weeks without trial of Mrs. Hain and three other members of the branch after they were arrested while putting up anti-Republican posters in 1961, and the constant intimidation of the party's non-White members.

The efforts of the Minister to try to frighten a legal political party which opposed him were deplorable, but were "of course entirely consistent with the Nazi-like outlook of the Nationalist Government," Mr. Hain said.

CONTEMPT

"We can assure him that his latest attempt at intimidation will be treated with the contempt it deserves. Liberals will not be frightened off by Mr. Vorster's bullying tactics," he added.

FOOTNOTE: Mr. Hain was dismissed from his post as a top Provincial Administration architect in 1963 because of his political affiliations. The office in which the warning was administered to Mrs. Hain was directly above the Marriage Office at the Pretoria Magistrates' Courts — the office in which Mr. and Mrs. Hain were married 14 years ago.

To equate political violence with any particular racial group is to shut one's eyes to the evidence

Repression breeds violent reaction

By W. V. Hain

THE brutal murder of five innocent people near Engcobo, together with Paarl's night of horror, have been taken by many Whites as confirmation of a deeprooted fear: that Africans are essentially violent and brutal people.

This fear is a powerful factor in South African political life, for there are many of goodwill and advanced political thought among Whites who nevertheless baulk at the prospect of extending political power to non-Whites on a significant scale, because of this fear. Yet as a racial fear it is both illogical and unfounded.

There are really two forms of violence — political and social.

Political violence is an attempt to attain political aims by violent means, and in this sphere South African non-Whites have a record of non-violence unparalleled by others in similar political circumstances. For political violence by non-Whites was virtually non-existent prior to the banning of the ANC and PAC and to the introduction of the Sabotage Act last year.

This has been so despite the fact that non-Whites, especially Africans, live under conditions which are not approached today outside the Iron Curtain countries and which *are not equalled in any other state in the world*: the sudden and arbitrary arrest; the constant and severe police surveillance; the humiliation at the hands of petty officials; the harsh control over individual movement; the complete lack of effective representation. How and why Africans have refrained from violence in such circumstances is a mystery for which Whites should be profoundly thankful.

PROVOCATION

In contrast, Whites have often resorted to political violence under conditions of far less provocation.

The type of activity indulged in by the I.R.A. in Britain and Ireland, for example, was very similar to the acts of sabotage which have taken place here recently, but with only a fraction of the provocation to which our non-Whites are subjected. And the same may be said of the fellow-travellers of the present Minister of Justice during the war and of Greek Cypriots during the Cyprus dispute.

For out-and-out acts of political killing and terrorism by Whites in recent years one need look no further than the exploits of the Palestine terrorists or the O.A.S. in Algeria.

But non-Whites need not delude themselves, for the record of non-Whites in other countries has given no more cause for congratulation than has the record of Whites, where violence is concerned. To equate political violence with any particular racial group therefore is to shut one's eyes to the evidence.

Social violence — assaults, armed robberies, murders, etc. —is certainly more prevalent among non-Whites in South Africa than among Whites, and with very good reason. For social violence is the direct result of social conditions and circumstances, prominent among which are ignorance, frustration, poverty, overcrowding, insecurity and fear. When such conditions exist, as they do in large measure among our non-Whites, then violence is almost inevitable.

Social violence is not peculiar to the non-Whites of the world, but occurs in equal measure among all underprivileged groups. Thus, it is as dangerous after dark in the slums of Naples or New York as it is in Orlando and Atteridgeville.

Significantly, in the bad old days of American gangsterism the hoodlums and killers came principally from the minority racial groups — Italians, Germans, Irish — which (together with Negroes) at that time comprised the underprivileged communities of the U.S.A., crowded together in slummy tenements, looked down upon and discriminated against by the older Americans. Since then these groups have made their way and have largely been supplanted in their earlier violent roles by more recent minority groups such as Central Europeans and Puerto Ricans, who, in terms of economics and acceptance, stand today where their predecessors stood 30 years ago.

The point about social violence is that its causes are known and understood and can therefore be eradicated, but before this can be done both the will and the means to eradicate them must be present.

ALLIED

In South Africa social violence is closely allied to politics, for the fact that so many non-Whites are condemned to live under the social and economic conditions which breed it is directly attributable to their lack of political rights.

Whites-only rule has resulted in a progressive increase down the years in non-White frustration, insecurity and ignorance, and has acted therefore to promote social violence among non-Whites. Successive White governments, both here and elsewhere in Africa, have made it increasingly obvious that no large-scale alleviation in these conditions can be expected until non-Whites share in the making of the laws which govern them. And in making it virtually impossible for them to bring about this state of affairs peaceably in this country, the present Government has ensured that political violence, which has hitherto been a stranger to the non-White South African scene, will in future become part of our lives.

The irony of our situation is that it is White fear of the very violence which results from the political straitjacket in which they are keeping non-Whites, that is perhaps the greatest single factor in their stubborn

BEES AMONG THE BEANS

Pretoria Liberal leader fined

Pretoria Reporter

THE chairman of the Pretoria branch of the Liberal Party, Walter Vannet Hain, 38, was yesterday fined R30 (or 15 days) in the Pretoria Magistrate's Court for being in a proclaimed African area without permission.

Hain pleaded guilty to being in the Marabastad location on April 4.

Frans Ignatius Maritz van den Berg, 26, a member of the fund-raising committee of the Liberal Party, pleaded guilty to a similar charge and was also fined R30 (or 15 days).

Constable G. de Kock said that he found ain and Van den Berg in a van in Jerusalem Street, Pretoria. Hain told him their van had broken down.

An offence

In the van were an Indian woman, a Chinese, and some Coloured people. Constable De Kock said he arrested them as they had no permits to be in the location. It was an offence for Whites to be in the location between 6 p.m. and 6 a.m. The names of the other people in the car were taken and they were allowed to go.

Hain said he was taking the people to Hatfield. He thought it was not an offence to drive through the location, as long as he did not stop.

The magistrate, Mr. D. J. de Villiers, said that the accused had offered a reasonable explanation for their presence in the area, and the court accepted it. The fact remained, however, that they had been in the area, and were guilty of an offence.

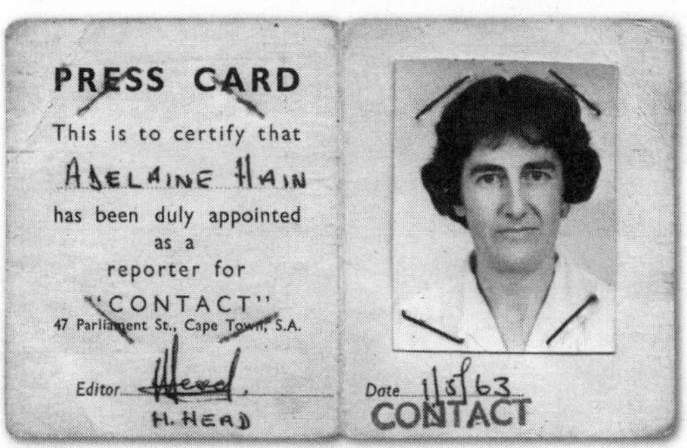

Ad's press card for Contact, *liberal news and comment magazine, 1963.*

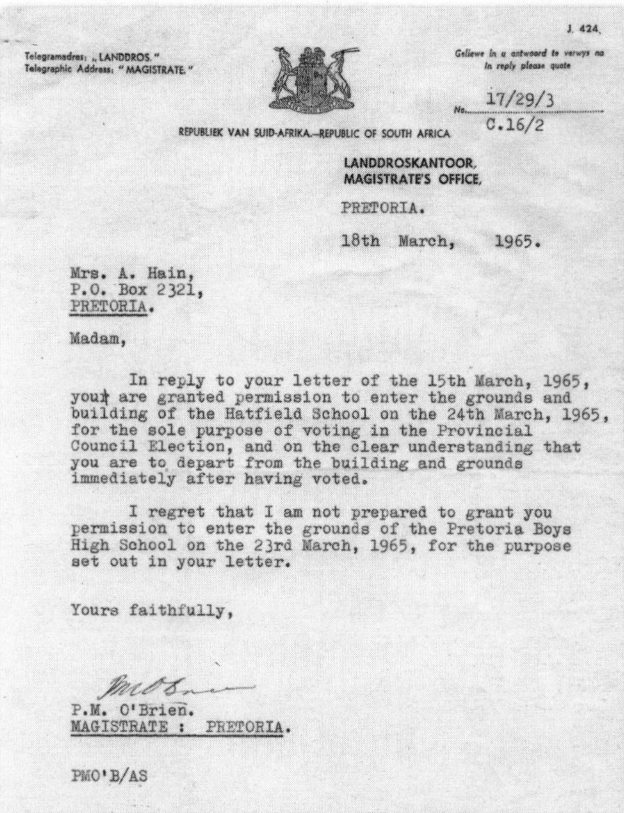

J. 424.

Telegramadres: „LANDDROS."
Telegraphic Address: "MAGISTRATE."

Gliewe in u antwoord te verwys na
In reply please quote
No. 17/29/3
C.16/2

REPUBLIEK VAN SUID-AFRIKA.—REPUBLIC OF SOUTH AFRICA

LANDDROSKANTOOR,
MAGISTRATE'S OFFICE,

PRETORIA.

18th March, 1965.

Mrs. A. Hain,
P.O. Box 2321,
PRETORIA.

Madam,

In reply to your letter of the 15th March, 1965, you are granted permission to enter the grounds and building of the Hatfield School on the 24th March, 1965, for the sole purpose of voting in the Provincial Council Election, and on the clear understanding that you are to depart from the building and grounds immediately after having voted.

I regret that I am not prepared to grant you permission to enter the grounds of the Pretoria Boys High School on the 23rd March, 1965, for the purpose set out in your letter.

Yours faithfully,

P.M. O'Brien.
MAGISTRATE : PRETORIA.

PMO'B/AS

Official government correspondence with Ad, granting her limited permission to enter Hatfield School, 1965.

D.I. 63.

Telegramadres
Telegraphic Address } "INTERIOR."

Meld in u antwoord:
In reply please quote:

No. P 968.

REPUBLIEK VAN SUID-AFRIKA.—REPUBLIC OF SOUTH AFRICA.

Navrae
Enquiries }

DEPARTEMENT VAN BINNELANDSE SAKE,
DEPARTMENT OF THE INTERIOR,
PRIVAATSAK 114,
PRIVATE BAG 114,
PRETORIA.

Tel. No.......................................

17 -3- 1966

REGISTERED.

PERSONAL.

Mr. W.V. Hain,
203 Northwards,
Arcadia Street,
Hatfield,
P R E T O R I A.

Sir,

I forward herewith Departure Permit No. P 03080 issued to you in terms of section 5(6) of the Departure from the Union Regulation Act, No. 34 of 1955, to enable you to leave the Republic permanently, and have to invite your attention to the provisions of section 6 of the abovequoted Act, which reads as follows:-

> "6 Any person to whom a permit endorsed as provided in sub-section (6) of section 5 has been issued and who has left the Union for the purpose of proceeding to a place outside the Union, shall -
>
> (a) if he thereafter returns to the Union be deemed for the purpose of section 2, to have left the Union without a valid passport or permit;
>
> (b) for all purposes become a prohibited person within the meaning of the Admission of Persons to the Union Regulation Act, 1913 (Act No. 22 of 1913), in the Union with effect from the time he so left the Union."

2. In terms of section 15(1)(c) of the South African Citizenship Act, No. 44 of 1949, as amended, a South African citizen ceases to be a South African citizen should he, for purposes of admission to the Republic of South Africa become a prohibited person.

3. Your British passport is returned herewith.

Yours faithfully,

SECRETARY FOR THE INTERIOR.
(PASSPORT SECTION).

Conditions for departure from South Africa.

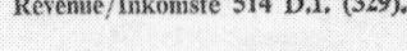

Revenue/Inkomste 514 D.I. (329).

R2

REPUBLIC OF SOUTH AFRICA • REPUBLIEK VAN SUID-AFRIKA •

P. 03080

REPUBLIC OF SOUTH AFRICA.
REPUBLIEK VAN SUID-AFRIKA.

PERMIT IN TERMS OF THE DEPARTURE FROM THE UNION REGULATION ACT, 1955.
PERMIT KRAGTENS DIE WET TOT REËLING VAN VERTREK UIT DIE UNIE, 1955.

This permit is issued to
Hierdie permit is uitgereik aan

Mr./~~Mnr.~~ WALTER VANNET
~~Mrs./Mev.~~
~~Miss/Mej.~~ HAIN.
of
van PRETORIA
for
vir ONLY ONE
departure from South Africa/South West Africa.
vertrek uit Suid-Afrika/Suidwes-Afrika.

DESCRIPTION OF HOLDER.
BESKRYWING VAN HOUER.

Place of Birth
Geboorteplek SOUTH AFRICA SEE OVERLEAF.

Date of Birth
Geboortedatum 29th DEC. 1924

Nationality
Nasionaliteit S.A. CITIZEN

The validity of this permit expires on
Die geldigheid van hierdie permit verval op 6th SEPTEMBER 1966

Given at
Uitgereik te PRETORIA this
op hede die 7th

day of
dag van MARCH 1966

Secretary for the Interior.
Sekretaris van Binnelandse Sake.

Passport Officer/Paspoortbeampte.

IMPORTANT

Wal's permit for departure from South Africa, 1966.

Revenue/Inkomste 514 D.I. (329).

P. 03079

REPUBLIC OF SOUTH AFRICA.
REPUBLIEK VAN SUID-AFRIKA.

PERMIT IN TERMS OF THE DEPARTURE FROM THE UNION REGULATION ACT, 1955.
PERMIT KRAGTENS DIE WET TOT REËLING VAN VERTREK UIT DIE UNIE, 1955.

This permit is issued to
Hierdie permit is uitgereik aan

~~Mr./Mnr.~~ ADELAINE FLORENCE
Mrs./~~Mev.~~
~~Miss/Mej.~~ HAIN.
of
van PRETORIA
for
vir ONLY ONE
departure from South Africa/South West Africa.
vertrek uit Suid-Afrika/Suidwes-Afrika.

DESCRIPTION OF HOLDER.
BESKRYWING VAN HOUER.

Place of Birth
Geboorteplek SOUTH AFRICA
Date of Birth
Geboortedatum 16th FEB. 1927 SEE OVERLEAF.
Nationality
Nasionaliteit S.A. CITIZEN

The validity of this permit expires on
Die geldigheid van hierdie permit verval op 6th SEPTEMBER 1966
Given at
Uitgereik te PRETORIA this op hede die 7th
day of
dag van MARCH 1966

Secretary for the Interior.
Sekretaris van Binnelandse Sake.

Passport Officer/Paspoortbeampte.

IMPORTANT

Ad's permit for departure from South Africa, 1966.

Index

Also available from Biteback Publishing

OUTSIDE IN
Peter Hain

'Disarmingly understated … refreshingly honest … Peter Hain has lived life to the full, which is more than most of our politicians can say.' John Kampfner, *The Observer*

Peter Hain has always spoken his mind – whatever the topic, whatever the cost. Growing up as the son of anti-apartheid South Africans, Hain was first in the public eye aged fifteen, reading at the funeral of a close comrade hanged in Pretoria. Living in exile in Britain during his late teens, he led campaigns to disrupt whites-only South African sports tours. His political notoriety resulted in two extraordinary Old Bailey trials and a letter bomb.

480pp paperback, £12.99
Available from all good bookshops or order from
www.bitebackpublishing.com